When the Snakes Awake

When the Snakes Awake

Animals and Earthquake Prediction

by Helmut Tributsch

translated by Paul Langner

The MIT Press
Cambridge, Massachusetts
London, England

Originally published as *Wenn die Schlangen Erwachen;* © 1978 by Deutsche Verlags-Anstalt GmbH, Stuttgart.

This book was set in Baskerville
by The MIT Press Computergraphics Department
and printed and bound by The Murray Printing Co.
in the United States of America.

Library of Congress Cataloging in Publication Data

Tributsch, Helmut, 1943–
    When the snakes awake.

    Translation of *Wenn die Schlangen erwachen.*
    Includes bibliographic references.
    1. Extrasensory perception in animals. 2. Animals, habits and behavior of.
3. Earthquake prediction. 4. Earthquakes. I. Title.
QL785.3.T7413   001.9′4   82-7148
ISBN 0-262-20044-9   AACR2

To the observers of nature without name, title, or career
for their contributions to the progress of science.

Contents

Preface   *ix*

Acknowledgments   *xiii*

1
Animals as Earthquake Predictors: Superstition or Salvation?   *1*

2
Reports and Documents About Abnormal Animal Behavior Before Earthquakes   *12*

3
Is There a Characteristic Behavior?   *66*

4
Signals From the Earth   *75*

5
The Sensitivity of Animals   *95*

6
Circumstantial Evidence for Charged Particles   *108*

7
Searching for the Causes of Electrostatic Phenomena   *122*

8
Earthquake Fogs   *132*

9
Earthquakes and Light Phenomena   *143*

10
Earthquake Sensitivity and Weather Sensitivity   *155*

11
Discoveries and Rediscoveries   *173*

12
Earthquakes in Scripture and History   *185*

13
Needless Deaths and a Lost Opportunity   *203*

14
The Response of Science   *207*

Tables   *219*

References   *239*

An earthquake laid the foundation for this book—a not especially remarkable earthquake when compared with some others. About 1,000 people lost their lives and around 100,000 lost their homes. These are relatively insignificant figures when one considers that in this century alone more than 1.5 million people have lost their lives through earthquakes. Possibly as many as 655,000 perished in the last great earthquake of Tangshan, China, and 700,000 more people died in only four other quakes. One earthquake report from medieval China shows just how violent the earth can become and helpless man is: The quake of 1556 that scourged Shansi province claimed 830,000 victims.

This one insignificant quake that struck the province of Friuli in northeastern Italy on May 6, 1976, acquired a special meaning for me for purely emotional reasons. A member of a native German-speaking minority, I had grown up in the rugged mountains in one of the small villages the quake reduced to ruins. My parents had continued to live there until that fateful night when they had to abandon the ancestral home. I had been working in South America at the time of the earthquake, and I immediately left for my native village to find out just how extensive the destruction had been.

To return to these places that held so many different memories for me and that were now ruins was depressing. But what left the most profound impression on me was meeting and talking with the people living there, most of them peasants, whom I had known since childhood. Driven from their farms, they were living in tents, hay sheds, and roughly built shelters in constant fear of additional tremors. The talks I had with them motivated me to carry out my study and to write this book. When they would describe to me the course of the catastrophe and their own fate, they would often bring the conversation around to a strange phenomenon they had observed that they thought might interest me since I was a scientist: Animals had acted very strangely before the earthquake. "If we had only understood them!" an old woman said to me, and her words kept going through my head.

I knew very little about the reasons for these mysterious phenomena myself. I had occasionally read brief reports of them in newspapers, and I also knew that the peasants of the earthquake-plagued Andes believed seriously that animals can predict earthquakes. They believe this so firmly that they keep birds expressly to be warned of a coming earthquake by their excited behavior. I may even have run into this phenomenon myself, by pure chance. Around the first part of January 1972 I had spent a terror-filled night in Managua, Nicaragua, which was shaken by about half a dozen medium to heavy quakes that kept sending people into the streets in panic. After midnight, when it had been quiet for an hour and a half, my friend and I went back to our hotel. Suddenly a dog's excited barking broke the stillness of the night. Barking loudly, the dog ran down the street toward our hotel (which was at an intersection) and then turned around and tore back up the street, still barking furiously. "Surely we are not going to get another earthquake," I said jokingly in an allusion to what I knew was a folk belief. Another quake struck, in fact, only 20 seconds after I had spoken.

After I had talked with the peasants of my native area, whom I trusted completely, the conviction grew in my mind that the unusual behavior of animals before an earthquake could be a genuine phenomenon. How does one explain to simple people why so much money and creative intellectual effort can be devoted to the exploration of the moon and the atomic nucleus when such basic needs as protecting people from nature's violence cannot be met—when, in fact, suggestions for it are not even taken seriously? It may be that not enough information about abnormal behavior of animals before earthquakes is available. But who has made a serious effort to carry out statistical analyses or experiments to confirm or to disprove this phenomenon?

Earthquake premonition by animals does not fit into the rational world of science, and as a phenomenon it has an added disadvantage in that it cannot be examined at will. It has become too hot to handle without ever having been seriously tested scientifically. It is considered to be an image conjured up by people looking back on a shattering experience. Any scientist interested in studying this problem would risk not only his reputation but also any chance of getting support. After I had talked with the people of my village it became clear to me that injustice had been committed here and that science had failed. I decided then to do something to change this, regardless of the consequences to myself. I have now redeemed this promise as my contribution to the victims of the earthquake.

I knew from the beginning that there would be only one way of luring scientists out of their reserve and of forcing them to take a position: I would have to produce such a solid piece of work about the abnormal behavior of animals before earthquakes that it could not simply be dismissed as speculation. To accomplish that I would not only have to amass a convincing number of reports about this phenomenon from many countries, but (more important) I would have to advance a hypothesis about its possible causes. Only with a scientific hypothesis that could give order to a multitude of observations would it be possible to test the reality behind earthquake folklore about animal behavior and to learn whether it springs from an actual geo-physical phenomenon. In my attempt to attract the interest of science to earthquake folklore I have taken the side of those simple, scientifically untrained people who have seen the warning signs, who have ex-perienced the earthquakes, and who have had to bear the tragic con-sequences.

Against the scientific rules that demand that basic observations of nature must be as precise and reliable as possible, I have adopted these people's faith in what can be seen and experienced so that I might be better able to defend their case. I do not expect a single observation made by some peasant in another century to be persuasive. What I do expect to be persuasive are the close agreements among observations made by many people from different cultures and oc-cupations and, above all, the deeper scientific meaning behind them that we are trying to find.

Acknowledgments

Too many people have contributed to this study, directly or indirectly, for me to list them all. Peasants and workers entrusted their experiences to me, collaborators in libraries and museums abetted my search for ancient documents with valuable hints, and scientists gave me information from their specialties. I hope that someday the treasure of buried knowledge they helped to unearth will redound to their own benefit.

Among the seismologists and geophysicists I am, above all, obliged to P. Molnar, W. Brace, and W. Lee for sponsoring my visits to earthquake research centers in the United States and for giving me access to information from the People's Republic of China.

Very special thanks are due to my parents, who helped me follow up and confirm reports of earthquake precursors in Friuli despite their tragic and psychologically difficult circumstances.

A valuable contribution was made by my wife, Christine, who patiently prepared the maps and helped me with the proofreading.

When the Snakes Awake

1

Animals as Earthquake Predictors: Superstition or Salvation?

A reunion in Friuli

For me the challenge and adventure of earthquakes began in a small town on the eastern flank of the Peruvian Andes. The front page of a newspaper I bought from a street vendor showed a village in the mountains that had been turned into a field of rubble by a quake. Search parties were digging for survivors. It was one of those great tragedies we tend to think happen only to strangers, but I quickly realized that I knew the site of the disaster very well. The village in which I had grown up and in which my parents still lived was only about 20 kilometers (12 1/2 miles) from the epicenter.

By the time I was driving homeward through the destroyed Friuli countryside, I knew that my parents had escaped with only a scare but that their old house was a broken-down ruin. As prepared as I was to see some depressing sights, I was still shaken when I finally got to look at the peasant village in which every stone had once been familiar. A dozen of the sixty-odd houses in the village had already been bulldozed flat, and the rest, gaping with cracks, had been braced temporarily and were in danger of collapse. The people who had lived in them were now living in army tents and in roughly built huts in the fields, and salvos of aftershocks were still shaking the countryside. The world these people had known had collapsed.

I had known many of the villagers since my early youth. Even though I had to look after the affairs of my family in the ensuing two weeks, I did get a chance to talk to most of them. As they told me of their experiences, life and color began coming into what at first had been an abstract calamity whose specific attributes were a 6.5 on the Richter scale and a time of 9 P.M. on May 6, 1976.

Eyewitness reports unmistakably drew the outlines of a phenomenon that is as old as the history of earthquakes and has just as long been enigmatic and controversial: the premonition of earthquakes by animals. Some peasants had been calming their cattle in the barn or checking to see why the dog was barking when the earthquake struck. Others remembered that cats had not appeared for their feeding on the evening of the quake. There had been no living tradition about earthquakes, because destructive earthquakes happen too far apart in time. Thus, the peasants had no preconceived notions about earthquakes. The animals had shown such vivid fright that the peasants later asked me, as a scientist, to explain why animals could recognize a coming earthquake.

Once I had gotten over my initial confusion and surprise over these reports of animal earthquake premonition (which I had never taken seriously) and looked at the tragedy around me, I decided to make a careful collection of these observations. I wanted to see whether they were consistent with one another and with analogous older reports. Most of the information about the behavior of animals before the earthquake was collected in my home village of San Leopoldo, formerly known as Leopoldskirchen. Other reports came from surrounding communities (Pontebba, Apua, Malbourgetto) and from the area of the epicenter.

For two days before the quake and two days afterward the weather had been sparklingly clear. Daytime temperatures had climbed to nearly 30°C (86°F). There had been no atmospheric disturbances. Other than the fact that it had been uncommonly warm and dry and oppressively close on the day of the great quake, people had noticed nothing out of the ordinary. The only thing worth mentioning had been the singular behavior of animals. Many peasants who had been working in the fields had noticed that the woods that cover the mountains down to the village of San Leopoldo had been surprisingly noisy. Again and again the rough-sounding call of the roe deer could be heard, a rarity at that time of the year. Late in the afternoon of the day of the earthquake, some witnesses were startled to see something they had never seen in this game-poor region: On the steep grassy slopes a few hundred meters above the village about fifteen roe deer were crowding together as tightly as they were able. A short distance away stood four red deer. One man who had watched the animals through binoculars had noticed that they had kept their heads down but had not been grazing. Usually, wild game would come down into the valley in herds only in the harshest winter or during the most severe thunderstorms.

Domestic animals, too, had changed their behavior that day without apparent reason. Chickens, who proverbially roost early, could not be persuaded to go into their coops. In some farmyards it took until 8 P.M., two hours past the usual time, to get them into the coops. One peasant, when asked what he had been doing shortly before the quake, said he had been chasing a recalcitrant rooster around the barnyard. On another farm, when the people rushed outside just as the great quake's minute of trembling started, they found the chickens already fluttering around all over the garden. They had evidently gotten out of the coop somehow before the quake had started.

At the time of the quake not a single cat was to be seen in the entire village, according to several people. These animals, otherwise numerous, had disappeared without a trace. Two to three days after the quake they returned, just as mysteriously. Several cats that could be depended on to show up at 7 P.M. for their evening meal had not shown up on the day of the quake. Two mostly wild cats that had been coming to an old woman's house at the same time every day to be fed before slipping back into the woods did show up, but seemed very nervous. They accepted no food, and they ran away from their benefactress.

A cat living at another farm had recently had kittens. On the day of the quake she had carried them from the attic and quartered them in the vegetable garden. A somewhat similar case was reported to me by a family in Ospedaletto, very near the epicenter. This family's two cats, which had been raising kittens, both carried their litters from the house into the garden just before the earthquake. When the man carried some of the kittens back inside to their nests, the anxious mother cat carried them back out again. One woman remembered that her cat had been trying to leave the house immediately before the earthquake hit. The cat kept jerking its ears, and ran nervously around the house.

Also noteworthy is the report that in a different community people living on a farm became quite irritated to see mice and rats running around freely while their five cats were nowhere to be found. The rodents had evidently left their hiding places after the cats had sought the great outdoors.

Two people living in a remote Alpine cottage noticed not only the repeated calling of roe deer but also the wailing of a wild cat.

Many peasants remembered their cattle kicking up a commotion. After they had been fed and watered, the animals began lowing and tearing at their chains for no apparent reason. This kind of behavior was reported to have started about 15–20 minutes before the quake.

The various witnesses agreed rather closely as to time. Some observers later thought they had noticed unusual behavior as much as an hour before the quake. One peasant, who rushed into the barn on hearing the commotion, found his six cows vigorously bellowing in concert and furiously flapping their ears and whipping their tails.

The unusual behavior of dogs, which was noticed abut 20 minutes before the earthquake, astounded many observers. An innkeeper told me that his two dogs had suddenly started to bark furiously in the yard and had pawed at doors and windows. When he tried to let them in, they refused to come, slunk back, and ran in circles howling. As soon as the door was closed again, they started pawing it desperately and jumped against it. The innkeeper tried again, but could not lure them into the house. While he was trying to calm his four-footed friends—it was a few minutes before the earthquake—he noticed that the fields and the woods were resounding with bird calls even though it was already dark. He was able to make out the call of the cuckoo clearly. When the earthquake struck, his dogs ran away in panic. One returned three days later and the other after five days.

Other dogs had behaved just as strangely, except that they had not run away. One bitch dragged her puppies out of the house into the open before the earthquake. One woman, whose dog had always slept in the house, could not lure the animal back in on the evening of the earthquake. A peasant woman who lived alone did manage to get her little dog to go into the house about 10 minutes before the quake, but he snarled and barked so much that she decided to take him for a walk despite the late hour. When the quake came, the dog was under the sofa, trembling and curled up into a ball. In another case, a dog that had been especially good-natured until then bit the boy he usually played with. This happened late in the afternoon of the earthquake.

Among other precursors of the approaching earthquake were the strange sounds made by yard fowl and wild birds and the timing of these sounds. On one farm the chickens set up such a shrieking just before the quake that the people thought a fox had gotten into the coop. They rushed out to the coop with sticks in their hands. Around midnight on May 8, about 2 hours before a particularly heavy aftershock, a man lying in his tent heard cocks crowing and another man was surprised to hear blackbirds calling at that time of night.

At least two people had noticed, independently of each other, that during the seemingly endless series of aftershocks their roosters would signal a shock regularly by making a sound which they rendered as "Krrr . . . Krrr . . . ." These are the same sounds a rooster makes to warn the flock of hens of an approaching hawk. One man seriously considered killing his rooster because he couldn't take much more — each time the bird gave forth its "Krrr" sound, the man without thinking would dash headlong out of the now rickety house.

Caged birds behaved in remarkable ways just before the earthquake. Owners of canaries in six houses in three different villages reported the same observation: About 10–15 minutes before the quake, the birds began jumping around and calling out. Then they would flap their wings energetically and fly around inside their cages. One observer reported that his birds kept flying up against the ceiling of the cage. One woman threw a blanket over the cage but was unable to quiet her birds. Of four birds in one cage only two survived the earthquake, and one bird died in another cage. The causes of their deaths remain a mystery. The birds may have succumbed to overexertion when they tried to fly.

One woman told me about a water container in the cage of her parakeet that she had usually filled daily. The bird drank from it and bathed in it, using up about half a container per day. On the afternoon of the earthquake, she noticed that the container was empty. It could not have been the heat, because her stone house stayed fairly cool. She refilled the tub only to find it empty again a little while later. Since the bird could not have drunk all that, it must have been bathing all the time. After the earthquake, the observant woman thought she could detect heavy water consumption on the part of her bird before each of the many aftershocks, and she used the water level as her private earthquake forecast.

The many aftershocks allowed the people in the earthquake zone to repeat certain observations, and they accumulated an astonishingly rich store of details in this manner. For example, a man who moved into his bee shed after his farm was destroyed noticed that the beehives were a lot noisier than usual just before a quake. Animals seemed to sense danger in the air as the many aftershocks continued weeks after the great earthquake. Chickens, for example, roosted later than normal, and cats came home only long enough to eat.

More than four months after the main earthquake in Friuli, a second destructive earthquake struck the area on September 15 at 11 A.M. With a force of 6.1 on the Richter scale, it was noticeably weaker than the first quake had been. When I checked around, I found markedly fewer recollections of excited animals than there had been before the big quake. This may, in part, have been due to the fact that at the time of the tremor many peasants were working in their fields, far from the domestic animals. Besides, the animals must have been used to the phenomena after the hundreds of aftershocks.

Apart from isolated reports of barking dogs and fleeing cats, two additional observations are worth mentioning. Two peasant women were talking between their houses when they noticed the noise made by a swarm of sparrows that were fluttering around one of the gables. One of the women remarked that she hoped this was not a sign of another impending earthquake. They had just changed the subject when the earth shook again. The other observation concerns the unusual behavior of swallows. Having left on their fall migration several days before, they returned to the village and their nests on the morning of September 15. About half an hour before the quake, they all flew away again—this time for good.

In view of this plethora of unusual observations of animals made by the peasants shortly before the catastrophic Friuli earthquake of May 6, 1976, the question naturally arises of why the peasants did not become wary and suspicious. The explanation is simple: Their own animals represented only a small segment of the total phenomenon, and the great herd of roe deer approaching the village was such a peaceful sight that the observers—even after the earthquake—did not make the connection with the earthquake (only I suspected that).

When a scientist comes up against a totally inexplicable, mysterious phenomenon, he is inclined to be cautious. If he is smart and concerned about his reputation, he will take no public position on it. But when the phenomenon is one on which life and death may depend, and when those enigmatic observations made under tragic circumstances are passed on to him by people whom he knows and trusts, then he cannot escape serious conflicts of conscience.

The prejudices of science

The sociologist of science Stephen Toulmin was of the opinion that in the development of scientific advances, much as in the development of species in the course of biological evolution, changes result from the selective propagation of variants. His colleague Thomas B. Kuhn also inclines to the view that the laws governing scientific progress are similar to those that govern natural selection. In any given historical situation, and within the available options, the fittest are selected. The question of whether that choice is the best that could have been made is not even asked.

Comparing scientific development with natural evolution is an attractive exercise. Science sometimes shows leaps of development that may be compared to mutations in biology; sometimes there is faulty evolution that leads into a blind alley, which compares to the extinction of overly specialized animal species; and sometimes there are independent rediscoveries of similar principles, a phenomenon that can be found in nature time and again. Just as animal species evolve almost explosively in a new and for them favorable direction when they suddenly discover a new range or niche, so science skillfully exploits every opportunity that a generous society or even such emergencies as wars or supply crises may offer.

These governing criteria should be kept in mind when the following questions are asked: Why did modern earthquake research, throughout its stormy development in the twentieth century, close itself to the rich oral tradition of earthquake predictions? Why did earthquake research stubbornly insist that the detailed reports of unusual animal behavior before earthquakes, of springs that turned muddy, of odd displays of light, and of other such phenomena were nothing but figments of the popular imagination, when they reappeared after every great disaster through hundreds and thousands of years? Why have many recognized earthquake researchers denied time and again and in a very unscientific manner that there is even the possibility of a measure of truth in these reports, without ever having seriously collected the relevant documents or scientifically analyzed the phenomena?

Many explanations could be advanced for why scientists tend to be reserved and reticent when faced with old folk wisdom. Since scientists are bound to know that earthquake survivors' recollections will be colored by the shock and suffering they went through, could it be that this condemns these recollections to be met by disbelief? However, it would seem that the many existing reports and assertions about mysterious earthquake signs that agree with one another deserve at least an earnest attempt at contradicting and weakening them. The suspicion that such prejudices of science cannot be blamed entirely on the difficulty involved in observing and studying these phenomena, but that these prejudices should rather be ascribed to complex criteria governing scientific circles and to "environmental influences" in the evolution of science, is confirmed by the remarkable example set by the collective earthquake watch in the People's Republic of China.[1-4]

China breaks the spell

In June 1974, China's National Earthquake Bureau issued a warning that a serious earthquake should be expected in Liaoning province in the next year or two. This prediction had been preceded by an investigation of four years. The investigators had carefully studied the 2,200-year earthquake history of the region, and their conclusion that geological changes were imminent was buttressed with precise seismological, geodetic, and geomagnetic measurements.

This warning had two immediate consequences: The scientific observation network was expanded (partly through the use of portable measuring stations), and the people were mobilized. The latter move had been the backbone of the national earthquake prediction program since 1966. With the guidance of experts, amateur groups were organized and trained in thousands of industrial plants, schools, animal breeding institutions, and agricultural communes. Their task was to recognize signs of imminent earthquakes and to pass them on to a central clearing house.

Comparatively few of these groups were charged with measuring physical data, such as periodic changes in electric ground currents, and these measurements were carried out under very simple conditions. Most of the more than 100,000 honorary observers were to watch for the mysterious portents that according to 3,000-year-old Chinese tradition were supposed to announce the coming of a catastrophic earthquake. The volunteers were constantly impressed with the importance of their task through flyers, lectures, personal instructions, school lessons, and radio broadcasts. Radio Tientsin, for example, broadcast the most vital information in the form of a dialog between Teacher Tung and young Red Guards,[5] according to which the most widespread and most noticeable sign of an approaching great earthquake is "unusual behavior" of animals. With the use of numerous examples it was explained how animals would become excited, how they would signal their fears loudly, and that they would leave their burrows or try to break out of their stables. Also, the inexplicable clouding up of well waters and the appearance in them of bubbles and vile smells, sudden rises or drops in the groundwater level, and changes in temperature or chemical composition of the water were to be taken seriously as earthquake precursors. In addition, it was said that lightning bolts out of clear skies should not be overlooked, nor should lightning bolts coming from the ground. The latter, it was said, would appear as stripes, columns, or fireballs colored mostly red or blue. Also, strange noises coming from the ground, faraway growling thunder, or noises resembling those made by a moving tractor or by a storm could point to an imminent earthquake.

The efforts that had gone into the training of these many observers bore fruit: In the middle of December 1974 unusual animal behavior was suddenly noticed in the Tantung area. Snakes came out of hibernation, crawled from their burrows, and froze to death on the snow-covered surface. Rats appeared in the open in large groups and were often so confused that they could be caught by hand. Cattle and fowl, too, were strangely excited. In the same area, and at the same time, the water in the springs became cloudy and frothy and the groundwater table changed.

A special session of the National Earthquake Bureau predicted that a small earthquake would happen north of where the big one was expected. It happened on December 22, 70 kilometers (45 miles) north of Haicheng. Immediately after this quake, preparations were made to evacuate and care for the people and to minimize property damage. Efforts to collect earthquake signs were intensified. Regular observation centers were set up at fowl-breeding stations, at ranches, and in those rural communes that had many animals. Throughout January 1975, reports of unusual animal behavior kept coming into the central bureaus. More than twenty species of animals, among them snakes, rats, chickens, dogs, cats, horses, deer, and tigers, were said to have been seized by fear. At the beginning of February the number of these reports suddenly climbed steeply. Increasingly it was the larger animals, such as cattle, horses, and pigs, that were panicking. Different animals expressed this differently. Geese flew into trees, dogs barked as if mad, pigs bit each other or dug beneath the fences of their sties, chickens refused to go into their coops, cattle tore their halters and ran away, and rats appeared and acted as if drunk. Even three well-trained police dogs acted beyond all recognition. They refused to obey their handlers, howled, and kept their noses close to the ground as if sniffing something out.[2]

Groundwater anomalies began spreading. The wells of the Tingchiakou production brigade became artesian wells. Gas bubbles appeared in the pond water of the Shiaotze River Commune. The ice broke and water squirted up as if from a fountain. Dozens of other wells turned cloudy, foamed, and showed distinct changes in water quality.

A series of small earthquakes were detected in the first days of February. Their numbers rose quickly at first, but then gradually decreased through the fourth of the month. By then everything was ready. By 10 A.M. on February 4, there was no doubt in the minds of the experts that a big earthquake was imminent in the Haicheng area. By 2 P.M. evacuation was well underway. People were housed in previously prepared emergency shelters, animals were led from their stables, motor vehicles were parked away from buildings, and valuables were removed from the buildings. To entertain the evacuated people and to keep their spirits high, movies were shown outdoors.

At 7:36 P.M. the anticipated earthquake finally came. It reached an intensity of 7.3 on the Richter scale. Worst hit was the area around the epicenter near Haicheng, where about half a million people lived. At least 50 percent of the buildings were either destroyed or severely damaged. Without timely evacuation, tens of thousands might have died. As it was, there were few victims. Most of those were people who had put too little faith in official earthquake predictions to put up with February temperatures outdoors. Some stubborn individuals were moved out of their houses and into the safe outdoors by force, official reports have revealed.

After the successful prediction of the Haicheng earthquake, a number of foreign commissions of experts tried to analyze the scientific reasons for this remarkable achievement. The most detailed examination has been that presented by the ten-member Liaoning Earthquake Study Delegation from the United States.[2] It was impossible in the aftermath to reconstruct the precise scientific logic of short-term earthquake prediction, but since long-term earthquake prediction cannot be applied to short-term prediction, and since the results of other geophysical measurements hardly suggested clearly identifiable processes that could be useful scientific earthquake predictors, only three phenomena remain as reasonable choices: the dramatic rise in the number of cases of abnormal animal behavior, the distinct changes in the groundwater level, and a swarm of small earthquakes that preceded the main event (a swarm whose greatest density was detected on the morning of the day of the earthquake). The preshocks alone could not have justified sounding an earthquake alarm, since they were indistinguishable from ordinary small quakes which often appear in swarms. Consequently, the many reports of observed anomalies in animal behavior and in wells must have played a big role in the final decision. Some Western scientists did not exclude altogether the possibility that the dramatic rise in reports of abnormal animal behavior and changed water levels in wells just before the Haicheng earthquake had been a manifestation of mass psychology without foundation in reality, but if that is the case the whole successful prediction of the severe earthquake remains a riddle.

In their discussions with foreign seismologists and in their scientific papers in Chinese journals, Chinese earthquake researchers leave no doubt that they believe in the phenomenon of anomalous animal behavior before earthquakes, even though they admit that they do not understand it. An elderly Chinese seismologist told the American seismologist Clarence C. Allen of the California Institute of Technology that observation of animal behavior is "the best method for earthquake prediction thus far." This opinion is reflected in the amount of space devoted to this phenomenon in Chinese earthquake literature. To understand its enigmatic manifestations better, I shall try in the following pages to trace it back into the remotest corners of the earth and into the early history of man.

2

Reports and Documents About Abnormal Animal Behavior Before Earthquakes

Europe

In Europe the knowledge that animals can perceive coming disasters before humans can goes back at least as far as recorded history. How else can we account for the geese that were kept at the Capitol in ancient Rome to announce approaching danger with their honking? Why did the ancients believe in the ability of sacred birds to divine the future? As early as 469 B.C. a rabbit was mentioned as having had a premonition in connection with an earthquake in Sparta.[6]

The first precise description of animal behavior before an earthquake dates from 373 B.C. and concerns the city of Helice in Achaia, the region of ancient Greece bordering the Gulf of Corinth. Helice was destroyed that year by an especially violent earthquake, sank into the ground in the course of the geological upheavals, and was swallowed forever by the sea. Five days before this thriving city sank from sight, reports the Greek historian Diodorus [Diodorus Siculus (fl. first century B.C.), a historian whose works are partly based on authors now lost— Tr.], all animals that had been in it, such as rats, snakes, weasels, centipedes, worms, and beetles, migrated in droves along the connecting road toward the city of Koria[7] the inhabitants of Helice were said to have been much puzzled. This episode (which has the best possible historic documentation) would later provoke condescending smiles. But did Diodorus really invent the story? What reason would he have had for doing that? Or did reports of the flight of the animals from the port city actually reach him?

Pliny the Elder, the Roman writer and scientist who at the eruption of Mount Vesuvius in 79 A.D. paid for his scientific curiosity with his life, describes four signs of a coming earthquake in section 83 of the second book of his Natural History.[8a] One of the signs has to do with excited animals: "Even the birds do not remain sitting fearlessly." Though Pliny divulges no further details, this piece of testimony confirms that the phenomenon of unusual animal behavior was known to ancient Rome.

Documents of the period from the decline of the Roman empire until the Middle Ages in Europe are scarce, and it would require a great deal of patience to search through these writings for anything about animal behavior before earthquakes. These documents are dispersed over many libraries and are often hard to read. Still, such descriptions can be found, even if they do occasionally contain a strong admixture of superstition. Here, for example, is a report out of Württemberg from the year 1095: "Fearful souls saw in the heavens all manner of wonderful signs, such as bloody clouds, burning torches, a great flaming sword, battling armies, and besieged cities. In many cases the fowl left human habitations to go and live wild in the woods and mountains."

Alongside episodes intermingled with superstition and fantasy, older European earthquake reports contain persuasive examples of animal earthquake premonition. In the city museum of Villach (in Carinthia) hangs a painting that, while not remarkable as a work of art, is remarkable for another reason. It depicts a dog that evidently was being idolized and into whose face the painter seems to have tried to paint every possible noble quality. The painting is an act of recognition and gratitude for the dog that saved the lord of the castle and his two sons from certain death in an earthquake by its unusual behavior. The date was December 4, 1690. The *Mährenberger Chronik* (a local chronicle) divulges the following details, which I repeat here in their entirety because they give a memorable sketch of how brutally a quake affects human lives:

At Schneegg, Neutreffen, in the castle of Lord Grotta von Grotteneck, the calamity happened in such a way that those who were present and were saved were able to describe it as eyewitnesses. Sitting by the stove was the elderly lady, Eva Rosina von Grotteneck, born Freelady von Aichlburg, who had sent her eldest daughter Sidonia to fetch something from a chamber. Lady Grotta's nurse was keeping the smallest child quiet in the cradle, while the young lady herself happened to be in the administrative building. The whining of the dog, which belonged to the elder lady, had attracted the two sons, Seifried and Franz, to the window niche. When the two looked down from the window to see what was going on, floor and ceiling collapsed with such force that the two sons of Lord Grotta were only able to hear the old lady cry out "Jesus, Mary." The old woman, together with the nurse and the child, were crushed by the falling rubble and buried by the debris. Miss Sidonia, who had been on the stairs on her way back, dropped into the depths along with the stairs, but she was saved. Also, the two brothers, in danger in the window niche, were able to save their lives without injury. Eleven persons and as many horses lost their lives through this calamity.[9]

This account of the disaster offers no further details on what that whining dog had been doing down below, but other reports offer greater detail. They are summarized by Joseph Wagner in the *Album for Carinthia* for the year 1845:

On December 4, 1690, at quarter to four in the afternoon, an earthquake moved the broad region between Venice and Prague. . . . At that moment the Lord of Grotteneck was standing on the ground floor of the new castle at Treffen. Suddenly his loyal dog whined and jumped against the barred window as if he wanted to break through it. The lord, alerted by the carrying-on of the dog and suspecting that the cause for it was outside, opened the window and looked out while holding onto the window bars. Suddenly it raged below and above him, floors and rooms collapsed and only he and the dog, covered by the window arch, found safety; but, alas, the spouse, children, everything living, was buried in the rubble. In the castle at Treffen the portrait of the dog is still being preserved. On its collar one can read the letters A.S.B.G. (probably Adam Siegfried Baron v. Grotteneck).

The earthquake of 1690 had been the strongest in Carinthia since the one of 1348, which had brought the Dobratsch peak of the Villach Alp crashing down. The city parish church in Klagenfurt was turned into a tangled ruin, and in Villach many dwellings were damaged and many people killed.

While searching for more reports of abnormal animal behavior in old European literature, I thought it might be worthwhile to leaf through the works of the great French natural scientist Georges-Luis Leclerce de Buffon (fl. eighteenth century). In his *Histoire de la Terre* (published in 1749) there is indeed an interesting piece of information about earthquakes and animals.[10] Buffon refers to Le Gentil and his work *Voyage autour du monde* (voyage around the world), and quotes him in these words: "I have . . . already made several observations about earthquakes. The first sign is that half an hour before the earth moves all animals are seized with terror; horses whinny, tear their halters, and flee from their stalls; dogs bark; birds are terrified; rats and mice come out of their holes, etc."

The strongest earthquake to shake Europe in the last few centuries happened in 1755 in Lisbon. It was so powerful that as far away as

Sweden the bells were rung by the earth's motion, and its effects were felt in large parts of Africa and as far away as the Americas. In this catastrophe, too, there are reports of unusual animal behavior. Some can be found in the writing that the German philosopher Immanuel Kant devoted to this shocking event. In a very general way he summarized the contemporary store of experience with noticeable earthquake signs: "The cause of earthquakes seems to spread its effect even into the surrounding air. An hour earlier, before the earth is being shaken, one may perceive a red sky and other signs of an altered composition of the air. Animals are taken with fright shortly before it. Birds flee into houses, rats and mice crawl out of their holes. . . ."[11a] Concerning particularly the Lisbon earthquake, Kant has this to report: "Eight days before the tremor the ground near Cadiz (south of Lisbon on the Atlantic coast) was covered with a multitude of worms that had crawled out of the ground. They had been driven forth by the ostensible cause (mists expelled by the earth). In the case of some other earthquakes the harbingers had been vigorous lightning bolts in the air and apprehension observed among animals."[11b] Other reports about the Lisbon earthquake purport that, 20–30 hours before, the cattle had been highly excited and irritability and restlessness had been spreading among people.[12,13]

The next European earthquake from which documents about unusual animal behavior are available happened in 1771. Here we are actually dealing with a long series of quakes that shook the Alba region in Liguria. In January and February 175 earthquakes were counted. We have a report about effects on humans and animals: "Before the tremors, the animals were highly excited, and after the strongest ones some persons perceived a hissing and ringing in their ears, as well as anxiety and fatigue."[14]

A memorable account of the earthquake fear of animals was written by Deodat de Dolomieu, who was reporting some observations about an earthquake in 1783 in Calabria: "The warning by animals of the approach of earthquakes is a singular phenomenon and ought to surprise us the more because we do not know through what senses they perceive it. All species sense it, especially dogs, geese, and chickens. The howling of dogs in the streets of Messina was so loud that an order was issued to kill them."[15] Another account, probably based on different sources, describes the same gruesome episode: "In Messina, 1783, [the dogs'] howling became so unbearable that they were killed. They continue to howl even when there are no more shocks."[16]

Another memorable story of animal behavior, in the great Neapolitan earthquake of 1805, was published in a nineteenth-century periodical as a letter from an Italian correspondent and quoted in Wittich's dissertation "*Curiosities of Physical Geography*":

I must not omit in this place to mention those prognostics which were derived from animals. They were observed in every place where the shocks were such as to be generally perceptible. Some minutes before they were felt, the oxen and cows began to bellow, the sheep and goats bleated, and, rushing in confusion one or the other, tried to break the wicker-work of the folds; the dogs howled terribly, the geese and fowl were alarmed and made much noise; the horses which were fastened in their stalls were greatly agitated, leaped up, and tried to break the halters with which they were attached to the mangers; those which were proceeding on the roads suddenly stopped, and snorted in a very strange way. The cats were frightened, and tried to conceal themselves, or their hair bristled up wildly. Rabbits and moles were seen to leave their holes; birds rose, as if scared, from the places on which they had alighted; and fish left the bottom of the sea and approached the shores, where at some places great numbers of them were taken. Even ants and reptiles abandoned, in clear daylight, their subterranean holes in great disorder, many hours before the shocks were felt.

Large flights of locusts were seen creeping through the streets of Naples toward the sea the night before the earthquake. Winged ants took refuge during the darkness in the rooms of the houses. Some dogs, a few minutes before the first shock took place, awoke their sleeping masters by barking and pulling them, as if they wished to warn them of the impending danger, and several persons were thus enabled to save themselves.[17]

What is remarkable about this account is that behavior patterns are reported—with perfect assurance and as if it were a matter of course— for a great variety of animals that are the same ones later mentioned in Chinese information brochures. The behavior patterns, though they differ from species to species, are characteristic of the behaviors the Chinese brochures give for each animal family. Another reporter, named Poli, observed essentially the same phenomenon.[16] He reports that several minutes before the first perceptible shocks came, in places where the shocks would turn out to be the strongest, cattle roared and braced their forelegs on the ground, sheep bleated and tried to break out of their pens, fowl were making loud agitated noises, and on several occasions dogs awakened their masters.

The thread of the European experience with the phenomenon of earthquake premonition by animals (and people) was picked up again in 1808 when a wave of earthquakes shook the Italian province of

Piedmont. According to earthquake researcher Bossi, nervous people were seized by an inexplicable restlessness, a sort of trembling and racing of the heart, some time before the tremors.[14,18] He reports: "The inhabitants often had been alerted 10 minutes before the tremor by animals. Dogs, cats, sheep, and goats gave no particularly distinct signs. Horses seemed more sensitive; a few minutes before the earth shocks, they showed restlessness, became excited, and threw themselves down. They kicked and stamped their feet. Even birds reacted with extreme excitement to the earth tremors and flew in an unsteady manner."

The next report about the earthquake sense of animals is short, but is describes the phenomenon unmistakably. This document concerns the Ligurian earthquake of May 26, 1831, and contains this information: "Shortly before the earthquake the general restlessness of fowl, cats, mules, etc., was noticed."[14]

In his book *The Great Neapolitan Earthquake* (London, 1862), Mallet reports some interesting observations made about the southern Italian earthquake disaster of 1851: "On August 14, 1851, it was the donkeys who first announced through frequent and loud braying that an earthquake was imminent. . . . A dear friend of mine told me that animals in general, but pigs in particular (a peculiarity also noted by some people in Potenza) exhibited signs of depression and uneasiness ten days before an earthquake. There were three pigs in a pen near the monastery kitchen. After the evening meal, hearing some unusual grunting, he went out to see what was happening and found them furiously excited and biting each other like dogs." (ref. 19; also quoted in ref. 20) This very phenomenon was observed on February 2, 1975, two days before the great Haicheng earthquake in China, and was correctly interpreted then as a sign of an impending earthquake. About a dozen young pigs, fighting in their sty, bit each other's tails off.[21]

The most reliable and complete reports of abnormal animal behavior in Europe's earthquake history come from the Italian researcher and earthquake pioneer Giuseppe Mercalli. He was professor of vulcanology and seismology at the University of Naples at the turn of the century and at the time of his death in 1914 he had been director of the Vesuvian Observatory. Before the end of the nineteenth century this scholar had studied numerous Italian and other European earthquakes, had written several books on the subject, and had given his name to an earthquake scale (still in use) that relies on subjective impressions and the extent of damage. Mercalli belonged to an earlier generation of seismologists who could not rely on automatic recording instruments and whose ideas about the processes within the earth were still far from clear. Whenever an earthquake happened, he and his colleagues, attentively and with open minds, would go around the countryside asking questions. With painstaking attention to detail they collected observations about the warning signs, the progress, and the results of the catastrophe. They supplemented their personal inquiries with questionnaires sent to the mayors of all communities affected by earthquakes, to railroad station masters, and to heads of weather stations. After the Ligurian earthquake of 1887 alone they evaluated 1,000 questionnaires. That Mercalli was very shrewd about where to obtain the best information is shown by the many reports of village priests he quotes. Hoping to learn from seemingly unimportant or inexplicable phenomena, the researchers recorded not only reports of earth movements, earth noises, light displays, or earthquake damages, but also those of abnormal animal behavior.

The largest collection of reports about the reaction of animals can be found in "The Ligurian Earthquake of February 23, 1887," which Mercalli wrote with his collaborator T. Taramelli.[22] This report contains, under the heading "Physiological Phenomena in Animals," the following information: "In more than 130 localities, as far as it is known to us, a condition of unrest and fear among domestic animals was noted which expressed itself in unusual cries, restlessness, flying by fowl, attempts to flee into the open, etc., generally a few minutes before the earthquake. These phenomena were observed in the following localities, which we have ordered by provinces. . . ." The 130 places are then listed. The animals, mostly yard fowl, dogs, cats, horses, donkeys, cattle, and birds, are named in parentheses. Special reports about the time that the restlessness began and how it was observed are given for only about two dozen places. The rest are apparently covered by the phrase "a few minutes before the earthquake" in the introduction. Among the two dozen detailed reports are five that mention expressly that the paniclike reactions of the animals were observed only a few seconds before the earthquake. The remaining detailed reports document animal behavior that began a considerable time before the quake or describe especially remarkable incidents. Following are some examples of the latter. (It should be borne in mind that the quake happened on February 23 at 6:20 A.M.)

On some farms in Carru, on the evening of the 22nd, about 12 hours before the quake, it had been impossible to drive the chickens into their coops. This refusal of fowl to go to their sleeping places continued through the 23rd and the 24th, after the main earthquake.

From Rivoli came reports that chickens had acted extraordinarily scared since the day before the earthquake.

In Alfiano Natta abnormal behavior by cattle was noticed as early as the evening before the earthquake. From San Marzanotto came the report that dogs had been barking without letup since several hours before midnight, which would mean 8–9 hours before the earthquake. In Savona dogs, donkeys, and roosters barked, brayed, and crowed without letup throughout the night from the 22nd to the 23rd. In Mondovi, too, animals exhibited abnormal behavior throughout the night of the 22nd to the 23rd. In Lucianasco people had noticed 10 minutes before the earthquake that birds were becoming excited, and in Pietrabruno the same observation was made 30 minutes before the quake. From San Maurizio Canavese came a report that a parrot that usually slept in a net hung from a beam was found at 3 A.M. sitting in a ring hanging from a wire. Professor Guasti of Florence told how on the morning of the 23rd his parrot beat its wings so vigorously just before the earthquake that the commotion woke the professor. The parrot seemed highly agitated, but did not make a sound. When Guasti invited the bird to perch on his finger, which it usually liked to do, the parrot refused, flipped over, and dangled upside down on the chain. The professor thought his parrot was sick.

The horses of a mail coach traveling on the road from Ceva to Ormea stopped suddenly and the driver was unable to get them going again. While he was trying to get the horses to continue, the earthquake struck. In Camale, the woman who owned the hotel heard some unusual noises from the horses while she was in her bedroom. She opened the window and called out to the stablehand to see what was the matter. As she was closing the window, she felt the quake.

In Bordighera some horses tore their bridles and escaped. In San Stefano di Mare various kinds of animals tried to escape from the stables. In Serravalle Scrivia a peacock screeched loudly and continuously starting a few minutes before the quake. In Pieve d'Asti chickens flew the coop before the earthquake, and in Costigliole d'Asti and Villastellone they broke windows trying to escape. In Aramengo dogs howled piteously. In Vado the frogs would stop their croaking a few seconds before each tremor as if on signal and resume it a few minutes later.

The report of Mercalli's and Taramelli's investigation also contains two eyewitness accounts from France. A dog in Nice had howled throughout the night of the 22nd to the 23rd without letup, and a man in Villefranche observed some unusual excitement among birds that same night.

To get a good overview of the reports of unusual animal behavior in the Ligurian earthquake zone, I have entered information gathered by Taramelli and Mercalli onto a map (figure 1). I was able to find only about 80 percent of the localities named. Those communities in which the phenomenon appeared hours before the quake are marked with distinguishing symbols.

Mercalli's work on the later earthquake in Calabria on November 16, 1894, has fewer reports of animal anomalies.[23] Still, there is this: "The priest of Riviconi says that in the nights preceding the earthquake the dogs barked and howled. The priest of Polistena wrote to me: 'With the following tremors we observed that horses were predicting them a long time in advance by kicking and with signs of agitation.'" Interestingly, an animal anomaly was observed before a short tremor that preceded the main quake by about 35 minutes. Mercalli noted: "A woman from Barnara told me that she first heard a goat bleating persistently and then felt a shock which came from below and was very short." The remaining reports are without time notations and refer generally to the earthquake night of November 16, which saw many aftershocks. The reports show to what extent animals' nerves are strained in an earthquake disaster. Birds became so excited that they broke out of their cages and fled, swarms of thrushes and other small birds were seen migrating, and geese and ducks sought the outdoors. Dogs started to make noise before aftershocks. They ran away when the tremors started, and afterwards they would bark as persistently as if they were trying to corner an invisible thief.

The chain of reports of unusual animal reactions before earthquakes does not break in the twentieth century.

One day in 1910 in Landsberg, Bavaria, all the bees left their hives at 9:30 A.M. and buzzed around in great excitement.[20,24] The beekeepers did not know what to make of this, and barely noticed the weak quake that happened between 9:32 and 9:36, according to the records of the earthquake observatory in Munich. It took 15 minutes for the bees to calm down enough to return to their hives.

In 1932 the inhabitants of the western Greek islands of Cephalonia, Zakinthos, and Ithaca were roused from their sleep by a chain of strange events. The village dogs suddenly ran out into the streets and began to howl. Cats and goats, too, left their houses and stalls and ran off in panic. These signs turned out to be precursors of a short, intense quake that shook the earth a few hours later and brought many houses crashing down.[25] The earthquake of Sofadhes, Greece, which happened on April 30, 1954, was also predicted by frightened

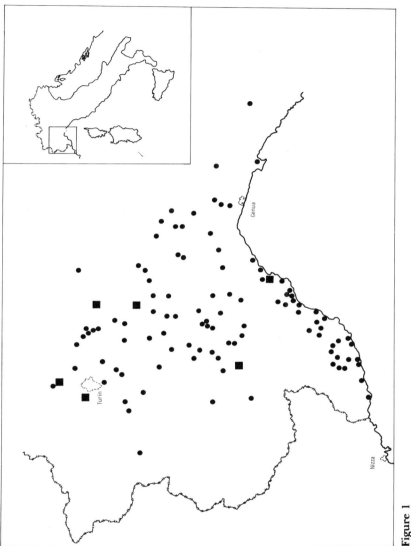

Figure 1

Map showing some of the communities in Liguria where the earthquake researchers Taramelli and Mercalli collected detailed reports about unusual animal behavior after the quake of 1887. Such behavior usually precedes a quake by several minutes, but in many cases it was reported to have occurred 3–12 hours before (the places of such occurrences are marked with squares).

animals. About half an hour before the disaster, storks began to fly around and seemed very excited.[26] Many villagers, who may have known of the possible meaning of this behavior from old traditions, sensed a disaster and took the precaution of moving into the open, where they survived the earthquake without injuries.

The eyewitness observations from Friuli mentioned in chapter 1 are not the only ones documented for the earthquake of May 6, 1976. Similar reports, recognized as genuine by other interested and scientifically qualified collectors, were obtained from other parts of the earthquake zone. There were, for example, numerous reports of anomalous animal behavior in southern Carinthia, where the damage caused by the Friuli earthquake was minor. These reports inspired Robert Samonig, a natural-history teacher and lecturer at the Academy in Klagenfurt, to organize a popular movement similar to the one in China whose aim would be to predict earthquakes through animal observations.[27]

In Friuli itself, extensive inquiries into earthquake premonition by animals were conducted by Giorgio Matteucig, a professor of zoology at the University of Naples. I visited him in Naples to compare experiences. Because his family came from the earthquake-ravaged Natisone valley in Friuli, Matteucig, too, had personal motives for making the effort. He did not let the skepticism of his colleagues sway him, he was ready to believe the reports of mysterious observations made by simple people whom he knew, and he was happy to put his training at the disposal of the inquiry. He paid out of his own pocket for the thousands of questionnaires he distributed in the villages of Fruili. The effort shows in the richness of the reports that he collected, parts of which were published in Italian newspapers.[28,29]

Some of the examples of unusual animal behavior collected by Matteucig follow: Before the earthquake of May 6, a peasant near Pizano noticed a swarm of fireflies on the right bank of the Tagliamento river, flying just barely above the surface. Near Cividale on the morning of May 6, the bulls at a breeding farm suddenly stopped their mating activities, and it took much effort to calm the excited animals down. Some bulls tore their nose rings out. The watchman at the fortress of Osoppo, Valentino de Cecco, said that a peacock kept near the kitchen had been showing signs of nervousness and restlessness at nightfall as early as three days before the quake. A peacock in the Via Ampezzo in Udine had to be taken away because the neighbors protested; it would shriek at the approach of each tremor until the nerves of the abutters were thoroughly frazzled. Reports of excited dogs, cats, donkeys, horses, chickens, and swine that tried to flee from their shelters

were numerous. Many dogs began barking shortly before the earthquake, and some residents of Gemona, in the epicenter, reported that
their lives had been saved only because they had been chasing dogs
who had broken their chains justs before the earthquake. Some people
noticed many snakes, and others saw worms crawling on the surface.
Even moles did not seem to feel comfortable under the ground. On
the day of the earthquake, they did not throw up any hills but burrowed
along just below the surface in rows of tunnels. One informant remembered that trout were swimming around very excitedly before
the earthquake, and another was astonished to see herds of roe deer
in unusual places. Many people noticed the bawling of the roe deer
in the woods, or heard songbirds singing at night. Some vintners in
Rocca Bernarda and in the Natisone valley noticed that two or three
days before the earthquake there was an unusual clouding of wine in
barrels, which normally would have indicated renewed fermentation.

These reports from the Old World show that valuable experience
about earthquake premonition by animals has been accumulating for
two millenia. Why has this knowledge, bought with such great sacrifices,
remained untouched — indeed, rejected and smiled at? Have other
cultures had similar experiences with these phenomena?

China

It was not so much the successful prediction of the great Haicheng
earthquake of February 4, 1975, which bordered on the miraculous,
that attracted the attention of the world; it was more the news that
observations of animal behavior had been one of the most important
methods. This event brought into public view a phenomenon that had
long been ridiculed as superstition and fantasy in Western countries,
despite the occasional anecdotes in the press after catastrophic quakes.

Could animals really sense the coming of an earthquake, that proverbially unpredictable and incalculable display of nature's violence?
Or were these positive reactions merely a product of the imagination
of people who had first been alerted by other earthquake precursors?
The next earthquake in China seemed to prove the skeptics right. On
July 28, 1976, a catastrophic earthquake struck the Tangshan area
without warning. Even though geologists had been predicting that a
severe earthquake would occur in that area within two years, they
were unable to alert the population in time. Human losses were great;
the number of 655,000 dead has been mentioned.[30] Did the animals'
senses fail, or was it a failure of human organization? Did the earthquake
give off warning signals but with too little time, or were the signals

obliterated by unfavorable weather? Too few eyewitness reports have found their way out of China into the West to provide us with possible answers to these questions. Also, little is known about what it is that underlies the sixth sense of animals, except for some suppositions. At least one report—from the news agency ANSA—did mention animals in connection with the severe earthquake of Tangshan.[31] According to that report, many Chinese had been wide awake when the earthquake struck. They had been roused several minutes earlier by the loud barking of dogs. It had been 3:43 on a rainy, windy morning. Who pays attention to the behavior of animals at such a time of day, especially in a city of a million people?

Since the destructive 1966 earthquake in Hsingtai, the Chinese authorities have made great efforts to develop methods of predicting earthquakes. In their search for a key alarm, they unearthed the ancient Chinese lore about animals changing their behavior before earthquakes, sometimes drastically. The knowledge of this strange manifestation is not only rooted in the traditional Chinese folklore, but surfaces again and again in the context of documentations of earlier earthquakes from the chronicles of dynasties going back 3,000 years. The chroniclers thought it worthwhile to inform posterity that before earthquakes "creatures on land and in the water showed unusual behavior."

In the opinion of Chinese experts, frequent mention of abnormal animal behavior in connection with earthquakes is not necessarily valuable from a scientific point of view, because the classical style of Chinese writing is terse and succinct to the point where it is sometimes difficult to tell whether the anomalies happened before or during an earthquake. There are, however, many unmistakable proofs that for centuries the Chinese people had been using abnormal animal behavior—besides other phenomena—to prepare for impending earthquakes. One example is a report about the great earthquake of 1739 in the Yinchuan-Pingluo area of Ningsia province, which reached intensity 8 and was followed by a series of smaller quakes that went on for years: "There were every year smaller earthquakes [compared with intensity 8] in Ningsia and people got used to them. Generally, there were more earthquakes in spring and winter. When the water in the wells suddenly became murky, when there were noises like cannon shots that were protracted and indistinct, and when dogs barked in unison, then [the people] prepared without delay for this [earthquake] plague. . . ."[32]

The documents of the dynasties comprise about 35 million words. They have been evaluated for material pertaining to earthquakes, and the most important data have been collected in the *Chronological Tables of the Earthquake Data of China*, published in two volumes making up 1,653 pages by the Seismological Committee of the Academia Sinica.[33] These volumes contain documents on about 1,000 destructive earthquakes in China. Modern Chinese earthquake experts often admit that they do not understand why the animals react abnormally, but they insist that the phenomenon is real and that the skillful organization of an observation and alarm system based on it will lead to successful earthquake predictions. The conditions in China are very favorable to the observation of animal behavior; more than 80 percent of the people live in agricultural communities in close proximity to domestic animals whose habits they know well.

As the following reports from China show, the belief that this phenomenon could serve to predict earthquakes is fully justified. It is possible to point to at least ten earthquakes in this century that, according to Chinese records, were unquestionably heralded by abnormal animal behavior. In at least four of these the reasons for the abnormal behavior of animals were recognized before the earthquakes occurred. At least, that is what emerges from written Chinese sources available for analysis.

The cases in point are articles in two Chinese scientific journals, *Acta Geophysica Sinica*[37] and *Scientia Geologica Sinica*.[1,34] Also, there are excerpts from the *Chronological Tables of Earthquake Data of China*;[33] a report from the *Proceedings of the Lectures by the Seismological Delegation of the People's Republic of China*, which was published in Japan;[3] an illustrated brochure about observing animal behavior to predict earthquakes, published by the Seismological Office of Tientsin;[35] the book *Earthquake Questions and Answers*,[21] written for the general public and published by the Geological Bureau of Peking; a Chinese report about forecasting the Haicheng earthquake;[4] and a book by a Chinese expert on earthquake forecasting.[36]

The following selections from Chinese reports of unusual animal behavior before earthquakes give a good view of the nature of the observed phenomenon and the quality of the documentation.

Page 1343 of the *Chronological Tables of Earthquake Data of China*[33] contains the following entry about the Daguan earthquake in Yunnan province, which happened on July 31, 1917, and had an intensity of 6.5: "One month before the earthquake, fish in Daguan floated to the surface. Several days before the earthquake, the water level in the river rose greatly and thousands of fish jumped to shore." Animals are also mentioned in an analysis of the earthquake of Haiyuan (in Ningsia Hui province), which unleashed a force of 8.5 and took the lives of 200,000 people. This report, too, is kept brief: "In addition, there were also anomalous reactions of animals before the 1920 great earthquake, especially cattle, dogs, wolves, and chickens. The reason for animal anomalies before large earthquakes may be due to stimulations of (1) high frequency vibrations before the earthquake, (2) electric and magnetic phenomena immediately prior to the earthquake, and (3) changes in shape of ground and certain special gases escaping from the soil."[37] There is also this interesting but brief report about the earthquake of Xingtai in Hopeh province on March 8, 1966: " . . .3 to 5 days before the March 8, 1966 Xingtai earthquake in China many rats ran away from grain storages and peasant houses and disappeared even though the ground was covered with snow."[36]

Many examples of unusual animal behavior have been reported in connection with the earthquake that struck the Bay of Bohai on July 18, 1969. Here the efforts to mobilize the broad mass of the people to recognize earthquake precursors apparently bore their first fruits. The earthquake manual of the Geological Bureau of Peking says: "When people used precursory animal anomalies to predict earthquakes, they attained better results. For example, two hours before the July 18, 1969, Bohai earthquake of magnitude 7.4, keepers in the Tientsin Zoo accurately predicted this earthquake based on several animal anomalies."[21] An illustrated brochure issued by the Seismological Office of Tientsin[35] explains which anomalies are meant. Under the heading "People's Zoo in Tientsin," and under the subheading "Actual example of using animals to predict earthquakes" it says: "Since 1968, workers in the People's Zoo of Tientsin have participated in earthquake prediction work. In the morning of July 18, 1969, they discovered several animal anomalies; they took notice and held joint discussions. They believed that these animal anomalies might be precursory phenomena before earthquakes, and were not due to other causes. They reported immediately to the Seismological Office of Tientsin. At noon of the same day a magnitude 7.4 earthquake occurred in Bohai (Gulf of Chihli)." The animals whose unusual conduct tripped the alarm are pictured in the brochure. Under the photo of a tiger it says "A northeastern tiger had low spirits, lay on the ground and did not want to get up." Next to the picture of a panda is this caption: "A giant panda did not want to go to the playground to play. Holding its head with its forearms, it screamed strangely." Over a picture that shows fish (loaches), leeches, and turtles is the legend "Loaches, leeches, and turtles suddenly swam up and down and rolled over continuously." Next to the picture showing a yak we read the following: "A Tibetan yak did not eat grass. Contrary to usual behavior, it rolled over and over." Beside a picture of swans is this comment: "Water-loving swans stayed on land far away from the shore, pointed their feet towards the sky, and refused to enter water."

And then there is this report concerning the earthquake of January 5, 1970, in Yuxi, in Yunnan province: "Before the . . . (Yuxi) earthquake, although it was not the growing season for fish, many peasants discovered that groups of fish migrated from deeper water regions to shallower water near the shore with many floating on the surface and jumping continuously. In the epicentral region and vicinity, many loaches and eels occasionally came out of the mud bottom."[36]

Even a relatively mild quake, a tremor of intensity 4.9 that happened on May 25, 1970, in Tangshan, was announced by abnormal animal behavior. The observations made there are described as the second example of a successful earthquake prediction in the Tientsin brochure. Above a picture showing a peasant trying to calm a pair of prancing horses it says: "On May 24, 1970, an animal keeper at a certain production brigade in the Tangshan area discovered that livestock refused to enter barns or eat grass. He remembered that a similar phenomenon occurred a year earlier before the Bohai earthquake. He reported immediately to his brigade leader that there would be an earthquake. Subsequently a magnitude 4.9 earthquake occurred there on the early morning of May 25." What makes this report so interesting is that a catastrophic earthquake of magnitude 8.2 happened in the same area on July 28, 1976. For all its great force, it was not predicted in time. Although animal alarms were not altogether absent, they came too late or were not distinct enough. Did bad weather jumble the equation? Did rain neutralize the alarm signals?

A separate group of unusual biological reactions that might precede an earthquake is mentioned in the earthquake information book of the Peking Geological Bureau[21] in connection with the earthquake that occurred in 1971 in the area of the mouth of the Yangtze River. The same reactions appeared before the earthquake of Haicheng in 1975. As if nature were being ironic, flowers, shrubs, and trees bloomed in winter as harbingers of terror, death, and destruction. Under the heading "Do Plants Have Reactions Before Earthquakes?" we read:

Normally when one talks about anomalies before earthquakes of living beings one means animals. Do plants show anomalous reactions before earthquakes? For example, early sprouting, early blooming, re-blooming, etc. These types of examples do not seem too numerous, and very few people mention them. Actually, some plants do have anomalous reactions before earthquakes. For example, before the December 30, 1971, earthquake of magnitude 4.75 near the estuary of the Yangtze

River, flowers bloomed on the top axis of a good Chinese cabbage and on the leaf tops of Chinese green vegetables. Shepherd's purse usually blooms in spring, but it bloomed early in the middle of December. In another commune potato vines also bloomed, and bamboo sprouted in September of the lunar calendar. In late November of the year before the February 4, 1975, Haicheng-Yingkou 7.3 magnitude earthquake some apricot trees bloomed.

There may not be a direct relationship between plant anomalies and earthquakes, but they may be related to changes in temperature and weather. One evidence is that in the above examples, temperatures before earthquakes in those localities were higher than usual. Some people believe that there is a relationship between electromagnetic phenomena induced by earthquakes and reactions from living beings; they have carried out certain long-term observations of white willow trees and desert date trees. However, up to now, these phenomena are still under study, and it is too early to talk about real application in earthquake prediction.

The role of animal behavior in modern Chinese seismology is outlined in an official report[34] that was prepared by Y. Liu (director of the National Seismological Bureau of China), published in the official Chinese scientific journal *Scientia Geologica Sinica*, and distributed by the Chinese seismological delegation at the UNESCO session on earthquake crises. It confirms the forecast of the Bohai earthquake of 1969 and tells of another similar example:

Facts have proved that the forecasters of the masses are in a position through simple observation methods to give rather good prognoses. A few examples follow: Two hours before the magnitude 7.4 Bohai earthquake on July 18, 1969, a feeder at the zoo in Tientsin had noticed the anomaly in behavior of tigers and other animals and suggested to the Tientsin seismological department: "a big earthquake may be approaching." A mass's prediction team in Chetotang production brigade in Kangting, Szechwan province, had made a fair prediction on a magnitude 5.8 earthquake occurrence on September 27, 1972, according to such phenomena as a fall in the indigenous terrestrial electricity, the panic of chickens, pigs refusing to enter pigsties, horses and sheep running about frenziedly and other anomalies in the animals' behavior. In the course of prediction and taking precautionary measures against the Haicheng earthquake in Liaoning province in 1975, the masses provided numerous phenomena of anomalies in animals' behavior, and results of their observations on subterranean water and indigenous terrestrial electricity [current and voltage changes between electrodes planted in the ground], and played a great role in an impending earthquake prediction by the professionals. . . .

The most detailed Chinese reports of abnormal animal behavior can be found in connection with the Haicheng earthquake of February 1975. This is not surprising, because the prediction of that earthquake was a sensation for seismology and a great triumph for the leaders of Liaoning province (who received much-deserved recognition in the many reports). The first anomalies in the behavior of animals, remarkably, were registered a month and a half before the earthquake. Engineer Chu Fung-ming of the Earthquake Bureau of Liaoning province wrote the following report:

In the middle of December, 1974, many anomalous phenomena in various wells and animal behavior were noticed by the public prediction forecast network in Tantung district. The following phenomena were noticed in many areas: (1) Snakes hibernating came out of their burrows and were frozen stiff on the snow; rats appeared in groups and were so agitated that they did not fear human beings (a member of Tanchengtung People's Commune of Tantung, Sun Tao-yi, discovered over 20 rats and could catch them with his bare hands), and other anomalous behavior was observed in domestic birds and animals. . . .

Asia is the only continent from which we have reports of abnormal behavior appearing more than a few days (in this case, a month and a half) before an earthquake and still being associated with the quake. It may be that in the rest of the world similar phenomena are simply not acknowledged because the observers lack sophistication and because the catastrophe does not happen. It is altogether possible that under certain circumstances an earthquake will make two or more "run-ups," which animals perceive, before it finally has its full effect. Among the episodes of anomalous behavior reported just above is a report of an earthquake swarm that happened on December 22, 1974, 70 kilometers (43 miles) north of Haicheng, and culminated in a quake of magnitude 4.8.[2]

The dramatic, untimely awakening of the snakes (photos of this animal tragedy were seen in China by foreign scientists) is confirmed in the information book *Earthquake Questions and Answers* put out by the Peking Geological Bureau.[21] This book also describes the behavior of animals during the last days before the convulsions of the earth escalated into the gale of the earthquake:

One and one half months before the February 4, 1975 Haicheng-Yingkou magnitude 7.3 earthquake, hibernating snakes came out of their burrows. During a time interval preceding the earthquake, quite a few geese panicked, screamed, refused to nest, and some even flew away. One to two days before the earthquake, pigs did not eat, climbed walls, and butted doors. On February 2, in a pigpen of a production brigade in the Panjin district, small pigs bit each other, a dozen or so small pigs chewed off their tails and ate them. In Dangtong, at the home of a commune member, a black hen flew up to the tree top at sunset on February 4. [The quake happened at 7:36 P.M.] At the home of a worker a female turtle suddenly rolled over, jumped out of the water and screamed. This was a little over 20 minutes prior to the large earthquake on February 4. A production brigade in Yingkou county had six cows. At 6 P.M. on February 3, four of them fought and butted horns, two of them dug the ground with their hooves. At 10:50 A.M. on February 4, deer in a deer farm at Anshan suddenly ran madly and pushed open the pen door. In the process of rushing out of the pen after the door was pushed open, a three-year-old deer, about 90 kilograms (198 pounds), broke its left front leg knee cap and right front leg bone. There are many other anomalous animal phenomena. The great worker-peasant-soldier masses observed such conditions and played an important role in successfully predicting this earthquake.

Another report that adds to and confirms other accounts of abnormal animal behavior before the Haicheng earthquake may be found in the Chinese book *The Southern Liaoning Earthquake*.[4] It describes the following event, albeit without without specifying any times:

In frozen sky and snowy ground, students from an elementary school discovered several snakes on the road after school. . . . They knew that snakes did not come out from their caves in cold winter. They asked "Why did the snakes come out today? Is this an earthquake precursor?" They reported immediately to their school's earthquake prediction team.

"Keepers . . . suddenly discovered that chickens flew blindly together. Even the heavy geese raised their necks, flying and screaming. They thought this was an earthquake precursor, and telephoned the seismological office.

The many observations of abnormal animal behavior before the Haicheng earthquake have apparently been carefully evaluated in China. This is suggested by a map, published as part of the work of Chu Fung-ming,[3] in which the geographic distribution of observed animal anomalies has been entered with great attention to detail. I have copied this map and added to it the fault lines in the Liaoning peninsula (figure 2). It yields some surprising information. The animal anomalies are clustered neither around the epicenter nor along the earthquake faults. Instead they appear in irregularly distributed clusters, large and small, separated by zones free from anomalies and arranged irregularly around the epicenter, which is also devoid of any reports

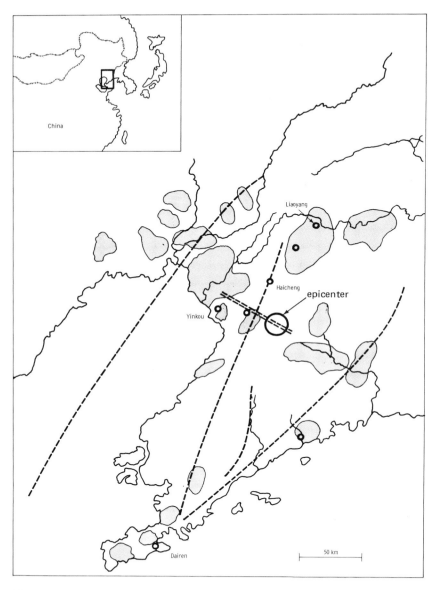

Figure 2
Plot of reports about unusual animal behavior before the Haicheng earthquake
of February 4, 1975. Areas with many such reports (gray zones) were not
equally spaced around the epicenter or along the fractures, but were distributed
irregularly.

about animal anomalies. This specific geographic distribution pattern of animal anomalies might suggest that it could have been mass hysteria set off by other earthquake signs that made people think they recognized strange behavior in their animals. Why else are there no reports of anomalies from a large area near the epicenter? Why would areas with and without anomalous animal behavior appear side by side in zones of equal earthquake intensity? Did geological conditions make the difference, or was it the local weather immediately before the earthquake?

It should be mentioned that, in areas where abnormal animal behavior was reported, Chinese earthquake watchers also noticed changes in water levels or the clouding of water in numerous wells before the earthquake. This is clear proof that some sort of geophysical process had been taking place in the ground before the earthquake. It is in this process that we should look for the primary cause of the panicky behavior of animals.

Chinese literature indicates that the problem of earthquake sensitivity is being examined in the most qualified scientific laboratories in the country. An allusion to this is made in the earthquake information booklet of the Peking Geological Bureau:[21]

In conclusion, physical and chemical changes (vibrational, electric, magnetic, meteorological, radon-content, etc. anomalies) associated with earthquakes usually can stimulate certain organs of some animals to give anomalous reactions. If there is an anomalous gravity change in a region, certain animals may feel it through their balance organ. A vibrational anomaly may be recognized by the hearing organs of certain animals. Scientists from the Biophysics Institute of the Academia Sinica, in their survey of animals in the epicentral regions, discovered that among several domestic animals raised in near natural conditions, there was a relatively good correlation between anomalous reactions of pigeons and earthquakes. What are the factors stimulating anomalous reactions of pigeons?

Through research, scientists discovered that there is a small body, which is sensitive to vibrations, located in the inter-bone membrane between the shinbone and muscle bone in the pigeon's leg. This small body is ellipsoidal in shape, smaller than a grain of rice, and barely can be seen by the naked eye. There are over a hundred of these small bodies with nerves connecting them like a bunch of grapes. They are very sensitive to vibrations; nerve currents can be generated if they are stimulated by vibrations with amplitudes of a fraction of a micron.

Scientists in the Biophysics Institute carried out an experiment using one hundred pigeons. Fifty of the pigeons had the connections of small bodies in their legs severed from the central nervous system; the other fifty remained intact. Before a magnitude 4 plus earthquake, those pigeons without disconnected small bodies were flying madly, whereas those pigeons with severed small bodies were basically calm as usual. This demonstrates that anomalous reactions of animals before earthquakes are related to their physiological structure (for example, sensing organs).

Here we discussed only an example of domestic pigeons; this does not mean that we have understood all the factors causing anomalous reactions of pigeons before earthquakes. In addition to pigeons, there are many species of animals which have anomalous reactions prior to earthquakes. In order to successfully and thoroughly predict earthquakes, we must carry out more research in this direction.

Unfortunately, no time is given for the earthquake in the report of the interesting experiment with pigeons. It is well known that birds can react very sensitively to vibrations. For example, it has been reported several times that a few seconds before distant thundering of cannon becomes audible, or a few seconds before a sonic boom, birds stop singing and fly up in fright. They evidently register the weak earthquake waves that are caused by the explosion and travel through the air faster than sound. Birds and other animals also seem to react to the P waves of an earthquake, a special kind of wave (compression waves oscillating in the direction of travel) that travel faster than S waves and cannot, ordinarily, be sensed by humans. (They are, of course, registered by seismographs.) Though many big earthquakes are preceded by miniature quakes,[38] there surely must be many very small quakes that are not followed by big earthquakes. If animals were to react to them all, they would be agitated more often than they are.

There are probably significantly more earthquakes in China with reports of animal anomalies than we know about, because it is difficult to get reports out of the country. In addition, more earthquakes than we were able to find out about were evidently recognized beforehand and predicted. That, at least, emerges from a published remark made by the director of the National Seismological Bureau of China, Y. Liu: "In the course of the past few years, we have succeeded in predicting a considerable number of earthquakes with intensity 5. . . ."[34]

Once the Chinese leadership had made its decision to incorporate earthquake folklore into the evolving mechanism of earthquake prediction, it became necessary to mobilize the broad masses of the people and to train specifically gifted persons for the leadership role of responsible earthquake amateurs. Most of these collaborators were recruited from among workers, peasants, teachers, students, telephone operators, broadcast and weather-service employees, and animal caretakers. Their numbers gradually grew to more than 100,000.[34] Information and training brochures were written in language that anyone could understand to prepare these amateurs for their work and to keep them abreast of developments. These brochures are of great interest because they summarize the most significant insights gained from the various methods employed in earthquake prediction.

In the illustrated booklet *Earthquakes* put out by the Seismological Office of Tientsin,[35] there is a section about the use of animal anomalies for the prediction of earthquakes. One picture shows a pretty little Chinese village. Drawn into the picture, in contrasting darker color, are many animals that may be expected to behave unusually. Fish jump from the village pond, a horse has become wild, a dog barks, a rabbit runs in a curious manner, rats escape through the door of a peasant house, chickens have sought out an elevated spot on a wall, pigeons sit on the ridge of the roof or are flying, and a hog runs from its sty. Even a snake can be made out. Above the picture is written "It is easy and simple to use animals to predict earthquakes." Next to that we read: "In general, certain organs of animals may acutely detect various underground changes before earthquakes. Both historical and recent surveys of large earthquakes prove that animals have precursory reactions." Beneath the picture is a caption whose typography suggests that it may be a song or a poem:

Animals are aware of precursors before earthquakes,
Let us summarize their anomalous behavior for prediction.
Cattle, sheep, mules and horses do not enter corrals,
Rats move their homes and flee.
Hibernating snakes leave their burrows early,
Frightened pigeons continuously fly and do not return to nests.
Rabbits raise their ears, jump aimlessly and bump things,
Fish are frightened, jump above water surface.
Every family and every household joins in observation
The people's war against earthquakes must be won.

What is remarkable about this summary is that, in 1973, it described the phenomenon of hibernating snakes waking up, a phenomenon that appeared again so dramatically one or two years later before the Haicheng earthquake. This shows how reliably the pattern of animal behavior before earthquakes repeats itself. It has also been reported that, several days before the Hsingtain earthquake in 1966, people noticed that snakes had crawled out onto the snow-covered ground.[36]

In the information book *Earthquake Questions and Answers* put out by the Geological Bureau of Peking,[21] the answer to question 98 (out of

113) is given as "a song written by the masses of people in the epicentral region of our country." The question is "What anomalous reactions do the animals have before strong earthquakes?" The answering song repeats some of the animal reactions described above, but adds a few new ones:

Animals have precursory behavior before earthquakes,
Observation and preventions by the masses are very important.
Cattle, sheep, mules and horses do not enter corrals,
Pigs do not eat, and dogs bark madly.
Ducks do not enter water and stay on shore.
Chickens fly up in trees and scream loudly.
Snakes come out of burrows in freezing sky and ground,
Big cats pick up little ones and run.
Rabbits raise their ears, jump aimlessly and bump things,
Fish panic and jump above water surface.
Bees move their hives making noise,
Frightened pigeons stay in the air and do not nest.
Every family and every household joins in observation,
To gather anomalies for earthquake prediction.

This song is followed by an enumeration of animal species that show unusual behavior before earthquakes:

Animal species that have reactions before earthquakes include tigers, wolves, deer, pandas, yaks, swans, loaches, turtles, eels, leeches, frogs, dogs, cows, mules, donkeys, pigs, sheep, rats, geese, chickens, ducks, cats, rabbits, monkeys, snakes, fish, pigeons, sparrows, eagles, bees, and ants, etc. Among them are those walking on ground and those that fly in the sky and swim in the water. People living in epicentral areas observed that burrowing animals such as rats and snakes, etc. were more sensitive than animals living above ground, and small animals appeared to be more sensitive than large animals. According to the survey of four major regions of China by the combined team from the Biophysics and Zoology Institutes of the Academia Sinica, preliminary results show that 58 species of wild and domestic animals have relatively reliable anomalous reactions before earthquakes.

From such brochures, from newspapers, from primers for grade-schoolers, from students' books, from wall posters, and through school instructions, evening courses, and radio lectures, several hundred million Chinese learn the details of this mysterious, unknown phenomenon that has been passed down in folklore and that, when combined with other observations, can help save human lives. It is astonishing that the Western world knows of this phenomenon only by hearsay and that many scientific observers would rather view the Chinese efforts with amusement than take them seriously.

For precisely this reason I report here a few additional details of observations and experiences from the Middle Kingdom about animal behavior before earthquakes. For example, there is a rule of thumb that dogs begin to suffer from anxiety 1–10 days before a heavy earthquake.[36] They bark in unison and without apparent reason, day and night. Occasionally they try to climb onto roofs of houses or they dig holes into the ground as if they were trying to chase some small animal there. Generally, they refuse to sleep in doghouses or in doorways and often flee outside the village altogether. Since they react so sensitively and stubbornly to earthquakes, few of them are ever killed by collapsing houses. Cattle, horses, mules, and sheep, which show similarly pronounced nervousness before big earthquakes, reduce their intake of nourishment and water noticeably or stop eating completely. They also scream constantly, refuse to go into their corrals, and try to flee. Even the sluggish and voracious pigs become nervous and restless and lose their appetite. They, too, refuse to go into their pens; if they find themselves in them, they try to break out, and when they succeed they run around blindly and grunt. Chickens start to show fear 2–3 days before a big earthquake; they refuse to enter their coops and show no interest in feeding. Sometimes they fly up into trees or onto other high resting places, or else they fly around blindly and shriek. According to Chinese experience, roosters seem to be less sensitive than hens. Roosters are said to cackle sometimes before earthquakes, like a hen that has just laid an egg.

Ducks seem to be somewhat less adept at earthquake prophecy than chickens. But they, too, seem restless and frightened, fly around blindly, and cry. They also refuse to go into the stalls at night, and they avoid the water. If they happen to be in the water, they become frightened and fly ashore. Among birds, pigeons react especially sensitively to signs of earthquakes. Two to three days before a big earthquake, they stretch their necks high, hold their heads rigid, and give the impression of being frightened. Sometimes they emit a lot of sudden calls, which sound more drawn out than usual. They refuse to seek out their nests, and when danger approaches they fly away, even at night.

Sparrows and crows also show abnormal behavior 3–5 days before an earthquake. Whole flocks of them can be seen flying around crying and excited. They, too, refuse to seek out their nests, and under some circumstances they are apt to disappear from a village entirely 2–3 days before an earthquake. Even insects can react sensitively toward an approaching earthquake. Depending on the force of the coming earthquake and other circumstances, bees may leave their hives as a swarm 10 or more days before a quake. Ants, too, resettle sometimes, and the population density of locusts can change drastically in some places.

Chinese peasants know that unusual behavior is a reliable sign of a coming earthquake only when it appears in many animals simultaneously, because changes in the weather, illness, changes in the environment, or the seasonal changes in their drives can throw animals off their daily routines. Moreover, not all animals of the same species are equally good at predicting earthquakes; as with people, there are distinct variations among individuals in the intensity of their instincts. Mothers with young, according to Chinese experience, seem to be especially sensitive.

Can China's impressive treasure of experience, can a tradition thousands of years old, can the earnest efforts of hundreds of millions of people be devoted to the apparition of a phantom? Or are we in the West closing ourselves to a natural phenomenon because we do not understand it, because we don't want it to be true?

To observers with a skeptical view of the popular methods of earthquake prediction, the gruesome Tangshan earthquake tragedy of July 28, 1976, has become an argument that seems difficult to refute. How could a natural event of such proportions roll over an army of well-trained observers without any signs proclaiming the disaster in advance? Are the time of the disaster (3:43 A.M.) and the bad weather enough to dispel any doubts?

Not until 2–3 years after the disaster did the veil of secrecy begin to lift enough to reveal something about the course of the disaster. Foreign visitors spoke with eyewitnesses, and Chinese experts described their investigations. In this context, a report[209] by Shen Ling-huang of the Chinese news agency is very revealing. It says that Chinese scientists—biophysicists, biologists, geophysicists, chemists, and meteorologists—visited the ruins of Tangshan and 400 surrounding communities shortly after the earthquake in order to question survivors. In the process they collected reports of more than 2,093 cases of unusual animal behavior that had preceded the earthquake by a brief period. Some of the observations involved goats that did not want to enter their stables, cats or dogs that hauled their young into the open, pigs that squealed strangely, excited chickens that fled from their roosts into the open in the middle of the night, rats that left their nests, and fish that flitted around in the water. The inquiry revealed that the number of observed animal anomalies increased toward the epicenter. They usually reached their peak sometime within the 24 hours before the earthquake and continued until the disaster struck. A typical eyewitness report was given by a cattle breeder from the People's Commune of Kaokechuang, which lies 40 kilometers (25 miles) from Tangshan. When he went to the stables before dawn, he found his two horses and his two jennies in the highest state of excitement. They would not eat, they jumped around, and they kicked. Finally they tore loose and stormed outside. A blinding white flash of lightning illuminated the sky and a thundering noise was heard. It was the earthquake of Tangshan.

A Japanese scientist who was in China at the time of this great earthquake told me the following story, which was later printed in great detail in Peking's largest daily newspaper: A train was rolling along at full speed in the vicinity of the epicenter when the conductor saw a strange light in the sky. He brought the train to a stop immediately, just before the earthquake began to rattle the rails. The engineer of a second train that was also moving at that time noticed nothing unusual, however, and hurtled blindly toward disaster.

These mysterious earthquake signals were by no means the only precursors of the approaching geological cataclysm. Between 30 and 40 percent of all the stations that had been taking measurements of electrical ground resistance in northern China registered distinct anomalies. At the same time, the number of observations of irregularities in wells and springs rose rapidly. Whereas 59 reports of unexplained changes had come in between the tenth and the fifth day before the earthquake, 665 such changes were reported in the last five days.[210] As is shown by recordings salvaged from the rubble of the Tangshan seismological station, no tremors worth mentioning had preceded the main quake.

It will probably never be explained why the relatively numerous signals of this catastrophic earthquake were not evaluated properly. A crucial factor may have been the political changes that were taking place in China at that time, which reached into the scientific hierarachy of the earthquake watch. Western experts have heard that alarm reports from seven earthquake stations were ignored and that no appropriate earthquake alert was issued.[211] Even if this were not quite true, the disaster at Tangshan would be no reason to doubt the predictability of earthquakes.

Japan

The *Nihon Jishin Shiryo,*[39] a newly edited collection of old Japanese earthquake reports, contains the following story about an incident that occurred before the earthquake of November 11, 1855, which left Edo (now Tokyo) in ruins:

There lived a man in Edo who was so enthusiastic about fishing that he pursued this sport every day. Thus, on the evening of November 11 he betook himself to the river in the hope of catching some eels. To his surprise he noticed there a considerable number of catfish splashing around in the water in great excitement. He remembered an old tradition that speaks of catfish becoming very active before impending earthquakes, forgot his beloved sport, and hurried home. A skeptical neighbor, who also fished, succumbed to the temptation of a rich harvest and remained. When the careful man reached his home, he began—to the amusement and later to the horror of his wife who thought little of old stories—to drag all the furnishings into the garden. After a while the expected earthquake did indeed take place. The fisherman who had believed in the catfish legend retained his furniture and his household effects, the other one probably only a few catfish.

Catfish and earthquakes have been linked for many centuries in Japan. In the Middle Ages it was even believed that giant catfish living underground were responsible for moving the earth now and then. This mythological idea has found artistic expression in many multi-colored Japanese wood block prints (*Nishiki-e*).[40] Does the catfish legend illustrate a connection between animal behavior and earthquakes? The earliest preserved handwritten documents that associate catfish with earthquakes are from the seventeenth century. It is impossible today to trace the origin of the Japanese belief that catfish, which normally lead a sluggish life in muddy river and lake bottoms, become excited and active before earthquakes. We only know that eyewitness reports describing such unusual behavior surface again and again in Japanese earthquake documents.

Several such reports connected with the severe earthquake of August 31, 1923, have also become known.[41,42] For example, a high official of the ministry of education is said to have noticed catfish in a restaurant pond jumping around in great agitation on the day before the earthquake. He asked a member of the restaurant staff about it and was told that the fish had developed their unusual temperament only recently. Later he told this story to a painter friend, who remembered that some catfish he kept in a tub as models for drawings had also been jumping around wildly. Another ministerial official received a welcome present, courtesy of the earthquake. On the day before, this avid sports fisherman cast his net in a pond south of Tokyo and ended up going home with three buckets of catfish, each measuring about

30 centimeters (nearly a foot). Another unusual catfish catch was registered in the vicinity of the city of Kochi two weeks before the Nankaido earthquake of December 21, 1946, which had a magnitude of 8.1.[43] Four or five days before the Fukui quake of June 28, 1948, unusual numbers of catfish were seen in rivers and along the coast.[43] At the beginning of June 1964, reports of astonishing hauls of catfish, and of overactive specimens, came out of the communities of Ageichi and Tsuruoka, which were hit by the Niigata quake on June 16.

In 1932 two scientists of the Biological Station of Asamushi, S. Hatai and N. Abe, decided to take a closer look at this famous or notorious fish.[44] They built an aquarium, fitted it with mud and roots to make it as homelike as possible for a few catfish (*Parasilurus asotus*), and fed it directly with water from a small creek. In this way the aquarium was connected with the animals' natural environment, and therefore with the earth, through both the inflow and the outflow. Since catfish while away their days lying in the mud or hovering among the roots without moving, the two scientists had a splendid experimental opportunity to test the nerves of the catfish. They began a systematic search for the stimuli or environmental influences that would shake the composure of these fellows. The results were not encouraging at first. All attempts seemed to founder before the equanimity of the catfish. But as time passed it occurred to the two scientists that these animals sometimes reacted quite vigorously when the base of the aquarium was tapped. They would then leap, turn, or thrash with their fins. The unexpected result of long and patient observation was the discovery that these animals would become hypersensitive about 6–8 hours before one of the local earthquakes. The intensity of an earthquake did not seem to affect the behavior of these curious fish significantly. They reacted vigorously to even the smallest earthquake as long as the epicenter was near enough. The researchers, who were later joined by S. Kobutu,[45] finally ventured their first earthquake prediction, which they tacked to the station's bulletin board. Their success rate eventually reached a proud 80 percent, even though the experiments were adversely affected by changes in the weather and other environmental influences.

What were the physical or chemical signals underlying the earthquake premonition of these catfish? There was no longer any doubt that the fish were put under stress through some earthquake precursor. When the scientists isolated the aquarium from the natural environment of the catfish by stopping the inflow of water, the ability of the fish to prophesy earthquakes dwindled drastically. This pointed to something electrical as an alarm signal—a hypothesis supported by evidence that catfish were sensitive to electrical signals. It was actually shown that there were certain correlations among rapid changes in electrical potential in the aquarium, approaching earthquakes, and the behavior of catfish. It is easy to see why a fish would be sensitive to rapid changes in electrical potential; the current pulses generated by them penetrate its surface better than direct current does. Direct current produces electrochemical reactions that increase resistance. But do changes in potential or current in natural bodies of water always indicate earthquakes? The Japanese scientists think they have found that they do, with reasonable probability, provided that in these changes we are dealing with pulses in which the generated changes in potential are reversed immediately. Catfish often reacted to just such voltages with anxiety. Unfortunately, these interesting experiments, which got their impulse from the Tokyo earthquake of 1923 that killed 70,000, were carried no further and were not repeated. An early Japanese flowering of animal research associated with earthquakes, to which the earthquake researchers Terada, Suyehiro, and Musha made valuable contributions,[46-49] wilted away. Only the Chinese successes with animal observations for predicting earthquakes have revived interest in the old earthquake folklore in recent times.

The severe quake of 1854 off the Japanese Pacific coast reached a magnitude of 8.4 and sent a flood rolling over the coast of central Japan. When people afterwards went to look over the beaches littered with wrecks, seaweed, and marine life, they could not cease marveling: The beaches were strewn with fish that even the oldest and most experienced fishermen had never laid eyes on in their lives. The strange shapes led them to suspect that nature's violence had torn them from the darkest depths of the ocean and had thrown them into the sunny upper reaches and thus to their deaths (ref. 39). But why is it that these strange creatures are never seen except when their dead carcasses are found drifting on the surface? How can a brief tidal wave lift them out of the still depths and transport them miles away onto strange shores? After all, it is not the water that wanders great distances as mountainous waves, but the rhythm of its motion. Perhaps, in dim premonition of disaster before the violent quake, these exotic animals fled from their depths and crowded into shallow coastal waters, where they were overtaken by the flood.

Thus, the threat of an earthquake was hanging over Japanese fishermen when on September 1, 1923, off the coast of the Izu peninsula, they found deep-sea fish of the cod family near the surface. (Similarly, the catch in November 1963 of a giant deep-sea fish of the genus

Regalecus that was tumbling around in shallow coastal water preceded the Niijima quake. Also, in May 1968, deep-sea fish of the genus *Alepisaurus* and *Nemichys* went into fishermen's nets in shallow water before the submarine quake off Hokkaido.[50] It may have seemed like superstition when on September 1, 1923, the fishermen, having seen many deep-sea fish drifting on the surface, suspected disaster and hurried to shore.[43] But the heavy quake of Kanto, which came a few hours later, vindicated their ancient tradition.

Many marine animals sense a coming earthquake through some mysterious sensory perception and try to dodge the epicenter. In their flight, masses of fish often crowd against the coast, where they anticipate the catastrophe in great excitement. In panic they try to move out of their dark deep-sea home and are not averse to pressing on into the hostile environment of the light-filled ocean surface. Sometimes they are seized by a mysterious illness, drift dying on the surface, sink to the bottom, or swim in a peculiar manner.

The history of the fisheries of the island country of Japan is rich in unusual incidents and observations, which, remarkably, were always more frequent before great earthquake disasters. Many of these incidents are described in the reports of the Imperial Japanese Earthquake Investigation Commission[51] and in newer collections of data based on those reports.[39] The Japanese earthquake researcher K. Musha included 21 examples of unusual behavior of fish before earthquakes in reference 48 and 131 examples in reference 49. The earthquake scientist T. Terada[46] and the widely known fish expert Y. Suyehiro[47] contributed to the knowledge of this phenomenon in the early 1930s, when the terror of the Tokyo earthquake was still deep in the bones of people and when marvelous earthquake signs such as odd animal behavior seemed worth an investigation. In 1957, Musha collected many of these animal anomalies in a book titled *Earthquake Catfish*. Other anomalies are described in more recent work by Suyehiro.[43,50,52]

These bold studies by individual Japanese scientists do not by any means reflect the attitude of most contemporary seismologists. A 1976 book about earthquake prediction by T. Rikitake of the Technical High School of Tokyo[42] states the professional attitude best. Rikitake describes numerous examples of abnormal animal behavior and such other popular traditions as unusual light displays and weather phenomena in his second chapter, but does so under the revealing heading "Earthquake predictions—various legends." He writes: "It has often been reported that animals and fish behave unusually before an earthquake. . . . Very likely the desire of mankind for a prediction of a catastrophic earthquake is so great that some people yield to temptation to regard such things as true. . . . Not that we believe in all these legends, but it is important for scientists to look into things which might contain some truth without being biased." Such skepticism is a very safe and comfortable attitude for science. There is no need to prove that folk traditions are based on a real phenomenon or that they are without foundations. Unless they are given a boost by science, reports of unusual animal behavior before earthquakes will simply remain unproven anecdotes even when entered in serious documents and collected from reliable observers.

The aforementioned catfish were not the only marine animals to announce the coming of the Edo earthquake of November 11, 1855. Near Yokohama many crabs left their wet habitat for some unknown reason and crawled ashore.[43] Other ocean dwellers, too, seem to find their element uncongenial before an approaching earthquake. In 1854 a violent quake of magnitude 8.4 loosed a distructive tidal wave off the northeast coast of Japan. Was it a coincidence that shortly before the catastrophe—as it says in an old document reproduced in the *Nihon Jishin Shiryo*[39]—one could catch great quantities of eels on the beaches of the area that was later devastated? Experience indicates otherwise; before the Sanriku earthquakes of 1896 and 1933 great quantities of eels crowded against the seashore.[42] Before the catastrophic quake of 1896, whose tidal wave took 270,000 lives, so many eels crowded onto the beach that one man caught 200 of them.[39] Before the disaster of 1933, these hardy and quick animals had been so frightened out of their usual behavior that children were able to catch them on the beach with bare hands.[42] Before the Sanriku earthquake of 1896 people noticed an unusual number of sea urchins[49] and were surprised to see sea snakes and trout swimming up the rivers.[43] Some fishermen near the city of Fukuoda in 1896 saw large numbers of fish jumping high above the wave crests. While the fishermen were still puzzling over this strange spectacle, the sea became ruffled and the fish suddenly disappeared. The fishermen stopped their work and returned home in time for the earthquake.

Fishermen on the Pacific coast of northeastern Japan have a proverb that says "Sardines bring disaster, but squid save people."[42] This proverb sums up an old piece of folklore which says that great schools of sardines will crowd against the coast to be caught easily just before an earthquake and its ensuing tidal wave. Afterwards, the upper layers of the ocean will be full of squid, evidently driven out of the depths by earthquake signals or by the quake itself. By then the danger is generally over. Historic reports clearly confirm the old proverb. Before the Kanto quake in 1923, fishermen caught giant quantities of sardines near the Boso peninsula. Before the earthquakes of 1896 and 1933 at Sanriku schools of sardines appeared along the coasts. In one bay in Miyagi prefecture, where sardines are rarely seen, schools of disturbed sardines fled into shallow water only 20 centimeters (8 inches) deep before the 1933 quake. Before the Kanto quake, too, many sardines were observed near the coast in the Kanagawa region. Some of those began, out of some strange, deep anxiety, to swim up the fresh-water rivers. An unusual school of bonitos was noticed at the mouth of Tokyo Bay before the Kanto quake, and before the Tonankai quake of 1944 large numbers of these fish swam into nets off the Kii peninsula. This same phenomenon of the sudden appearance of vast numbers of fish near the coast was also observed in 1946, making it possible to predict the ensuing Nakai earthquake (December 21, 1946) on the basis of older experiences that matched the newer observation.[42] It is also worth noting that on Oga Island in the Sea of Japan, before the severe earthquake of 1939, 15-kilogram (33-pound) tunnys were caught from the beach. They had never before been seen so near the coast. The experienced fishermen on the coast of Iwate prefecture were no less surprised when they suddenly hauled in crabs of a species that they had never seen before in the area. This happened 15–16 days before the violent Sanriku quake of 1933.

When great schools of fish appear along some shores, they must have disappeared from other regions. Numerous reports from Japan confirm this. Before the Sanriku earthquake of 1896, for example, it was impossible to catch cod or shark in northeastern Japan. The same held true for other fish before the Sanriku quake of 1933. Several days before the Kanto quake of 1923 the fish harvest in Sagami Bay is said to have dropped drastically. Two to three days before the Niigata quake of June 16, 1964, which had a magnitude of 7.5, the squid harvest off Fukui also sank to a low point never reached before.[43]

In rivers and lakes, too, the living habits of fish evidently change before an earthquake. Otherwise it would be hard to explain why several hours before the 1948 Fukui earthquake one fisherman on the Kuzuryu River caught nearly three times as much as on a normal day, or why so many carp were caught in Yamanakako Lake immediately before the Kanto quake of 1923.[42] Before that same quake some men south of Tokyo, attracted by the many fish jumping out of the water of a pond, improvised a fishing method and filled half of a 70-liter (18.5-gallon) tub.

Aquatic animals seem to be beset by strange health problems before earthquakes. On the morning of the great Kanto quake of 1923, for example, the carp in a pond in Tokyo came to the surface and seemed exhausted as if they lacked oxygen.[42] In the rivers around Yokohama many fish died at the same time, seemingly under great torment.[43] On the morning of the 1927 Tango quake, native fishermen near the epicenter observed mackerel shooting up from the surface, something they considered highly unusual for this species. One day before the quake of Sanriku in 1933, near the fishing village of Kuji in Iwate prefecture, carp even jumped from the river onto the bank. In the area of the Nazenjii temple of Kyoto it was noted that goldfish would leave their stations near the bottom of the pond about 10–30 minutes before an aftershock, come to the surface, and let themselves settle back to the bottom only after the quake.

Fish in glass containers whose water was insulated from the earth did not show this astonishing rhythm.[43] This interesting observation admits of the conclusion that, in the question of earthquake predictors, we are dealing with signals of a chemical or electrical nature. Even plankton seems to react to these mysterious signals. As chance would have it, K. Tago at the Imperial Fisheries Experimental Station was collecting plankton at the mouth of Tokyo Bay on the morning of the great Kanto quake of 1923. The analysis of plankton distribution as a function of water depth showed a surprising anomaly: The surface layer of the water was unusually rich in plankton, while the middle layer was correspondingly sparse.[46] This observation was confirmed indirectly through investigations by Suyehiro.[47] This ichthyologist studied sardines caught on the evening before the Sanriku quake of 1933. Their stomachs were extraordinarily distended and contained mostly benthic plankton, which was completely contrary to normal conditions inasmuch as sardines take in surface plankton almost exclusively. Since the sardines had been caught on the surface and had mostly surface plankton in their stomachs after the earthquake, the bottom plankton must have risen to the surface before the earthquake.

Suyehiro also did some scientific work on the appearance of deep-sea fish in shallow waters in connection with earthquakes. He describes the case of a rare and slender eel-like deep-sea fish, *Nemichthys avocetta*, which was caught live along with several other deep-sea fish a few hours after the Sanriku quake of 1933 on the coast of Odawara. Since this uncommon creature normally lives on the bottom in deep seas, it had to have left its natural home before the earthquake in order to reach the coast by the time it was found. Another specimen of this genus of fish was found drifting near the coast of Hayama a few days before the quake of 1923.[43]

Japan has still more examples of such earthquake-caused migrations from the deep sea. Before the severe Kanto quake of 1923, a reddish deep-sea fish was observed drifting in Sagami Bay southeast of Tokyo, and on the western shore of the bay, near the Izu peninsula, there were sightings of unidentified deep-sea fish.[42] Before the Tango earthquake in 1927 many lobsters and squid, animals that normally live on the bottom, were caught in nets on the surface off the coast of Kyoto prefecture in the Sea of Japan.[42]

What signals does the earth, tensed up before an earthquake, communicate to the sea that it affects the lives and behavior of aquatic animals so profoundly? Is it low-frequency sound, which the ocean bottom, like a giant microphone, transmits to the sea? Are there chemical changes through gases that dissolve in the water, or is it turbulent bottom mud? Are there electric currents that bridge accumulated tensions?

Dolphins know how to identify the center of a submarine quake in time and avoid it. Unusual dolphin migrations were observed 2 hours before the severe Niigata quake. Swarms of these intelligent animals appeared unexpectedly on the coast of Sanri in Kochi prefecture as if they had been on the run from the earthquake that followed immediately.[43]

That fish avoid earthquakes through unusual migratory movements has not only been shown by some individual observations, but has been proved statistically by Terada.[46] This earthquake researcher followed up reports that the kinds of fish caught most often on the eastern shore of the Izu peninsula before the 1930 earthquake were completely different from those caught after it. Similar reports had surfaced in connection with the Kanto quake of 1923. It was observed at that time that, in the middle of the season for horse mackerel (*Caranx*), large quantities of full-grown mackerel (*Scomber*) were suddenly coming into the nets. This otherwise inexplicable deviation could have only been connected with the earthquake that followed immediately. Terada tried to follow the trail of the horse mackerel and examined the recordings of the Imperial Fisheries Institute concerning fish catches on the western side of the Izu peninsula in the year of the earthquake. He was greatly surprised. Horse mackerel had been caught only in March, in May, and from November to December. These had been exactly the months with distinct earthquake activity. For the year 1928 the harvest curve for young tunny, as well as that for horse mackerel, showed a noticeable similarity to the earthquake distribution curve.

On February 29, 1972, at 6:32 P.M., an unusually large school of flying fish went into the nets of Japanese fishermen. The catch was about ten times as plentiful as could have been expected in that season.

It coincided with a great earthquake of magnitude 7.4 in the waters of neighboring Hachijo Island.[52]

In 1934, the Japanese ichthyologist Suyehiro introduced a scientific article about abnormal fish behavior before earthquakes in these words:[47]

As we are so often visited by terrible earthquakes, the unusual phenomena of the natural world accompanying them have long been observed by many scientists as well as laymen. Accordingly, papers dealing with the abnormal behavior of fishes prior to an earthquake are exceedingly numerous all of which have been systematically embodied in the report of Mr. K. Musha.

Prof. T. Terada has recently made a statistical investigation of the effects of the Idu earthquakes on the horse mackerel and bluefin tuna fisheries. Prof. S. Hatai has studied biologically the responses of the catfish to earthquakes. All these studies equally prove the existence of a mysterious and instinctive reaction of the fish to earthquakes.

Decades have passed since these words were written, and no progress has been made. There have not even been serious efforts to collect new data, and the bellwether works on the subject have been neither continued nor confirmed. They have gathered dust in the bottom drawer of an expensive scientific curio cabinet. Modern science seems unable to take a stand on this question.

Because of the special geographic situation of the country and because of the dramatic quality of the phenomenon, most Japanese reports of unusual animal behavior before earthquakes concern ocean creatures. But there are also numerous documents of similar reactions by land animals in Japan. Two to three months before the Edo quake of 1855, it was noticed that sparrows did not return to their territories. Ten days before, the chickens and roosters in the area of the epicenter became restless and nervous and did not want to go back into their coops.[49] Three days before, cawing crows began seeking the open spaces. Rats had suddenly disappeared, and many grass snakes had left their holes and were moving stiffly and awkwardly on the cold ground when it finally trembled.

Reports of rats behaving very oddly before an earthquake and conspicuously departing the danger zone just in time are very numerous. The light wooden structures of traditional Japanese homes were easily penetrated and settled by these swift and hardy rodents, and many people had no choice but to resign themselves to the pervasive presence of the uninvited boarders. Perhaps they had been tolerating the rats in their living spaces because their presence, according to an old tradition, suffuses the home with security and peace. In the city of Nagoya there was even a restaurant named the House of Rats. It was famous for the rats that ran around freely and were tolerated. They were, after all, the attraction. On the evening of October 27, 1891, the number of scurrying rats became smaller and smaller until finally they had disappeared altogether. This drew considerable attention, and the family that owned the business spoke of a forewarning of a catastrophe.[49] Indeed, the great Nobi earthquake, which reached an intensity of 7.9, came the next day. Its epicenter lay only about 40 kilometers (25 miles) from Nagoya.

The strange behavior of rats before the Nobi quake did not escape notice in other places. In Oyama it was noticed that the rats had been particularly excited, that crows had left their rookeries in the woods, and that sparrows had fled their nests. Several days before the quake, it was noticed in Aichi prefecture that winged ants had suddenly dispersed, and a day before the quake the pigeons disappeared from their nesting places. On the eve of the Nobi quake, in Gifu prefecture, it was impossible not to hear the crying of the wild cats.[49] Even when domestic cats meow in an odd way and are uncommonly nervous, many people in Japan conclude that earthquake danger looms.[42] Accordingly, this Nobi earthquake is not without its traditional cat story. It seems that shortly before the quake a cat was running around the house so restlessly that the owner opened the door to let it out—just in time to let the family flee from the house, which had suddenly begun to shake.

Before the Sanruki earthquake of June 15, 1896, it was noticed that the rats could not be heard anymore. Did they make for the open spaces? In Akita prefecture, birds began to cry loudly and continued to cry for 20 minutes until disaster struck. In another city in the district in the same year, rats and weasels suddenly began to run around aimlessly. The following day the Rikuu quake struck with a force of 7.5. An hour before, in the area of the epicenter, the roosters began to crow and the hens to cackle.[42]

During the strong Omachi quake of November 11, 1918, the abbot of the Buddhist temple at Daitakji was riding on horseback in the area of the village of Sanga-mra, in the north of Omachi. His horse suddenly dropped to the ground. No amount of whipping would make the horse get up again, and the abbot racked his brains in vain over the cause of this strange behavior. Only after the earthquake had passed was he able to get his horse back on its feet.[53]

Before the Kanto earthquake of 1923, as before other quakes, the rats suddenly disappeared. One of the people who later told the story of their disappearance said that when he first heard about it, several days before the quake, he had predicted the catastrophe. He had remembered that this same phenomenon had appeared before the Edo earthquake of 1855.[42]

Numerous stories about extraordinary reactions of animals have been told in connection with the severe Sanriku quake of 1933. The first signs of it, that rats were leaving their usual places, had been noted a month before in Iwate and Miyagi prefectures. This phenomenon intensified one week to several days before the quake. One day before the quake, the seagulls left their usual places on Kabura Island. A few hours before the quake, it was noted in Ofunate in Iwate prefecture that a duck did not want to go back into its sleeping place.

A Japanese folk tradition says that snakes, millipedes, worms, and similar ground animals come out of their holes before an earthquake. Also, swarms of dragon flies are supposed to announce danger.[42] It is said that the time of return of migratory birds deviates strongly from the norm in an earthquake year, or that these birds do not return at all. Ants are supposed to cling together in bunches and wait, motionless.[36]

The only studies of reactions of land animals to earthquakes that have been conducted in Japan and that may be described as scientific were those of F. Omori, published in 1923.[53] They focused on the pheasant (*Phasianus versicolor*), which, according to Japanese popular belief, announces earth tremors through intense crowing before the tremors become perceptible to humans. Pheasants—because they are clumsy fliers and because they taste good—are always exposed to pursuit by predators, and they depend for their survival in brush and grass on sensitive hearing and a delicate sense for earth vibrations. Therefore, they would seem to have excellent qualifications as short-term earthquake forecasters. Omori used to spend his evenings reading and studying long past midnight. When he sat quietly in his house, he could clearly feel gentle tremors from small quakes, and he could plainly hear the crowing of a pheasant in the large garden of his neighbor. For three years, from December 1913 to November 1916, with unimaginable patience and with the help of a chronometer, he noted to the second every crowing of the pheasant and every perceptible tremor of the ground. Later, he would determine the exact time and the force of the tremor with a seismograph. In those three years he managed to register the crowing behavior of the sensitive bird in connection with 23 small quakes. In seven cases the pheasant crowed distinctly before a perceptible quake, and in four cases it crowed in time but the quakes were too weak to be sensed by a human. In six cases it crowed simultaneously with the onset of the quake, in five further cases it crowed later, and once it did not crow at all. Thanks to Omori's admirable patience and precision, we know now that sensitive birds can perceive the forerunners of earthquake waves—the fast P waves, which are imperceptible to humans. Frogs, too, according to Omori, can detect P waves. They will often stop their musical croaking abruptly before the onset of a tremor. This is the same phenomenon reported from Italy by Taramelli and Mercalli.[23]

Even though it is very useful to understand how animals react toward small quakes, the collected observations do not necessarily help us to understand better those animal anomalies that appear clearly and early before the actual trembling of the ground in severe earthquakes. With each full value of the Richter earthquake scale the intensity of an earthquake increases tenfold. The energy of great quakes is so violent that completely different physical processes may be at work.

Japan's long isolation from the rest of the world makes the presence in her culture of traditions about animal earthquake premonition all the more remarkable.

The Americas

The oldest known description of the phenomenon from the Americas comes from the year 1799 and concerns an earthquake that happened in Cumana, Venezuela. Measured against all the detailed reports from the Old World and from China this report supplies no particularly interesting details of earthquake fear by animals, and yet it is among the most valuable that have come to our attention. The observer was none other than the German natural scientist Alexander von Humboldt. It was in Cumana that von Humboldt experienced his first big earthquake, and he recorded—with the precision that distinguished him— his manifold scientific observations. Concerning the behavior of animals during the series of quakes, he wrote the following: "The most anxious ones paid attention to the conduct of dogs, goats, and pigs. The latter, who have an exceptionally sharp sense of smell and who are accustomed to rooting in the ground, announce the nearness of danger through restlessness and clamoring. We shall let it stand [without comment] whether they are the first to hear the underground tumult because they are nearer to the ground or whether gases that emanate from the earth have an effect on their organs."[54a] What scientist has the right to dismiss lightly the earthquake premonition of animals as a product of popular fantasy when the critical spirit von Humboldt himself reported this phenomenon and devoted some thought to its possible cause?

The next report I was able to find comes from Missouri and concerns the New Madrid earthquake of 1811. Just before the quake, a horse being ridden toward Henderson snorted piteously, let its head droop, and reared.[55] A story of another incident, which happened in 1812 in the area of Caracas, Venezuela, also concerns a horse. A Spanish stallion broke from his stall and fled into the upland. The people took this to be a bad omen, and a heavy earthquake did indeed follow.[42,56]

Especially interesting observations of unusual animal behavior have been documented for the year 1835 in the area of the city of Concepción in central Chile. By chance, the English research ship *Beagle*, with Charles Darwin on board, was lying at anchor off the coast when an intense earthquake struck. Perhaps earthquake premonition by animals would not now be ridiculed by scientists as a product of the imagination of people in shock from earthquakes if Darwin had been able to follow the earthquake precursors consciously. But he slept through them, along with his companion Covington, in a quiet grove. He only noticed the sudden, intense, unusual sea breeze and the quake.[57] The captain of the *Beagle*, Robert FitzRoy, fortunately had more to report. In his diary there is the remark that on February 20, 1835, around 10 A.M., great flocks of seabirds had flown inland over the city of Concepción. Many inhabitants are supposed to have regarded this as very unusual. Also, the dogs in the port city of Talcahuano are supposed to have fled from their houses and disappeared among the hills. At 11:40, a strong earthquake began. FitzRoy also indicates that horses and other animals exhibited signs of great anxiety and that birds had flown in all directions, terrified.[58] A mysterious flight of seabirds from the Chilean coast into the interior of the country apparently was also observed before the earthquake of 1822.

In 1868 the phenomenon of seabirds fleeing into the hinterland before an earthquake was also observed in the port city of Iquique at the edge of the Atacama desert in northern Chile. Many hours before this catastrophe devastated the city, it was heralded by the shrieking of gulls and by other seabirds leaving the coast in great flocks to fly far into the interior.[59] Only when severe storms threaten do seabirds exhibit similar behavior.

In 1853 an earthquake happened in Cuba. The natives there had long been keeping a species of snake, *Majita domestica*, as house pets. They believed that there was no danger in the air as long as the pet snake abided under the roof. Before the earthquake of 1853, these snakes are reported to have left their nests in their houses and fled outdoors.[20,60]

Probably the most detailed description of abnormal animal behavior before and during an earthquake comes from the quake that destroyed San Francisco in 1906. The reason for the wealth of information is plain: It is the result of systematic questioning. The reports were collected by Miss Finette Locke in the area between Santa Cruz and Santa Rosa, and the most important findings were published in the official report of the State Earthquake Commission.[61]

What was most frequently reported about the behavior of dogs in the San Francisco quake was that they had howled during the night before the earthquake. Before the aftershocks many dogs became alert and barked, whined, or ran for cover. In Santa Rosa, a dog ran around the house 10 seconds before the onset of the earthquake and then jumped out of an open second-story window to the ground. After the quake several dogs ran away and did not return for a day or more. Some barked at the time of the quake and ran around with their tails between their legs. Others became very excited and kept running around aimlessly for some time after the quake, and they repeated this behavior during the aftershocks. Still others ran back and forth at high speed. Some bitches took their pups into shelters. After the quake some dogs crawled into their sleeping places and stayed there for several days; others refused to eat.

Cats, too, became very excited during the San Francisco quake. Some ran around wildly with their tails bushy and their back hair standing on end; others hid in dark corners or behaved abnormally in other ways. In some cases they disappeared for several days after the quake. In Olema seven cats were not seen for two days, and in Alameda two cats disappeared for three days. Some of these carried their kittens away. During the aftershocks the cats seemed to register the tremors before people did. They cowered in fear and ran.

Several cases were reported of cows fleeing in panic before the observers felt the tremor. Other observers reported that cows that had to be milked were restless before the tremor and lay down as soon as they felt the trembling. Some cows gave less milk than normal. Cattle in the hills descended to lower elevations, and in some places they did not return to the hills for several days. Many ranchers reported that their cattle fled in panic. Lowing and mooing at the time of the quake were commonly reported, and in some cases were said to have begun before the quake.

Horses whinnied and snorted before the quake and galloped in panic when they felt the trembling. Some fell down from the trembling. Horses in harness became frightened and ran away, while others stood and whinnied. Some horses with riders in the saddle stumbled and fell, and others stood and trembled. In Santa Rosa a mule refused to eat for an entire day before the quake. A farmer in the same area noticed horses running around snorting and whinnying. He called to his son, who was with the horses, to ask what the matter was. He felt the earth tremble before the boy could answer. In a stable on Alabama Street in San Francisco all thirty of the horses reared up, snorted, and jumped before the stablehand, who had just fed them, realized what the problem was. All but five broke their halters and bore down on the stablehand, who had to hold them off with a pitchfork. Several horses in the pumphouses of the San Francisco fire department shied and tore loose from their hitches. In other stables, too, some horses tore loose and others lay down.

Restless and howling dogs predicted a heavy 1942 earthquake in San Juan, Argentina, a few hours before it happened.[25] Many animals are said to have fled into the plain beyond the city limits before this catastrophe.

An interesting episode happened on July 10, 1958, on the Situk River, 2 miles from Strawberry Point, Alaska, a few minutes before the severe Lituya Bay earthquake shook that region.[62] Several families were picking berries and fishing for salmon when some of the people noticed that terns and other birds seemed disturbed and were flying around noisily. Men who had been fishing in the river reported an increase in the number of bites. Just about every cast brought in a fish. One of the men present, Horace M. Disotell, described the situation as follows: "I noted that the birds across the river from us were making a lot of excessive noise. . . . I believe these birds were terns; at any rate, they flew before the first tremors were felt by me. They circled to a great height for small birds and continued to make their calls. I would say this was approximately two to three minutes before the first tremors were felt by myself. . . ."

The earthquake instinct of birds is given added support by an event that happened on August 17, 1959, at Lake Hebgen, Montana, a popular habitat and resting place for aquatic game birds and other birds. The phenomenon has been described as follows: "At noon on August 16, 1959, every bird began to leave the area and by nightfall not a bird was to be seen on the lake. This event was so unusual that it aroused both local and national scientific interest. At midnight the first shocks of Yellowstone's frightening earthquake began just west of the park."[63,64] This report has been criticized from the standpoint that reliable observation of aquatic birds during nighttime hours is hardly possible. But it is only necessary to turn one's attention to the next great quake in the Americas in order to add a reliable report of unusual animal behavior to our list. This report concerns the severe earthquake that happened on May 22, 1960, in southern Chile, which was followed by many aftershocks. The informant is E. F. Kilian, then the director of the Zoological Institute of the Universidad Austral de Chile in Valdivia and formerly a lecturer at Justus Liebig University in Giessen, Germany. Kilian admits freely that he cannot make any certain statements about animal behavior before or during the main quake. The shock that he and many colleagues experienced during the several-minute-long quake was so great that they cannot even remember whether they were able to stay on their feet or whether they kept falling to the ground. Therefore, Kilian concludes, observations made at the time of the great catastrophe can hardly be considered sufficiently reliable. However, during the long period of the weaker aftershocks it became possible to note certain behavior modes of animals repeatedly and reliably. Kilian reports the following; "Over a period of months it was possible to observe that the breeding horses kept in a stable of the university's experimental farm perceived the shock about 5 seconds before people did and that they reacted by whinnying and trembling. Horses in the open fled at even very small tremors, while sheep ran away only when quakes showed between 4 and 6 on the Richter scale. Tremors of magnitude 4 and higher caused panic among cattle. A ring-necked pheasant kept in captivity would announce every quake by his loud cackling (as in mating) about 10 seconds before people were able to sense it."[65] This alarm lead time of 10 seconds is remarkable for short, weak aftershocks, especially since we do not know how long before that the pheasant was able to notice a change in its environment without becoming excited. It is altogether probable that the intensity of these warning signals increases with the severity of the earthquake.

A similarly severe earthquake occurred on March 27, 1964, in Alaska's Prince William Sound, and a book by E. Engle describing this disaster mentions the following episode on heavily hit Kodiak Island: "Another rancher, Louis Beaty, had gone up into the hills at three that afternoon when his cattle had unexpectedly left their low-lying grazing ground hours before their usual time. He figured it was best not to quarrel with whatever instinct sent them to high ground, no matter what the reasons were behind it—and he was right." The earthquake came at 5:36 P.M., and a great tidal wave rolled over the lowland. Another sign of earthquake-related animal behavior is mentioned by Engle: ". . . on the day of the great quake and tsunamis, even the mammoth Kodiak bears came out of hibernation two weeks early. Tracks showed that they'd left their rock caves or protective quarters beneath spruce trees and headed out—on the run."

Few residents of the Parkfield, California, area will ever forget June 25, 1966, when a veritable invasion of rattlesnakes came into their towns.[67,15] What had happened that they should flee the surrounding dry grassy hills? No explanation could be found until two days later when the area was shaken by a medium-to-heavy earthquake. Panicky behavior by cows during this quake was also reported.[68]

Volcanic eruptions are special cases of earthquake activity in which the earth's crust is broken open by gases and liquid lava. They are generally accompanied by ground tremblings, and there is no reason why there should be none of the typical earthquake signs before volcanic eruptions. Anomalies in animal behavior before volcanic outbreaks are indeed frequent. A good example is the eruption of Mount Arenal in Costa Rica, which had been sleeping peacefully for about 400 years until one day in 1968 the cattle fled the rich pastures on its slopes. According to the story told by the locals to geologist Tom Simkin, who had gone there to study the aftermath, the mountain erupted shortly after the cattle fled the danger zone. An article describing this incident is accompanied by a photograph of a disturbed-looking bull.[69]

J. Derr, a scientist interested in earthquake lights, reports that a man he knew had observed extremely unusual behavior by a dog for at least a minute before an earthquake in Oaxaca, Mexico.[70]

During the night before the San Fernando quake in California in January, 1971, two police patrols reported independently to their dispatcher that rats were scurrying through the streets in great numbers.[71] The police officers believed that the observation was unusual enough to be reported since they had not even known that there were any rats in San Fernando. They were not the only ones to see this strange migration.

There are also reports of excited animals in connection with the earthquake that destroyed Managua, the capital of Nicaragua. Several hours before the tremor, monkeys became conspicuous by their chattering.[42]

Reports of horses that began to shy several minutes before an earthquake have come out of Hollister, California, in connection with a relatively weak quake (magnitude 4.71).

These examples from the New World illustrate that reports of ab-normal animal behavior are not limited to lands where traditions are deeply rooted; they also arise in societies that have by and large lost their associations with old traditions.

The rest of the world

The independent appearance of similar reports of abnormal animal behavior before earthquakes among diverse cultures and peoples sup-ports the argument that a credible natural phenomenon underlies such observations.

Egypt is rarely racked by earthquakes, but many of her old mon-umental buildings carry their scars. There was a quake on October 12, 1855, and it is reported that in lower Egypt and in Cairo dogs announced it with loud barking and donkeys with unusual braying 2 hours beforehand.[72,13]

In 1867, in Java, all the roosters are said to have crowed shrilly and fled the settlements, which were subsequently turned into ruins.[59]

In April 1905 the inhabitants of Lahore, Pakistan, were baffled by a sudden strange change in the behavior of elephants. A vigorous earthquake a few hours later provided an explanation for the excite-ment.[59]

There is also an animal anecdote connected with the surprise eruption of Mount Hekla in Iceland in 1947, which came one fine morning at 6:40. A couple living nearby told scientists who were investigating the circumstances of the eruption that they had been awakened between 2 and 3 A.M. When the woman went into the kitchen and turned on the light she saw that their old dog, which normally slept outside the kitchen door, was standing in the middle of the floor, obviously very frightened by something.[69]

A Russian book on earthquakes[73] reports that several days before the 1948 Ashkabad earthquake, which reached considerable intensity, ants ran from their hills, bees flew from their hives, and snakes scurried from their holes like lizards. A Soviet earthquake researcher told an American colleague that just before the earthquake, sheep were being driven from the mountain pastures into the valleys. The many snakes that were crawling around on the ground caused much disorder in the flocks.

From the Kamchatka Peninsula comes an interesting report of an observation made in the winter of 1955–56 and made public in the West by the Soviet geophysicist Vladimir Olchenskov.[74] A mighty vol-canic eruption took the lives of hundreds of people in that sparsely settled region, but not one of the bears hibernating in the area came to harm. They had left their winter lairs and wandered away long before scientific instruments registered any sign of volcanic activity.

A well-supported case of unusual animal behavior occurred before the eruption of Mount Kilauea on the island of Hawaii on February 28, 1955. On February 26, the dogs on the Nanawale ranch ran around excitedly and developed a need to dig holes in which they then sniffed as if they were pursuing small animals. Gordon A. MacDonald, then the director of the Hawaii Volcano Observatory, was notified. MacDonald and his colleagues had been suspecting for months that a volcanic eruption was coming because, among other signs, the micro-quake activity in the area was rising. The scientists spent most of February 27 in the area of the ranch, examining the terrain. They found no signs of developing cracks, and they smelled no volcanic gases even when they sniffed the holes that the dogs had dug. However, the next morning the volcano erupted no more than 400 meters (about 1,300 feet) from where the dogs had been digging.[69]

One morning in 1965 the inhabitants of Taal, in the Philippines, were awakened at 2:30 by noises made by frightened dogs, cats, and cattle. Some people are said to have heeded the alarm reaction of the animals and fled. The volcano later erupted and devastated their homes with ash, lava, and mud.[69]

We are not accustomed to thinking of earthquakes in Antarctica, and yet that continent has them. In fact, there is even a report of unusual animal behavior in connection with one of these quakes. The incident occurred in 1967 on the Palmer Peninsula. On December 4 the penguins and skuas deserted the terrain around the scientific base there for no apparent reason. Several hours later, tremors reached magnitude 4.7 on the Richter scale.[75,13]

In April and May of 1976 there were earthquakes of magnitude 7 in the Uzbek Soviet Republic. North of Buchara, on the day before the catastrophe, great swarms of bats were observed flying around during the day.[76] It might be expected that, among all animals, these highly specialized night hunters, who often live in mountain caves in intimate contact with the pulse beat of the earth, would react most sensitively to earthquake signs. No other observations of bats have become known to me, but people from the highland of Anatolia in Turkey have told me that, besides the howling of dogs and the rest-lessness of cattle, the appearance of bats during the day is highly valued there as a sign of the coming of a severe earthquake.

It is likely that much positive information about unusual animal behavior before earthquakes has already been collected in the Soviet Union, because serious efforts are apparently being made there to observe this mysterious phenomenon systematically and to apply it to earthquake prediction. That, at any rate, emerges from an article by A. Werner titled "Russian scientists use animals to predict disasters." The article, which appeared in the Canadian weekly *Midnight* and later in the book *California Superquake*,[74] referred to statements made by the Soviet geophysicist Vladimir Olchenskov when he announced the establishment of a chain of animal alarm centers in the earthquake-prone area of Uzbekistan. Some of Olchenskov's remarks draw an interesting picture of the experiences and the hopes connected with the unexplained phenomenon:

For one who knows how to "read" the signs they give, animals are the most sensitive disaster barometers known to science. The warning centers are scientific observation posts of animals in natural or near-natural habitats. The observers simply watch the behavior of animals preselected for "disaster sensitivity" and report significant changes in their habits to a central data center where assessment is made of the information which is correlated with disaster reports of both past and future.

Some of the observation teams' reports would be hard to believe if they weren't so carefully documented.

Ants pick up their eggs and move out of anthills in a mass migration before earthquakes.

Shrimp crawl on dry land before a storm; jellyfish head for deep water.

Pheasants chorus an alarm before earth tremors.

Goats and antelopes refuse to go into indoor pens for months before earthquakes.

Tigers and other big cats do the same a few weeks before quakes occur.

These have not been isolated occurrences, but are part of a far-reaching [behavior] pattern in nature which our researchers out in the field have witnessed time and time again. There is no question but that animals have alarm systems which warn them to leave areas which are about to become dangerous to them.

These remarks recall the efforts of the Chinese, which were probably the model for the Soviet program. Also, Olchenskov's remarks are the first mention outside of China and Japan of animals seeming to sense earthquakes more than a week ahead of time. Until now I had been blaming such early signs on unsuccessful runups of the earth's crust.

Earthquake premonition in folklore

Modern psychology, anthropology, and archaeology have repeatedly suggested that profound knowledge about natural relationships and actual events are reflected in ancient symbols, legends, religions, and common-sense rules. Random ideas or fantasies are not carried through generations for hundreds (perhaps thousands) of years. To achieve a broad basis among a people, a tradition must have at one time expressed a profound relationship. It may, perhaps, have passed on an observation, reported an event, or given an enlightening explanation.

For exactly this reason, the many reports and scientific findings of anomalous behavior by catfish before earthquakes tempt one to consider the origin of the Japanese legend that quakes are set off by the underground motions of a giant catfish. If the catfish legend does indeed represent a transfigured and elaborated ancient experience with unusual catfish behavior before earthquakes, and if legends can indeed arise through such circumstances, then similar animal legends about earthquakes must have arisen elsewhere in the world.

Since reports from many countries describe how snakes, even in winter, leave their burrows before earthquakes and crawl around on the surface, there should be snake legends similar to the Japanese catfish legend. Such legends do exist. One was told by a native of southern Chile and written down by the earthquake researcher Montessus de Ballore toward the end of the nineteenth century. This legend accounts for not only the earthquake itself, but for the floods and landslides that often accompany it:

The Cai-cay is a very big snake, which is mistress of the sea, lakes, and rivers. She lives in an underground cave, and when she comes out, she causes the waters to rise, go over the banks, and flood everything. Her enemy is another snake called Treg-treg who lives inside a hill. She has the power to set herself in motion just when the water rises and she always seems to overpower it.

Often the two snakes fight. As soon as she sees she can't put her enemy's dwelling underwater, the furious Cai-cay tries to flood the dwelling by digging a hole into it to let the water in. However, Treg-treg with her powerful tail sends stones and earth falling down to fill in the excavation made by Cai-cay. This causes landslides which often fall onto the snake and smash her down. To free herself, Cai-cay shakes herself vigorously. These tremors cause earthquakes.[77]

Some of the oldest known documents offer ample support to the hypothesis that unusual animal behavior before earthquakes has lived in the consciousness of peoples since time immemorial. Out of ancient

Egypt, for example, comes the "Tale of the Shipwrecked," in which the appearance of a deity in snake form to someone stranded on an island in the Red Sea is accompanied by thunderous roaring and earth tremors.[78]

A similar incident has been passed down from the ambit of Greco-Roman culture: Ovid writes that when a Roman embassy visited the temple of Epidauros, the son of Apollo, Aesclepius, appeared in the shape of snakes, and his appearance was accompanied by the trembling of the gate pillars.[79]

In a fifth-century book of the annals of Ravenna, written descriptions of the earthquakes of 429 and 443 A.D. are followed by a picture of a monster in the form of a snake, which apparently is spitting at a helpless man who holds out his hand defensively against it. Antiquarians have no explanation for the snake, but they suspect that this is an old depiction of Typhon or a giant who was said to appear as a snake demon.[80]

In ancient Chinese mythology, it was a winged giant snake (the world dragon Lung) that set the earth trembling, and in India, significantly, it was an elephant.[81] People of the Altai region of central Asia believed that earthquakes were caused by the motion of giant fish upon which the world rests. Also in central Asia, quakes were said to be caused by the activity of a mighty subterranean frog. In the mythology of the Kirghiz and the Caucasus Tatars, a giant bull carrying the earth on its horns produced the earthquakes. Even the ancient Hebrews believed in an earth demon in the shape of a bull. The people of northeastern Siberia believed that an underground mammoth set off earthquakes by its movements. The original inhabitants of Kamchatka, on the other hand, assumed that the dog on which the earth spirit Tuila rode made the earth tremble whenever it would shake the snow from its back.[82]

The Tzotzil Indians of southern Mexico have a story that earthquakes are caused by a cosmic jaguar that scratches itself against the pillars of the world.[83]

On the island of Crete, which has known the violence of nature often, mythology associates the bull of Knossos with earthquakes. It is said that, in unrestrained fury, the bull roars exactly as the earth does during an earthquake.[84]

Among the Babylonians, the underworld goddess Erashkigal was considered the originator of earthquakes. Her cries (the rumblings that develop along with an earthquake) were compared to the roaring of the lion, the howling of the wolf, the coughing of the fox, or the squealing of the pig.[85] This comparison can only be linked with the panicky sounds made by animals before an earthquake.

Folklore and the store of folk experience accumulated by people who live or have lived in earthquake-prone countries is rich in knowledge of earthquake premonition by animals. Various cultures have held that certain animals could foresee natural disasters, and their behavior was taken into consideration in divining the future. The sacred birds of antiquity and the geese at the Capitol in Rome are witness to the trust of man in the more wakeful senses of animals, even though much superstition was brought into play in interpreting animal behavior.

That the landing of a swarm of bees on the top of the Capitol was considered a bad sign by the Romans may point to a very ancient experience. It was observed in China[23] and other countries that bees occasionally swarmed before earthquakes. The natives of Caracas, Venezuela, kept dogs, cats, and jerboas as oracle animals that would announce natural disaster in time by their restlessness.[56] And, as mentioned, country people in Cuba used to, and perhaps still do, raise pet snakes for early earthquake warning.[20,60] In the villages on the slopes of the Mount Etna and on other volcanos, peasants rely on the earthquake sense of cats. They like to keep several animals in the house, and when all of them disappear suddenly, the peasants, too, consider it prudent to leave.[65]

The popular belief that animals can sense an earthquake in time is also widespread in the Peruvian Andes. On a journey through the highland there I happened to read a report in a local paper in which a native family described how strangely their donkeys had behaved before a quake.[86] The animals had stopped and had become very stubborn, and a trembling had run over their bodies. The report also contained a brief description of the experiences of local peasants with animals before an earthquake:

The peasants who through daily contact have become familiar with the capabilities that some animals possess, maintain that [the donkey] is in a position to sense the nearness of an earthquake several minutes and sometimes several hours in advance. . . .

There is also an old deep-seated tradition in some of the villages in the Sierra according to which small birds announce the imminence of earth tremors and other natural phenomena with their calls. The calls are unusual when an earthquake approaches, which is why it is easy to tell the difference, say these [peasants].

An interesting cross-section of traditions about earthquake premonitions by animals can be found in the popular beliefs of an earthquake-plagued country like Chile.[77,87] "The dogs howl when an
earthquake approaches," one can often hear people say in Santiago
and in other parts of the country. In La Serena, farther north, this
additional rule applies: "When animals show unrest and seek the
company of people, then one should count on trembling very soon!"
There is an anecdote that elaborates on the event that started the
idea that animals become tame before earthquakes: "Many years ago
I heard an overseer on my father's hacienda tell of the great fright
he got on a certain occasion when he happened to be in a pasture
and suddenly found himself surrounded by about 100 animals. Among
them were a few wild cattle which on this occasion appeared to be
as harmless and as intimidated as the tame ones. The good man, as
he told me, soon got his explanation for the unusual incident. It was
not long before a heavy earth tremor struck."[77]

Some instances of Chilean folk wisdom refer precisely (and apparently
unintentionally) to the time of the event that started the particular
tradition. This is true of a series of proverbs that connect the nighttime
crowing of roosters with coming earthquakes. This nighttime activity
alone would be unusual behavior on the part of the roosters. But the
vernacular is so precise in the transmission of life-or-death observations
that it includes incidentals and ancillary matter—and by doing so it
unwittingly and unnecessarily limits the impact of its statement. The
following examples illustrate this point nicely. The proverb has arisen
in Santiago that "if the rooster crows before eight at night, it is a sign
that it will soon be trembling."[77] The basis for this folk wisdom can
be traced to the night of August 16, 1906, when an old woman alarmed
the residents of an apartment building where she lived by calling to
them "Get out, get out—the rooster has crowed and an earthquake
is coming." Immediately thereafter came the disaster that laid central
Chile in ruins. In the city of Rengo they have the proverb, "When
the rooster crows before ten at night, it is certain that there will be
a quake two hours later."[77] This rule probably goes back to a midnight
earthquake that was announced by a rooster who had begun crowing
two hours earlier. An earthquake rule that has come out of Coquimbo
is so detailed that it is almost comical: "If roosters crow three times
in a row on a Friday and if they repeat this threefold song three times
in a row, there will be an earthquake."[87] Obviously, all the roosters
once crowed at a certain time without letup before the onset of an
earthquake.

A popular perception about roosters crowing at night being associated with earthquakes has arisen independently in widely separated parts of Chile. In Santa Fé de Bogota it is considered a sign of a coming earthquake when three roosters crow together before midnight. (This same rule is also current on the Isola delle Femine and near Palermo, Sicily, but there it is not especially important that the crowing happen before midnight.) In La Florida, near Santiago, it is said that there will be trembling the same night if chickens that have already roosted jump from their perches and cackle.[87]

In Linares, Chile, people believe that cats feel the approach of an earthquake, become nervous and excited, and jump and run around the house before a tremor.

The tradition on the Isola delle Femine and in Capacci, Sicily, about the behavior of cats before earthquakes is a very interesting one. The cats, it is said, show unrest and cry, their hair stands on end, and sparks jump from their backs.[87] According to this description, it would seem as if the cats had become electrostatically charged before an earthquake. Cat fur, because it is very dry, is very easily charged, and for that reason it is used in physics instruction for electrostatic experiments and to prove that electricity can be generated through friction. Cats are said to be extraordinarily sensitive to electrostatic charges. I was told in Chile that this was the reason that, in days past, the crews of wooden ships, which collect small amounts of frictionally generated electricity, would keep dogs instead of cats to control the rats. It could happen to a cat that upon jumping ashore it would fluff up into a hairy ball, and sometimes the animals would be hurt by sudden electrical discharges.

An especially noteworthy piece of folk wisdom from Pitrufquen in central Chile says that before an earthquake the wild animals become gentle and pumas do not dare even to raise their heads. In Greece it is said of storks that they have the ability to predict earthquakes. A sudden gathering, with conspicuous circling high in the air above the sea near the coast, is often said to have been recognized as an omen of earthquakes.

A funny episode which Alexander von Humboldt observed around 1800 on the banks of the Orinoco River assures us that the forest Indians, those most experienced nature experts, knew (and probably still know) the phenomenon of earthquake premonition by animals:

On a certain day, the frightful mosquitoes disappeared. We congratulated each other and asked whether this happy condition, this sweetening of our work, was permanent. But soon we surrendered to imagined fears instead of enjoying the moment. We imagined that the order of nature had been disturbed. The old Indians, the ones familiar with the place, assured us that the disappearance of the mosquitoes could be nothing but the precursor of a great earthquake. We discussed this heatedly, we perked up our ears with each minor noise in the foliage of the trees, and when the air filled again with mosquitoes, we greeted their return with pleasure.

The Soviet geophysicist Olchenskov reports that on the Kamchatka Peninsula, which is often plagued by volcanic eruptions and earthquakes, the natives depend on bears for timely information about an impending volcanic eruption.[47] When these ponderous animals become sprightly and suddenly leave their accustomed hunting grounds, the people of the peninsula consider it prudent to move out of the affected area also. It occasionally happens that entire villages are evacuated or abandoned by people only because the bears have fled an area around a volcano. No bear is ever supposed to have come to grief in this region—which is among the world's most active volcanically— through a volcanic eruption or an earthquake. They are supposed to have always managed to leave the endangered area just in time. (As mentioned, during the period of intense volcanic activity from 1955 to 1956, when hundreds of people lost their lives, the bears interrupted their hibernation in time and decamped to a safer area.)

To find out whether the knowledge contained in these many popular traditions makes any sense—whether it agrees with the many historically documented reports of unusual animal behavior before earthquakes or leads to contradictions—it seems useful to extract the essential information from the various popular sayings and to summarize it in the form of rules for early detection of earthquakes. If these traditions are valid, an earthquake is on the way

• when four-legged animals show great nervousness without apparent reason (Peru, Venezuela),

• when birds become excited and give forth unusual calls (Peru),

• when dogs howl in unison (Chile),

• when roosters crow persistently at night (Italy, Chile),

• when roosting chickens leave their roosts and cackle excitedly (Chile),

• when wild animals appear to be tame and intimidated (Chile),

• when the many pesky flies suddenly disappear (Venezuela),

• when snakes leave their lairs and flee outdoors (Cuba),

- when birds flock together, fly high, and circle conspicuously (Greece),
- when bears leave their winter lairs prematurely (Kamchatka), or
- when cats cry nervously, run around houses excitedly, and then flee outdoors (Italy, Chile).

This list could have been composed by a Chinese earthquake bureau to guide amateur observers. The phenomena described either match or fit in with traditions and documented observations from the Middle Kingdom and those of other lands.

Folk wisdom about earthquake prediction by animals deserves respect. Many of the popular sayings are, after all, not just the fruits of individual observations, but have been repeatedly submitted to tests through generations. Would people who depend so much on nature take the trouble to keep watching animals if they saw no point in it and had never realized any benefit from it? Watching animals can be nerve-racking because of the occasional false alarm. Just how sincere the belief of country people in the earthquake premonition of animals can be was noted by one von Salis during an earthquake period in Calabria: "So firm did they believe in the sense of animals in the Calabrian earthquake time of 1783 that later it was only necessary for a donkey to bray or for a dog to howl to cause all people to rush out of their huts into the field."[16]

3

Is There a Characteristic Behavior?

I have gone to some lengths to collect the most representative eye-witness reports possible from all over the world and to reproduce them, sometimes word for word, to lay the basis for a critical discussion of earthquake premonition by animals. These reports comprise observations of simple peasants and those of scientists acclaimed in their time, personal experiences and the results of systematic inquiries, and reports from different cultures, ethnic groups, and epochs. To make it easier to analyze the contents of these 78 independent reports, I have put them in a table (table 1) that gives the date of the earthquake, the type and the time of the abnormal animal behavior, and the source of the information. As figure 3 shows, reports of animal earthquake prediction have come from all areas of the world that are prone to earthquakes. One thing critics should not be able to say is that such observations were only extensions of the earthquake superstitions of individual peoples. That the animals' earthquake sense is not an empty myth becomes evident when we compare some of the reported behavioral peculiarities. Examples of very similar behavior are encountered repeatedly.

Especially conspicuous is the intense fear that makes dogs bark for hours or all night long, drives fowl and cattle to flee in panic, and causes horses to shy. Puzzling, but apparently just as characteristic, are the efforts of animals to break out of their stables or to leave their burrows. Occasionally the opposite effect is observed: Game animals approach people, predators become strangely tame, and rats let themselves be caught. Are these fear reflexes, or is it that under some circumstances earthquake precursors have an intimidating effect? The reports of pigs biting each other like dogs and of cows fighting with one another seem to be in stark contrast with those of cattle crowding for protection around the herder and of rats running into the hands

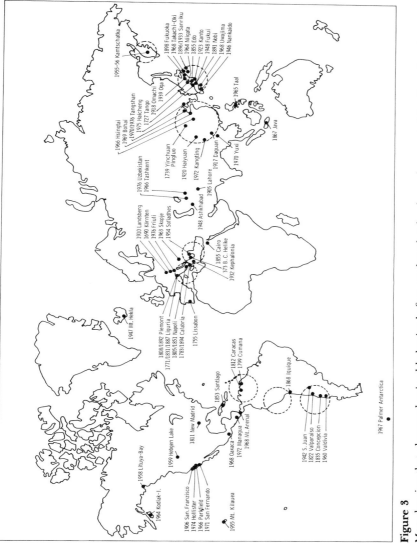

Figure 3

Map showing that abnormal animal behavior before earthquakes has been documented in all earthquake-prone areas of the world.

of their mortal enemy. In the former cases animals seem to show an excess of aggressiveness; in the latter, a lack of it.

This apparent contradiction could furnish weighty arguments to the critics who doubt that this phenomenon is genuine, but it does not present an insurmountable hurdle to understanding if we assume that those mysterious signals interfere with the animals' hormone balances. Then it would be mostly the threshold of stimulation, which would either rise or fall before an earthquake, that would shape the animals' responses to environmental influences.

Many of the so-called abnormal reactions of animals before earthquakes are actually not very abnormal and do appear on other occasions. They are unusual only under the given circumstances. Dogs bark when they suspect a burglar, and hordes of migrating rats, excited birds in the air, and crowing roosters can be observed in other circumstances. The Chinese observations that so many kinds of living beings with considerably different sensory ranges have reacted similarly to the unknown precursors, without yet being endangered by earthquakes, militates against a purely instinctual reaction.

This contrast between aggressiveness and tameness, which intrudes now and then, is joined by a second noteworthy peculiarity: There have been many earthquakes about which no conspicuous animal behavior before the tremors has become known. In addition, some animals that happened to be near people before some earthquake disasters were remarkably calm and seemed normal. This peculiarity might be connected to the fact that different earthquakes go through different phases of development and thus give off different warning signs. But the map from China that shows the geographic distribution of abnormal animal behavior before the Haicheng earthquake (figure 2) proves that before the same earthquake animals can act alarmed or normal, depending on their location.

Whether the unknown earthquake signal that can have a disquieting effect on animals depends on the geological makeup of the ground or on the momentary weather cannot be decided at this point. Aggressive animal behavior is more conspicuous than the peaceful kind. Were the animals in the white zones of the map in figure 2 more than ordinarily peaceful because of the approaching earthquake? Is there a connection between this phenomenon and the above-mentioned contrasts in aggressive behavior?

Before we pursue the reasons for animal earthquake premonitions, it will be useful to devote some thought to the average time span between premonition and quake. This will determine how the underlying physical processes can be used to save human lives.

The sparse reports of abnormal animal behavior before 78 earthquakes permit no reliable statistical analysis. It is also hard to estimate how the intensity of an earthquake, which increases tenfold with each unit on the Richter scale, influences animal behavior. However, a general and reasonably realistic figure for the earliest average starting point of the phenomenon was achieved like this: All 78 quakes were considered equal, and the animal anomaly that appeared first was selected. All reports of unusual animal behavior that preceded quakes by more than 10 days were ignored because they may be connected with earthquake forerunners and not with the main event. In all cases where reported times were vague, approximated minimal values were assumed. In all incidents of abnormal animal behavior that occurred between 3 and 10 days before a quake (they amount to nearly 10 percent), the time span was arbitrarily reduced to one-third so as not to give them too much weight. Time spans from 1 to 3 days are given in 24 percent of the reports, which indicates that they are representative and must be given full consideration. If we look for the average point of time of the first appearance of uncommon animal behavior in these reports, which in the above manner have been sifted somewhat for improbable deviations, we find that it is 21 hours. If one could comprehend the phenomenon, the conditions for saving human lives from earthquake disasters would be ideal.

We can do an interesting experiment with the average point of onset of restless animal behavior before earthquakes. If the examined phenomenon were not real but a product of the imagination of the people, then the mentality of individual peoples would be reflected in it directly. In one culture the median time span might be around 2 minutes; in another, 2 days. But, remarkably, the average point of onset in earthquake traditions deviates little from the world median. In Europe it is 18.5 hours, in China 25.5, and in Japan 23.5. In the Americas, interestingly, the earthquake apprehension of animals was, as a rule, noticed only 5.8 hours before the quake. In the rest of the world, however, the mean of 21.7 hours is remarkably close to the overall mean of 21 hours.

This side observation is another sign, albeit a minor one, that the earthquake premonition of animals is a true natural phenomenon. If we want to delineate the underlying reasons for it better, we should not pass up the opportunity to find out how animals react during the actual seconds or minutes of an earthquake itself. At that point, the unknown and nerve-frazzling alarm signal should have escalated to its peak. Does the animals' behavior then betray any peculiarities that will bring us closer to the secret of earthquake premonition?

It was a peaceful and idyllic scene in Friuli. An old man was driving a herd of young cattle down the road between the villages of Redona and Compone. The day was July 5, 1976, and the time was almost noon. It seemed as if nothing could disturb the serenity of the summer landscape, but without any apparent reason a wave of excitement suddenly ran through the herd and the animals ran away as if stung. The panicky chase led through rough terrain. Fifteen young cattle fell down a steep slope, broke bones, and died; then everything was peaceful again. No one could explain the event. Only the automatic recordings of an earthquake station threw some light on what had happened. At 11:51 A.M., at exactly the time of this mysterious incident, there had been a small earthquake. It was the 159th aftershock of the large quake of May 6, and it lasted 53 seconds. The tremor reached the modest value of 3.5 on the Richter scale and was barely perceptible to people in the open.[88] For the cattle, however, this quake meant an escalation of excitement and finally a tragedy. Why?

In our age many domestic animals are veritably flooded with vibrations. They feel them, for example, when trucks and trains rumble past, or when they themselves are being carried in vehicles. They rarely, if ever, panic outright. Do earthquakes harbor some secret? Is it less the vibrations than some physical processes that stretch the nerves of animals to the breaking point? Do these processes produce a primal fear whose causes we do not yet know? The animal psychologist H. von Hentig, in an article published in 1923,[20] seems to have been the only one so far to have tried to come to terms with this question (though he was unable to provide an enlightening explanation).

A deeper insight into the explosive instinctual behavior of animals, and into the mysterious reasons behind whatever brings it forth before earthquakes, can be gained if we try to reconstruct the various kinds of behavior from eyewitness reports.

From the observations about the earthquake behavior of dogs it is apparent that not all dogs act the same way. As with people, some react to a challenge with aggressive behavior, while others let themselves be intimidated. Restlessness often appears some time before an earthquake. Dogs whine and howl for no apparent reason. If they are lying on the ground, they will jump up and storm into the street, barking. But there have been descriptions of dogs that looked forward to an earthquake altogether lethargically. They would seek the nearness of the master, stare at him intently, or crawl under the furniture. If the quake is imminent or if the fateful chain of tremors is already in progress, the affected communities become the site of cacophonous barking and howling. Even a characteristic "earthquake whine" has been mentioned.[20]

A severe earthquake can disturb the normal instinctual behavior of dogs noticeably, and it can set off reactions that would never have been observed under any other conditions. They leap at doors barking loudly[89] without anyone standing behind them, or when outdoors they act as if they want to flush out an invisible enemy and bring him to bay.[23] Then, too, the fact that they occasionally leave settled areas[56,58] or that they fail to return to their owners and homes for days[90] is in stark contrast to their usual demeanor. It should be added, however, that many dogs have comported themselves courageously and sensibly during earthquakes. The zoologist Kilian tells about a smallish dog of uncertain breed that kept chasing the alternately opening and closing clefts in the ground and barking at them furiously.[65] The mechanical tremors of the ground alone cannot explain the highly disturbed behavior of dogs. Earthquakes rarely last more than a minute, but the mysterious excitement of dogs often begins long before and often continues for some time afterwards. And dogs generally do not panic when taken on trains or streetcars, where it is often difficult to keep standing.

There is much support for the proposition that the intensity of an earthquake often has no relation to the intensity of the reactions of animals. This is shown impressively by observations made in the zoological garden of Dresden on the occasion of a smallish quake that struck central Germany on March 8, 1872.[91] During the earth tremors—which were completely harmless to the animals—the elephant kept running back and forth whipping his tail excitedly, the antelope tried to jump over the high fence of its enclosure, and the bird house was suddenly filled with such a wave of crying, shrieking, fluttering, and other noises that visitors, young and old, ran outside in panic. What drove the birds, who were accustomed to frequent disturbances and who sat on swaying branches, out of their serenity?

A few interesting details about the demeanor of songbirds during earthquakes have been observed by Wölffing.[89] According to him, birds kept alone in their cages are supposed to have withdrawn into corners and emitted plaintive cries. When two or more birds were caged together, they would at first be totally still. This would be followed by a period in which the birds fluttered back and forth in apparent fright. This kind of panic could be seen among birds that showed hardly any restlessness when their perches were shaken on other occasions.

During a comparatively weak earthquake along the Rhine in 1846, birds fell from their perches, and there were reports of some of them dying.[92] On another occasion, von Hentig saw a tame jackdaw lying on its back as if dead, breathing heavily, with its wings spread and its feathers ruffled. When I asked around in Fruili, I was given reports of many songbirds having died. A peasant woman whom I know personally found two of her four canaries dead in their cage even though the cage had not been hit by any falling masonry. The remaining pair had—contrary to their habit—failed to build a nest in the spring of the earthquake year. The lasting terror that stays with many birds after an earthquake is documented in several reports. In connection with an earthquake that shook Algiers on August 21, 1856, it was reported that nightingales and other songbirds did not sing for a whole week.[20] During the great Neapolitan earthquake of August 1851, the earthquake researcher Mallet noticed that for more than a week no sparrows were heard twittering among the walls.[19] During a smaller quake, it was noticed that young storks made desperate efforts to fly. They failed and did not repeat their attempts until much later.[89]

Panic among domestic fowl has been noticed during smaller quakes in Germany. After the earthquake that shook the Altmühl Jura in Bavaria on June 2, 1915, it was reported that the chickens acted as if crazy, flapped their wings, and shrieked in terror as if a fox had broken into the coop. Near Kirchdorf, the chickens even tried to get out through windowpanes.[93] Wild birds in the open also acted excited. Swallows left their nests, sparrows tore away in all directions, jackdaws left their hiding places, and songbirds stopped singing. Ravens and jays flew up from their trees, crying loudly, and cackling pheasants fluttered down from their branches to the ground. When earthquakes are severe, the reactions of feathered animals are correspondingly more intense.

During the Calabrian earthquake of 1783, flocks of birds flew around restlessly and were reluctant to settle to the ground. On the occasion of the quake of Quintero in Chile in 1822, the shore birds cried weirdly all night long.[16] Roosters, which usually wait for others to sound off after they have crowed, crowed in a peculiar manner and completely without order during the quake of Lokris, Greece. Before the great Chilean earthquake of May 22, 1960, 500 young chickens and 300 yearling chickens in Angachilla had been laying an average of 230 eggs a day. The shock of the earthquake reduced the egg production of the 800 hens to 14 eggs the next day, and 20 days later they were still laying only 30 eggs a day. The chickens' red combs turned white.[65]

Cats show especially marked reactions during earthquakes.[89,93] They tremble all over and lay their ears back, and their hair stands on end. They meow pitifully and act crazy. It has been reported that during an earthquake in Lokris, one cat cried so hideously before each shock that the noise became unbearable. That mother cats try to carry their young to safety has been mentioned in old reports.[89,93] The phenomenon of cats disappearing for two and three days and then for several weeks coming home only to eat—reported to me repeatedly in Friuli—has also been observed in other earthquakes. Kilian reported that after the Chilean quake of 1960 his very affectionate tomcat would come into the house only to eat, even though it had not been in the house during the quake. The cat never got over this strange shyness, and died a year and a half later. After the San Francisco earthquake, cats also did not return home for days on end.[61]

Horses stamp the ground during an earthquake, snort, tremble all over, jump, and buck.[92] Harnessed horses shy and try to take off. Riders are thrown.[20] Like dogs, horses are said to spread their four legs during the movements of the ground, and to lower their heads. Often they fall to the ground. Cattle low, stomp, and rage. In Friuli the peasants told how cows in panic climbed the stable walls with their forelegs. Kilian reports that during the Chilean earthquake of 1960, bellowing cows and whinnying horses ran away in tight formations. In other cases, the animals would crowd together, with horses trembling hard.

There are also some old reports about the earthquake behavior of game animals. It has been observed that red deer and rabbits show their excitement by leaving the protective forest and brush.[89] On one occasion rabbits ran around a field with twitching noses during an earthquake and did not even take notice of the observer standing nearby.[20] During the Chilean earthquake of 1960, South American dwarf deer inside a large enclosure were observed running around aimlessly with their nostrils flaring. One of the animals ran to the caretaker and, trembling, licked his hand.[65]

The peripatetic scientist von Humboldt noted that forest animals became excited during an earthquake, and that sluggish crocodiles tried desperately to get out of the water onto dry land and into the forest.[54a]

Animals in the water seem to suffer more intensely from the consequences of earthquakes than do land animals. Many reports attest to the deathly torment of fish, their desperate attempts to leave their wet environment, and great losses inflicted on their numbers. The oldest document of fish dying as a consequence of an earthquake dates from 140 B.C. and is connected to a tragic event: A detachment of troops of Typhon, who had defeated Sarpedon, the general of Demetrius II, near Ptolemais, were marching along the Syrian-Phoenician coast drunk with joy. An earthquake struck and an immense tidal wave rolled over the soldiers. The just-defeated enemies rushed to the scene and found the bodies of the victors under mounds of dead fish.[94] I have already mentioned the dramatic dying off of fish during the Kanto earthquake of 1923 in the rivers around Yokohama.[43] Similar reports about mass destruction of fish have come from the earthquakes in Garga, Italy (January 23, 1746), Callao, Peru (March 30, 1828), and Chile (February 20, 1835).[16] What besides an earthquake could have caused the upwelling of Lake Constance in 1537, which killed a large number of fish? And after the severe earthquake in Calabria in 1783 the "*cicirelli,*" a species of fish that lives on the bottom buried in sand and that had been reserved as food for the rich, became the nourishment of the poor because they rose to the surface in great numbers.

Von Hentig concluded from his investigation in 1923 that an earthquake affects animals' internal secretions, and therefore their behavior, in such a way that the explanation of a triggering by mechanic vibrations is not enough. Animals are obviously reacting to another geophysical phenomenon—one that appears before the earthquake, and one that merely culminates in the quake.

4

Signals From the Earth

The earth's throes before a quake

Anyone who in deep winter crosses a bridge over a slow-moving river covered with ice floes should take a few minutes to watch and listen to the spectacle. The play of the floes, their swaying and turning, the manner in which they bump one another, push each other up or down, scrape against each other, slide past each other, and shatter one against the other, is an object lesson in miniature for physical events of great force: earthquakes. Only a thin crust, less than 100 kilometers (62 miles) thick—the thin skin of an apple—separates us from the white-hot viscous interior of the earth. Like the mud bottom of a dried-up puddle, this crust is broken up into many irregular plates. They drift along on the rotating earth, following the forces of inertia like ice floes in a river. Measured by human time scales, their movements are very slow. For example, America only drifts about 6 meters (19 feet) from Europe in 100 years.

The movements of the plates are not uniform. Again and again, there are jerking movements through which built-up pressures are relieved or lagging fragments move up. In a few seconds or minutes, billions of tons of rock are moved. For the earth these are only crackling noises in the mosaic of its surface plates, but for man they are disasters. About 50,000 earthquakes can be felt without instruments throughout the world every year, most so small that they are barely noticed.

The distribution of the plates, their average drift speeds, the contact zones along which they slide, and the critical areas in which buildups occur are rather well known to today's geophysicists. These scientists also can tell quite accurately where severe earthquakes will happen sometime in the future. The area around the San Andreas fault line, which burst apart during the earthquakes of Fort Tejon in 1857 and of San Francisco in 1906, has not moved since, for example. To keep pace with the plate movements in the larger surrounding area, there must sooner or later be a dramatic dislocation. In a giant area in southern California, between the Pacific and the Mojave desert, the ground has risen 25 centimeters (10 inches) in the last 15 years. This ground covers the region of the more than 1,000 kilometer (620 mile) long network of the San Andreas fault, of which 300 kilometers (186 miles) broke apart in 1857 and which has since been quiet.

By studying earthquake waves and the resulting geological changes, scientists can also tell what happens in the earth's crust during a quake. What they can only suspect is the chain of geophysical events that bring the tremendous built-up energies to a sudden discharge. These discharges seem to come like a bolt from out of the blue. Modern earthquake science, which has broken with older, traditional ideas about quakes, needed a long time to find suitable experimental starting points. Soviet scientists have made significant strides toward that. In 1949, after a severe earthquake in Tadzhikistan that killed more than 10,000 people, they were charged with the task of looking for earthquake signals that would help prevent another such catastrophe. After a search for data lasting almost two decades, they presented to the public an entire series of potential earthquake precursors. Electrical resistance of rock formations changed, radioactive radon appeared in springs in increased concentrations, and the ground layer over a future earthquake center became slightly deformed, like dough. But possibly the most remarkable discovery was that the velocity of propagation of microquake waves underwent a change before the earthquake. The compression waves (P waves) were slowed relative to the shear waves (S waves) by about 10–20 percent.

These fascinating beginnings were given a considerable boost by somewhat similar discoveries in Japan and later in the United States. As a result, scientists in countries concerned with earthquakes began to pursue investigations into these phenomena with much enthusiasm. The seismologists learned to handle a whole series of new measuring instruments. An interesting cross-section of the kinds of studies that are now being carried out can be seen along the San Andreas fault, where the U.S. Geological Survey maintains hundreds of measuring stations. Here we can find laser devices that measure distances across the earthquake fault, geodetic instruments that detect changes in altitude, clinometers that detect the slightest deformations of the earth's surface, and tension meters that register mechanical changes in the rock. These stations also have scintillation counters to measure the light that the radioactivity of radon causes to emanate from spring water, instruments that measure the electrical resistance of the ground, magnetic-field instruments, and gravity instruments that reveal changes in subterranean rock.

Stone under stress

In 1973, Yash P. Aggarwal, then a seismology student, discovered a change in the speed of seismic waves in the area of the Adirondack Mountains in upstate New York, which frequently has small quakes. Following up on the discoveries of Soviet scientists, he concluded that an earthquake was coming and estimated its intensity. Then he pinned his prediction on the bulletin board of his institute. A small earthquake of intensity 2.6 did indeed happen. It was the first successful earthquake prediction in the United States. Some time later, at Columbia University's Lamont-Doherty Geological Observatory, Aggarwal recalled to me the joy he had felt when he thought he was feeling the weak quake.

Seismologists are the only people whose eyes light up when they tell about experiences with earthquakes. The possibility of living through one personally, and perhaps having an experiment in progress at the time, fills them with rapture. They dream of the day when they will "snare the big one." The problems that have to be overcome before this goal is reached are truly discouraging. The origins of the great earthquakes that shake the entire planet usually lie deep beneath the surface, and it will require much careful examination to interpret correctly the symptoms that appear on the surface.

A big breakthrough in earthquake research was apparently achieved when A. Nur, Y. P. Aggarwal, L. R. Sykes, C. H. Scholz, and others [95-97] advanced the following hypothesis: An entire series of observed earthquake signs—from deformations of the earth's surface, through changes in the electrical resistance of the rock formations and in the speed of earthquake waves, to the increased presence of radon—can be traced back to dilation, a familiar loosening in the structure of rock that appears as a consequence of high pressures. Before rocks burst, they become shot through with a dense network of the finest of hairline cracks, which cause them to become distended. Water enters into these cracks and increases the electrical conductivity of the rock material, and because of the increased contact surface, more radioactive radon gets into the groundwater.

Dilation is a well-investigated phenomenon today. Many of the 282 geophysical changes that precede earthquakes which have been measured and collected in book form by the Japanese earthquake researcher

T. Rikitake have something to do with it. However, dilation is a long-term earthquake precursor. The stronger an earthquake turns out to be, the greater the area affected by it and the earlier dilation appears. In an earthquake of magnitude 3, dilation can be ascertained only about a day in advance, but in a quake that exceeds magnitude 6 the phenomenon may begin several years before. Thus, dilation points to a growing earthquake hazard and (in a relatively coarse way) to the strength of the quake that may be expected—but not to the exact time of the disaster. For immediate earthquake warning, the dilation phenomena are hardly suitable. It is not possible to keep people from their homes and factories for weeks or months without bringing the economy to a collapse. Besides, some complications have developed with the dilation theory. The anomalous changes in the speed of earthquake waves have not been observed before very many earthquakes, and when they did appear on occasion there was no noticeable deformation of the subsurface. Laboratory experiments also show that along existing fracture lines earthquakes can happen before the dilation stage is reached.

A much-discussed sign of an imminent earthquake is the microquake activity that appears several days or hours before some great earthquakes. But not all quakes show such typical precursors. Among 1,500 earthquakes in Japan whose strength exceeded 4, only 60 showed this sign unmistakably,[42] and in China between 1900 and 1949 about 21 percent of the major earthquakes exhibited this phenomenon[98] (whose cause, by the way, is still unknown). Microquake activity will acquire meaning for short-term earthquake prediction only when a way is found to distinguish these prequakes from the ordinary earthquake swarms of lesser magnitude.

No geophysical interrelationships are known today that would permit the forecasting of the more severe earthquakes within the span of a few minutes to a few days, so that human lives might be saved. But it is exactly this time span that is filled with unusual animal behavior, strange ground noises, startling light phenomena, and springs that have changed color and rate of water flow.

Earthquake noise

They [earthquakes] are. . . preceded or accompanied by a terrible sound that sometimes resembles a rumble, sometimes the lowing of cattle or the shouts of human beings or the clash of weapons struck together, according to the nature of the material that receives the shock and the shape of the caverns or burrows through which it passes, proceeding with smaller volume in a narrow channel but with a harsh noise in channels that bend, echoing in hard channels, bubbling in damp ones, forming waves in stagnant ones, raging against solid ones. Accordingly even without any movement occurring a sound is sometimes emitted.[8f]

This description of earthquake noises given by the Roman naturalist Pliny the Elder in the first century A.D. is, in my opinion, the best, most exhaustive, and most scientifically profound description that has ever been composed. Not only does it give a vivid image of the intensity and the character of the sound impressions; at the same time it explains in an understandable way how much the quality of sound varies with the structural form and the material composition of the environment. This remarkable description did not overlook the fact that earthquake noise frequently begins several seconds before tremors become perceptible, and that ground noises occasionally appear without earth movements.

It is interesting to compare the modern perceptions of this intensive acoustical experience. Charles Davison, who from 1889 to 1916 evaluated about 20,000 reports of earthquake noise, came to the conclusion that it was usually a dull-sounding rolling noise resembling distant thunder or the noise made by a heavy vehicle rolling past.[99] His seven-point scale also includes sound impressions that resemble the sounds made by a load of coal being tipped out and by a giant flock of partridges.

Several persons who told me their earthquake experiences compared the sensation to that of suddenly finding themselves on a mighty train that was hurtling over such bumpy rails that they were thrown about helplessly. The earthquake noise that accompanied the Ligurian earthquakes toward the end of the nineteenth century was compared by alert, technically trained observers to that of a train rushing past an observer in a tunnel.[14] An anecdote that a railroad engineer told the seismologist Mercalli shows how accurate this comparison is. It seems that a signalman happened to be in the 2,530-meter (8,300-foot) railroad tunnel between Joppoli and Ricadi, which runs through a rock formation, when the earthquake happened. The sound effect of an onrushing train was so genuine that the signalman gave the prescribed signals. He was terrified to hear the noise passing without seeing a train.

Despite the many earthquakes that happen every year, science has only very sparse information about the accompanying noise. The pride of earthquake researchers is a catalog of thirteen accidentally recorded tapes that reproduce, through the screaming of people and the falling of dishes, some "genuine" earthquake noises. Still, the representation of earthquake noise has been remarkably well developed thanks to careful laboratory experiments, accurate theoretical examinations, and a tape recording that caught several miniquakes.[100,101]

Since earthquake noises are generated when vibrations of the earth's surface transfer pressure waves to the air, the key to these sound phenomena lies in the knowledge of the vibrations that can be produced in the earth before and during a quake. We know today that there are many mechanisms that can evoke them. Earthquake waves themselves vibrate at frequencies between 0.1 and 10 hertz (Hz). This frequency range is followed (up to several hundred hertz) by the more rapid vibrations of the microquake. A human, whose hearing threshold lies around 16 Hz, could theoretically hear the waves of smaller earthquakes. On top of the frequency range of these microquakes are the frequencies (up to 3,000 Hz) of still other kinds of vibrations. These are produced by breaking rock.

Since sound is produced in all major earthquakes, this source of vibrations must not be neglected. Laboratory experiments, as already mentioned, have shown that before rocks break, fine hairline cracks appear in them. In this process, ultrasound signals are emitted at frequencies that can reach 100,000–1,000,000 Hz. The sound frequency varies with the size of the tears that are being produced and thus with the kind of rock in which the cracks appear. It follows, then, that almost any sound frequency may be emitted in an earthquake, from infrasound to the extreme ultrasound. But a concert of this kind would hardly have been compared to the growling of thunder or the passing of a train in a tunnel; rather, one might think of rattling tin cans, breaking glass, or screeching brakes. The reason for the great difference between generated sound and perceived sound in an earthquake is that rock swallows much of the generated sound energy. This muffling effect is not equally strong at all frequencies, but is proportionately stronger in the high frequencies. Whereas sound of 10,000 Hz travels 200 meters (656 feet) in typical bedrock, sound of 100 Hz covers 20 kilometers (12 miles). As sound travels through the bedrock, ultrasound frequencies are filtered out drastically, so that only the deeper earthquake tones remain. In order for ultrasound signals coming from the developing hairline fractures in rock to be detected, the events must be taking place 10–100 meters (32.8–328 feet) away. Since the origins of earthquakes generally lie many kilometers beneath the earth's surface, and since very shallow earthquakes are rare, ultrasound signals as earthquake signs are barely worth considering. This is confirmed by fortuitous tape recordings of three small earthquakes in 1975 in the Imperial Valley of California;[101] the measured acoustical frequencies are indeed limited to the very low frequency range between 50 and 70 Hz. However, earthquake noise is not always limited to this narrow frequency range. If a small quake happens in a bottom layer of granite or lava rock, people living above it may perceive very high-pitched noises. This is because small earthquakes produce high-frequency tones, and because these travel well through this kind of crystalline rock. A similar earthquake under a layer of ocean sediments, which swallows higher frequencies more easily, would sound muffled and deep.

The acoustical measurements of the Imperial Valley noises yielded a surprise bonus of a very special kind. Since antiquity, witnesses had always maintained that earthquake noise appeared several seconds before the tremors. (Even the Italian earthquake researcher Luigi Bossi experienced and described this phenomenon. According to his observations, aftershocks of the earthquake wave of 1808 in the Piedmont came with and without noises; when noises did appear, they preceded the earthquake by about 2 seconds.[14,18] If the dramatic descriptions of earthquake noise deserved to be taken with a grain of salt, then the claims that sound preceded the quakes deserved even more skepticism. But the measurements from the Imperial Valley confirmed these old reports. The earthquake noise began about 2 seconds before the onset of perceptible ground movements and was already waning as the latter were gaining strength. The explanation turned out to be the simplest one imaginable: The earthquake waves proper (the S waves), which are felt by humans and which oscillate at right angles to their direction of travel, are preceded by the compression waves, whose vibrations, much as those of sound waves, run parallel to their direction of travel. These P waves are about 70 percent faster than the S waves, and when they arrive at the surface from below they set the surface vibrating so that it radiates sound vertically into the air. The S waves from the same direction, on the other hand, cannot impel pressure waves into the air. But if the earthquake waves arrive at the surface at an angle, then only that part of the forces that move the ground at right angles to the surface will have an effect. Thus, people hear the earthquake wave that they cannot feel and feel the wave that they cannot hear. Only if an earthquake is stronger than magnitude 3 do the P waves become somewhat perceptible.

After scientists had poked around the secret of the sound-producing P waves for the first time, in 1975, the stories that country folk had recognized the phenomenon centuries ago and had used it prudently to save lives in the last seconds made sense. An observation made by Alexander von Humboldt in 1799 in Cumana, Venezuela, supports this view: "It is widely believed in Cumana that the most destructive earthquakes are announced by very weak oscillations of the ground and through a howling, and something like that does not escape people who are used to such incidents. In such moments you can hear the cry everywhere: Misericordia! Tembla! Tembla! Tembla! (Mercy, it is quaking, it is quaking), and it is rare that a false alarm is set off by a native."[54a]

If it is possible to hear an earthquake, it is possible to "hear" not only its distance, its intensity, and the direction of its source, but also the ground through which the sound travels and the earth surface that transmits it to the air. Water conducts sound much better than rock and also radiates it differently; its presence gives a different voice to an earthquake.

Acoustical earthquake alarms

In the town of Pontebba in northeastern Friuli, people had adjusted to the series of aftershocks that were following the second big earthquake of 1976. In the early hours of September 18 came a series of hard, muffled explosions, clearly from the earth's interior. They were not accompanied by real quakes, but they did cause windowpanes to break, metal enclosures to rattle, and cots to jump around. The people, already savaged by the earthquake, were suddenly nervous again. An old miner averred that the rumbles sounded like blasting underground, and in no time at all these phenomena were dubbed the "underground artillery." If a new earthquake had followed them, a connection between the two would surely have been made. But as it was, after two large quakes and countless aftershocks, the stored energy of the earth had been largely discharged. Was the worry of the people about these unusual ground noises justified?

The chronicles of this region make it difficult to deny a connection between ground noises and earthquakes. They report, for example, that a strong earthquake that occurred there on May 14, 1472, was preceded by the growling of thunder. Before the earthquake of February 19, 1855, constant thundering was heard for two days. Were these coincidences? In order to find examples of how reliably such an underground noise announces an earth tremor in some areas and how little it means in others, it is only necessary to leaf through the South American travel accounts of Alexander von Humboldt. At one point he reports, "In the city of Quito we no longer gave any thought to getting up at night when an underground roaring (*bramidos*), which seemed to come from the volcano Pichincha (two to three, sometimes seven to eight, minutes in advance) would announce a shock whose strength rarely bore any relation to the degree of uproar."[54f] Elsewhere he writes, "In 1784, the inhabitants of Mexico were as accustomed to hearing thunder under their feet as we are to hearing thunder in the air."

Historical reports of ground noises before earthquakes have been passed on from many other regions. One of the oldest comes from Constantinople, where an earthquake in 396 is said to have been preceded by a seven-day "roaring."[78] These long-term acoustic precursors of earthquakes do not exist for modern earthquake research because they have not yet been measured and because old traditions have not been evaluated for evidence of them.

Once again we have to turn to China. An impressive survey of the uses of earth noises in predicting earthquakes in the Middle Kingdom is presented in an article by the Lanchow Seismological Brigade.[32] Details of this unusual method of earthquake prediction, unknown to Western science, are also contained in the *Chronological Tables of Earthquake Data of China*[33] and in other Chinese articles about earthquake prediction.[102,103] According to these sources, the knowledge that in certain areas alarming earth noises appear minutes, hours, or days before an earthquake is at least 1,500 years old. The oldest written record of it dates from 474 A.D. and refers to the Yenmen-Chicheng earthquake in Shensi province. According to documents of the Wei dynasty there were "a dozen sound eruptions like thunder from above toward the west in Yenmen-Chicheng," and "after the sounds faded, an earthquake followed."

To have been distinguished as a dozen, these "thunderclaps" must have started at least several minutes before the earthquake. This could not have been the earthquake noise proper, which, when it accompanies the faster P waves, precedes the quake by only a few seconds. It was known as early as 1739, according to a previously mentioned document about the Yinchuan-Pinglu earthquakes in Ningsia province,[32] that thunderlike earth noises could be forerunners of earthquakes: "When the water in the well would suddenly turn muddy, when there would be cannonlike noise that was long and indistinct, when dogs barked in unison, then they [the people] would prepare themselves at once for this [earthquake] plague. . . ." The first prediction of an earthquake based on thunderlike noises, which is unmistakeably documented in the records of the Chinese dynasties and which has been collected in the *Chronological Tables of Earthquake Data of China*,[33] dates from December 11, 1855. It concerns an earthquake of medium intensity in Jinxian (in Liaoning province) that destroyed 567 houses. The original entries read as follows: "[The people] heard noises like thunder before the earthquake and took precautionary measures. They ran away from their houses and there were no dead, and the injured men, women, and children amounted to only seven persons."

A noise like rolling thunder began to growl from one to several minutes before the relatively weak earthquake of October 24, 1594, in Liaohaiwei in Liaoning province. About a day before the earthquake of Tancheng and Juzhou in Shantung province on July 25, 1668, which struck with a magnitude of 8.5, sounds were heard that resembled thundering water. Historic tradition has it that a servant sent out to inquire about the reason for the noise was unable to learn anything suspicious. In the similarly large Haiyuan-Xiji earthquake, which struck Ningsin province on December 16, 1920, noises were heard several days before. The Hoze earthquake in Shantung province, which struck on August 1, 1927, with magnitude 7, was preceded for some time (more than a few minutes) by thunder noise that lasted until the earthquake. Also, in connection with the Tonghai earthquake of January 5, 1970, in Yunnan province, which reached an intensity of 7.7, there are reports of earth noise. It was heard "several" to 20 minutes before. Several hours before the Luhuo quake in Szechwan province, which struck with 7.9 magnitude on February 6, 1973, earth noises were heard.

It appears that relatively few earthquakes are preceded by geophysical processes that express themselves through ground noise. Patient Chinese obesrvations have shown that this phenomenon appears frequently in certain areas, and that it repeats itself—and this is very important—before every earthquake. This was discovered by comparing various earthquakes that had happened at widely separated times in Liaoning and Ningsia provinces.

Apparently, the makeup of the ground governs the way sound is liberated. Ground noises that precede earthquakes happen more frequently in rocky, mountainous regions, according to Chinese findings, and are easier to hear where there is a lot of groundwater and many lakes and rivers, since water conducts sound better.

Earth noises associated with severe earthquakes in different regions are, as a rule, not alike. Before earthquakes whose magnitude exceeded 7, thunderlike noises, cannonlike salvos, sounds like tearing fabric, and echolike reverberating sounds have been noted. According to Chinese observations, only relatively shallow-lying quakes send noises in advance as warning signals. This is easy to understand because of the strong muffling effect of rock. Chinese experts believe that earthquake noises appear when so much broken stone and rubble has been accumulated in the fracture zones of the earth's crust, because of mounting tensions, that creeping is caused by diminished friction. They do not exclude the possibility, however, that electrical charges in the ground might contribute to the generation of ground noises.

Are there old reports from Western countries of ground noises preceding earthquakes? Consider the following obervations made during the Ligurian earthquake of May 26, 1831, which happened at 11:30 A.M.:

Before the earthquake towards 9 o'clock in the morning, a person at Ceriana heard underground growling which repeated itself and which was so strong that that person fled from the house, frightened; and at 7 o'clock in the morning of the same day a woman who had been mowing grass east of San Remo heard an underground snorting, like from a powerful gurgling of water. This frightened her so much that she did not want to continue her work, much as her mistress was urging her to. Finally, a strong noise was heard and copious flow of water (was observed) in a pond on the land of Giuncarello west of San Remo on the day that preceded the earthquake and on the 26th (the day of the earthquake).

Quakes and the earth's magnetic field

In our search for earthquake-related geophysical changes it will be worthwhile to give special attention to any possible disturbances of the magnetic and electric fields on the earth's surface. These fields are always present, and numerous animal species have learned in the course of evolution to extract valuable information about the environment from them. In order to decide whether unusual variations in the local magnetic or electric field can generate warnings of impending earthquakes, we will first have to carefully review existing scientific information about the connection between earthquakes and these fields.

The earth's magnetic field is maintained by complicated and only partly understood geodynamic processes in the fluid interior. Its arrangement is very close to that of an ideal magnetic dipole, much like that of a simple bar magnet. Therefore the strength of the magnetic field on the earth's surface depends very much on the latitude. At the magnetic poles it is about twice as strong as at the equator.

A simple permanent magnet generates magnetic fields of about 40 oersted. Highly developed modern magnetic materials and treatment methods produce permanent magnets with field strengths of 1,000 oersted and more. Compared with that, the magnetic field of the earth is relatively modest. At the poles it measures about 0.6 oersted, or 60,000 gamma, and toward the equator it decreases gradually to half that. Now, the value of the magnetic field on the earth's surface does not change only with the distance from the poles, but is strongly influenced by the nature of the material beneath the ground. During the cooling of the earth's crust, microscopic magnetic zones of rock that had been aligned with the magnetic field as it was then oriented became frozen in the congealing rock whose own magnetic field now overlies that of the earth. Variations in the magnetic field resulting from these magnetic properties of rock are usually on the order of magnitude of a few hundred gamma, and sometimes 1,000 gamma, per kilometer.

In addition, the earth's magnetic field varies with time. The causes of these variations are the solar wind (that stream of charged particles that comes to us from the sun) and the interplanetary magnetic field. The solar wind compresses the earth's magnetic field, and, since the earth rotates, the magnetic field at any given point oscillates with the changes of day and night. The range of this change in the magnetic field can amount to 30 gamma. A further variation in the earth's magnetic field comes about because the sun, whose surface is not uniformly constituted, rotates. That takes place in 27 days and causes magnetic field changes in the order of 10 gamma. Finally, magnetic-field variations just as big and sometimes twice as big are caused by solar eruptions, violent outbursts on the sun that briefly alter the strength of the solar wind and cause the so-called magnetic storms on earth. Not to be overlooked is the fact that in populated areas direct-current conductors of streetcars and rapid-transit trains or (in Italy and Holland) railroad trains spread strong magnetic fields. Two kilometers (1.2 miles) from the Berlin city transit, magnetic disturbances of 30 gamma were registered when trains would start up. Do magnetic-field changes caused by earthquakes make any impression at all on these natural and artificial variations?

The suspicion that earthquakes are coupled with magnetic-field changes goes back to the eighteenth century. Untold reports of magnetic-field changes during earthquakes have come to light, but only recently have reliable measurements been made. To exclude those field variations that are of no interest, two or more instruments separated by several meters are connected with each other. Magnetic disturbances from the ionosphere (which are caused by the solar wind) have similar effects on all instruments, whereas variations coming from beneath the ground should have differential effects on the magnetometers. The measurements showed that before earthquakes variations in the magnetic field can indeed appear. The orders of magnitude within which they move, however, are not impressive. Since 1973 the magnetic fields in earthquake-prone California have been registered at more than 100 measuring stations along the San Andreas fracture line by instruments spaced 8–12 kilometers (5–8 miles) apart. More than 30 earthquakes occurred in that time. Only three of them exceeded magnitude 3.6 and caused unequivocal magnetic-field disturbances. In two quakes with strengths of 3.8 and 4.3 the magnetic-field change amounted to 2 gamma; in the third, which reached magnitude 5.2, it came to only 1.8 gamma.[104] In the last case, the magnetic-field deviation began about two months before the quake and a month before the field began to level off. It is safe to say that there was no escalation in magnetic disturbance in that earthquake.

Systematic magnetic-field measurements before some bigger earthquakes have been performed successfully only in Japan and China. In China they were usually carried out by two or more stations separated by more than 100 kilometers (62 miles), whose measured values were compared later. This network detected a magnetic-field change of 20 gamma 8 months before the 7.3-magnitude Haicheng earthquake. As a result the Liaoning Peninsula, which is where Haicheng is, was declared a danger zone where a big earthquake could be expected in 1–2 years. Also, in the middle of June 1976, a month and a half before the fearsome earthquake of Tangshan, which the experts failed to predict, magnetic-field anomalies were detected in a zone that comprised the Tangshan-Peking area. They amounted to about 6.5 gamma.

The biggest magnetic-field disturbance ever registered before an earthquake was recorded in connection with the quake in Prince William Sound in Alaska in 1964.[105] It owes its measurement to a coincidence. When that colossal earthquake—it reached magnitude 8.5—struck and the city of Kodiak was destroyed by a giant flood wave, a magnetic-field-measuring instrument was taking readings in perfect safety on a hill where it had been set up by an oil company doing geological tests. Afterwards, the analysis of the recording trace showed that the magnetic field had increased considerably in strength before the earthquake in several brief, closely spaced spurts. The strongest of these pulselike magnetic-field deviations happened 66 minutes before the onset of the earthquake and reached the astonishing value of 100 gamma. No one knows yet what the mechanism is that led to these short increases in the magnetic field. It is tempting to think of a piezomagnetic effect—the generation of a magnetic field through changes in pressure in the rock—such as happens in a whole series of materials of crystalline structure.

A few other measurements can be added to these few lucky ones. They were taken in connection with volcanic eruptions and therefore recorded similar geophysical processes. These measurements, carried out on the North Island of New Zealand, yielded magnetic-field disturbances of 10–20 gamma beginning a day before and continuing sporadically during the eruptions.[106]

To get an answer to the question of whether animals are irritated by magnetic-field disturbances before earthquakes, we will not only have to prove that they react sensitively enough to magnetic fields; we will also have to explain how they distinguish these magnetic signals from other similarly large, and sometimes larger, variations of different origin to which they are exposed every day.

Quakes and the earth's electrical field

The surface of the earth has a constant electrical field. In fair weather, on flat terrain, it amounts to 100–300 volts per meter. At the tops of mountains or trees its strength is somewhat above that, but at an altitude of 10 kilometers (6.2 miles) it is down to 4 volts per meter. Since the air conducts electricity adequately, a vertical current flows constantly, intent on reducing the atmospheric electrical field. This current amounts to about 2×10^{-16} amperes per square centimeter (about 1.3×10^{-15} amperes per square inch). The entire electrical field would disappear within one hour if there were no mechanism of recharging it constantly. From the grandiose "Thunderstorm" research project, we know that it is thunderstorms, distributed worldwide and always active somewhere, that keep the atmospheric "capacitor" charged through the well-conducting ionosphere and the equally well-conducting earth surface. The latter is usually negatively charged. On the average, it carries 500,000 electrons per square centimeter (3.2 million per square inch). During precipitation or under the influence of outgassing, considerable variations appear in the atmospheric electrical field. The causes for these variations lie mostly with the appearance of charged clouds or their neutralization, and extreme values of 10,000 volts per meter are not rare.

Meteorologists know that many processes on the surface and in the ground influence the electrical field in the atmosphere, and lightning and light phenomena under clear skies have always been popularly recognized as predicting or accompanying earthquakes. Despite this, recent measurements of the electrical field above the spots where earthquakes originate have been made only in isolated cases. Only two attempts have become known, but because the earthquakes involved were comparatively weak they cannot be considered representative. The Japanese scientist G. Kondo, however, did find that during the Matsushiro earthquake swarm in 1966 significantly more earthquakes occurred at times of lowered electrical fields than under normal circumstances.[107] If these observations are correct, the processes that lead to earthquakes diminish the negative surface charge of the earth. In California, C. Bufe and J. Nanevicz are trying to carry out similar measurements for the United States Geological Survey.[108] They have observed suspicious field changes that preceded, by about one day, three earthquakes with magnitudes between 3.5 and 3.8. However, it was impossible to link these field changes conclusively to the quakes.

Springs and wells

From time immemorial, springs have been places of mysticism and magic. Legends have often surrounded their origin, mysterious water spirits were said to protect them, and people built temples around them, the better to converse with the gods. What makes spring water so fascinating is the unfathomable depth from which it bubbles forth. The priests at Delphi used the spring there to divine the will of the gods. Many other springs have helped attentive observers recognize the pangs of the earth before an earthquake.

The oldest traditions about spring water becoming cloudy before an earthquake, or changing in taste or in flow, go back to the sixth century B.C. Pherecydes, a Greek physicist and a teacher of Pythagoras, is said to have predicted an earthquake three days in advance by examining a spring. According to the Roman author Cicero, Pherecydes decided to make that momentous prediction after he "had seen the water scooped from an ever-flowing well."[109c] According to Pliny, Pherecydes recognized the approaching earthquake while drinking from a well.[8g] The scholars of antiquity seem to have taken it for granted that changes in springs indicated menacing developments in the interior of the earth. More than 1,900 years ago, Pliny expressly mentioned that when water in wells becomes cloudy and acquires a repulsive odor, it is a reliable earthquake omen. He was setting down an ancient observation, one not only made in the Roman empire but confirmed all over the world time and again.

To document this phenomenon, it is only necessary to leaf through old reports about earthquakes in different countries. Japan turns out to be a rich treasure trove. In the report of the Imperial Japanese Earthquake Investigating Commission,[51d] for example, is the story of a samurai who on the day of the earthquake of Takata in 1751 noticed that the usually clear water in one peasant's well had become cloudy. He discovered that the water of several surrounding wells had also become muddy and correctly predicted the earthquake for that evening. The earthquake of Edo in 1855, too, was foreseen by a samurai who found that water in a well had become clayey and its taste salty. He predicted an earthquake, but no one believed him.[39] Other Japanese legends and traditions suggest that it is not only the sudden appearance of clay in well and spring water that foreshadows an earthquake, but also the sudden decrease in flow, or a sudden rise or drop in the groundwater table. Reports of such earthquake precursors are plentiful in Europe, too. Four hours before the Piedmontese earthquake of April 2, 1808, the water in a mill canal near Lusera rose so suddenly that several women who had been washing their laundry had to run to high ground because the canal bank was inundatead.[14] One day before the Ligurian earthquake of February 23, 1887, the water volume of a well in Maranza receded noticeably, only to return stronger than before after the earthquake. A well in Antibes lost large amounts of water twelve days before the same quake. The water gradually turned white and then yellow. Groundwater was found only a few centimeters deep in the surrounding area, which is sandy and dry. Up to four days before the earthquake a clouding of the water and increased gas emissions were observed in the thermal springs near Pozzuoli.[14]

Similar observations have been reported from the Americas. How surprisingly similar some situations can be is shown by an event in Concepción, Chile, on February 20, 1835, which happened during Darwin's voyage in the *Beagle*: "Inland the town of Concepción was demolished in a matter of six seconds. Here too there was some little warning; women washing clothes in he river were startled to find that the water became muddy and rose with great rapidity from their ankles to their knees."[57]

Once more the Chinese authorities have been the first to give credence to an old popular tradition: They have tried to keep a systematic lookout for groundwater changes before earthquakes. In order to understand these phenomena better, they evaluated hundreds of historical reports. The earthquake records of the last 100 years alone have yielded a rich store of experience. An earthquake of magnitude 6 that occurred in 1856 in the border area between Hopei and Szechwan provinces was heralded days ahead by anomalies that suggested changes in the groundwater level. The 8.5-magnitude quake that devastated Haiyuen in Ningsia province in 1920 was preceded by the same sort of signs 3 days before. Two 1935 earthquakes in Taiwan province, with magnitudes of 7 and 6, were indicated 14 hours ahead of time by changes in well water. The quakes in Luenyuen (Hopei province, 1945, magnitude 6.3), Hangting (Szechwan province, 1955, magnitude 7.5), Tingchung (Yunnan province, 1961, magnitude 5.8), Hsingtai (Hopei province, 1966, magnitude 6.8), Tsunghai (Yunnan province, 1970, magnitude 7.7), and Sichi (Ningsia province, 1970, magnitude 5.5) were announced ahead of time by, respectively, 1, 2, 1, 1–10, several–10, and 1–5 days.[110]

The trouble taken with research and with installing measuring stations at springs and wells paid off: By January 1975, in the Liaotung peninsula, where a big earthquake was expected, wells had been equipped with measuring instruments and were being watched by watchmen who noticed the anomalies when they began to appear.[81] The groundwater rose in 55 percent of these wells and fell in 15 percent.[3] In 30 percent of them the water changed color, became muddy, or foamed, and in some of them the water boiled. On February 3, 1975, the water from a well of the Tingchiakou production brigade, about 10 kilometers (6.2 miles) from the epicenter, became clayey and oily. On the morning of February 4, the water from this well, which normally has to be pumped up 12 meters (39 feet), rose to the surface and artesian wells sprang up. The water coming out of them froze solid in the cold. The same thing happened with seven or eight wells in that same valley.[2] At 7:36 P.M. of the same day a severe earthquake shook the region. There were practically no victims. Together with the ominous increase in reports of unusual animal behavior and other signs, the quickly reported changes in groundwater tripped the disaster alarm. It was sounded at 2 P.M., 5 1/2 hours before the quake.

The Chinese efforts and successes in groundwater observation have stimulated similar studies abroad. In 1968, 1 1/2 hours before the Meckering earthquake in Australia, a rise in the groundwater level of 2.9 centimeters (slightly more than an inch) was observed 110 kilometers (70 miles) from the epicenter.[111] There is also a positive report of water-level changes before an earthquake in Przhevalsk in the Soviet Union in June 1970.[42]

A series of measuring stations are now in place along the San Andreas fault in California to automatically record any groundwater changes. The hope vested in these stations is not that they will announce the next earthquake in time. Instead, the instruments are expected to settle the question whether the positive experiences with an example of folk wisdom from China can be generalized and scientifically accepted. The attitude of non-Chinese earthquake researchers toward groundwater changes before earthquakes is generally one of wait and see, but they do find it worthwhile to carry out appropriate measurements for study purposes.[42] When the dust has settled over California after the next great earthquake, international science may have advanced a big step toward solving this question. Should the Chinese concepts about the meaning of groundwater changes be confirmed, then earthquake research will, it is fair to say, have reached the level of knowledge of the Greeks and Romans of two millenia ago.

The sea's warning signals

On February 15, 1783, according to a documented report by the earthquake researcher Giovanni Vivenzio, the sea off the coast of Calabria was unrecognizable even to experienced sea dogs.[112] Even though the air was totally calm and there was no sign of a storm, the open sea off Bivona and Pizzo was so turbulent that fishermen felt obliged to return to port. But near the beach the sea was again totally still. The inhabitants of the coastal village of Catro fled their homes when they suddenly saw the sea retreat from the bank. They thus saved themselves, not from the flood they expected (which did not come), but from a disastrous earthquake that devastated their homes a few hours later.

In 1793 a similar episode happened on the day of the Ajikazawa earthquake in the northeastern part of Honshu, Japan. However, the outcome was not so fortunate. On the morning of the earthquake the people living along the coast observed an unusual receding of the sea. They fled into the mountains, where they were shaken by the quake in the early afternoon. Terrified, they hurried back to the shore, where the tidal waves caught them and exacted their tribute.[42]

Another case of receding water driving cautious fishermen from their homes happened in 1802 on Sado Island in the Sea of Japan. The best-documented report of this kind, however, comes from the Hamada earthquake in 1872 in western Honshu. There the sea receded so far that it was possible to walk to an island 140 meters (460 feet) from the shore and to pick up mussels from the ocean bottom. Less than an hour later the earthquake and great tidal waves struck.

Several hours before the Tango earthquake of 1927 the sea level near some fishing villages is supposed to have dropped by a meter (3.28 feet). Such dramatic changes in water level have not yet been confirmed with modern automatic recording instruments, but this does not mean the reports are not reliable. Apparently, a deformation of the earth's crust that precedes an earthquake is responsible for the quake. Such a deformation can be read without instruments at the shore, where the sea acts like a carpenter's level. Chilean fishermen understood the meaning of the "indicator deflection" long before seismologists thought of recording such ground deformations with complicated instruments.[90]

Another interesting phenomenon that emerges from a survey of sea observations in connection with earthquakes or submarine quakes is that, shortly before the earthquake, the sea becomes absolutely calm. Many eyewitness reports confirm this phenomenon in connection with the Ligurian earthquake of 1887,[22] and Pliny writes that "tremors of the earth never occur except when the sea is calm and the sky so still that birds are unable to soar because all the breath that carries them has been withdrawn."[8g]

A friend of mine happened to be on the beach of Jesolo on the Adriatic when the second earthquake of Friuli occurred on September 15, 1976. The first thing he noticed was that the monotonous sound of the waves had suddenly stopped. There was just time enough to notice that the sea had become mirror-smooth; shortly thereafter the trembling of the ground was felt. This description indicates that calmness of the sea can appear only a very few seconds before an earthquake. It is thus reasonable to attribute this remarkable effect to the P waves, which vibrate in the direction of travel and whose tremors can be barely perceived by humans. The evenly circling motions of water molecules in the movement of waves apparently are so attenuated and mixed up by the pressure waves of an earthquake that they ebb away.

The state of earthquake research

Seismologists can now measure ground deformations that precede earthquakes on the order of 1 centimeter (0.39 inches) in 10 kilometers (6.2 miles). They can detect changes of 1 gamma in the magnetic field and 1 percent in conductivity of the ground over similar distances. Changes in pressure within the rock that amount to 0.0001 percent and changes in angle of less than 1/20,000 of a degree do not escape them either. Also, 20-percent variations in the radon content of groundwater over several months, 1-percent changes in the speed of earthquake waves, and gravity changes of 1×10^{-7} can be measured. And yet, until now there has been no way of detecting a uniform pattern that would show how changes in the earth's crust escalate into an earthquake. Dilation, which is responsible for a series of observed deviations, can be observed only in certain formations. Moreover, since we are dealing with long-term effects here, serious difficulties arise because the time of the disaster cannot be estimated reliably.

However, in judging the state of earthquake research we must not overlook the fact that the scientific search for such geophysical phenomena as ground noises, turbid spring water, altered groundwater level, and electrostatic fields (whose appearances shortly before earthquakes has been amply confirmed by many laymen's reports) is only now starting up slowly. The laymen's reports have been widely ignored until now. At the Fifth Japanese-American Seminar on Earthquake Predictions in January 1977 in Tokyo, Frank Press of the Massachusetts Institute of Technology said he was pessimistic about the prospects of observing enough earthquakes experimentally in the next 10 years to let scientists make reasonably reliable predictions based on the collected information.[113]

Under pressure from the Chinese claim that abnormal animal behavior played an important role in the successful prediction of the Haicheng earthquake in 1975, and recognizing that there is thus far no palpable physical earthquake sign that would facilitate short-term earthquake warnings, the United States Geological Survey (the American agency officially charged with earthquake prediction) called a conference in Menlo Park, California, on September 23 and 24, 1976, to test the credibility of the animal phenomenon.[114] Psychologists elucidated the problems with eyewitness reports, some biologists discussed the sensory capabilities of animals, and seismologists described possible geophysical earthquake signs. My ideas about the phenomenon, already worked out by then, were also presented for discussion. Amid all the skepticism about the reliability of many of the reports, the opinion prevailed that animals' senses are after all so sensitive that they could register various minor environmental changes before earthquake events. Therefore, the conclusion was, it might pay to pursue this phenomenon with scientific methods.

handl

The Sensitivity of Animals

Which are the alarm signals?

Big earthquakes are gigantic geophysical processes whose sources generally lie many kilometers deep within the earth's crust, and the areas they set trembling are huge. What we on the surface perceive are only pale reflections on the edge of these violent events. Just as in the planning and preparation of large-scale engineering projects small trial plants are useful for at least a proximate analysis of the complex interrelationships of many factors, so should spatially limited earthquakelike events on the earth's surface be able to render clues about signs that affect animals. Do we know of great rockslides, for example, that were recognized by animals ahead of time?

On November 10, 1881, the cats in the village of Elm in the canton of Glarus, Switzerland, left their houses and are reported to have run from the village in panic. The next day a rock mass loosed itself from Tschingel Mountain. About 10 million cubic meters (353 million cubic feet) thundered down, destroyed 83 houses, and killed 115 people. The cats all returned and looked in vain for their homes among the rubble.[65] I was told of another case by R. E. Whitehead at the Laurentian University of Sudbury, Ontario, Canada: During the years from 1960 to 1965 someone had been keeping a male pheasant in a barn about 400 meters (1,312 feet) from the excavations of a gold mine in Porcupine, Ontario. One spring this pheasant acted extraordinarily excited and crowed constantly for several nights in a row. Shortly thereafter about 100,000 tons of rock, mostly quartzite, irrupted into the underground caverns of the mine. This suggests that at least certain aspects of the earthquake fear of animals appear even on the occasion of comparatively insignificant rock breakages.

Laboratory experiments seem to confirm this. Recently W. H. Gawthrop and three colleagues at the University of Colorado at Boulder have examined the reactions of mice before the bursting of boulders that have been subjected to an hour of slowly increasing pressure.[115] Preliminary studies have shown that in several experiments two of the four observed mice showed clear signs of restlessness 1–2 minutes before the bursting of the rock and finally expressed fear by assuming rigid positions. The physical cause of these reactions, which obviously has something to do with the development of tiny cracks in the rock, has not yet been determined. Magnetic, electric, and ultrasound signals have been evaluated. In real earthquakes a whole additional series of possible earthquake signals would have to be considered. Venting ground gases, for example, could excite the animals, or perhaps changes in the groundwater table. Or could it be changes in atmospheric pressure or slight swaying of the ground? It is well known from laboratory experiments that rock that is bursting, or nearly bursting, emits sound covering a wide range of frequencies. Tiny hairline cracks, especially, generate ultrasound. So it might pay us to first examine closely the hearing sense of animals.

Weak vibrations

The British zoologist Maurice Burton reports the following observations:[116] In southern England a road carrying a constant stream of traffic runs close by a lake. Nothing out of the ordinary happens as long as passenger cars drive by. But if a heavy truck goes by, then without fail and always at the same place fish jump out of the water. At another lake, whenever doors are slammed in a house 100 meters (328 feet) from the bank, fish jump out of the water in one certain spot.

These observations show that fish react with fear to very definite vibration frequencies, and they bring to mind a phenomenon that may easily be observed in the woods. Squirrels or birds gambol high in the treetops without being the least bit concerned about the rustling of leaves or the creaking of branches in the wind. Frequently they ignore people walking around on the forest floor. But slap a tree trunk with the palm of your hand and the animals usually flee helter-skelter. Does slapping the tree produce sound frequencies similar to those that a small catlike predator makes when it jumps onto the trunk? Every hunter can tell a story of the sound sensitivity of shy forest animals. Sometimes coincidences have brought astonishing feats of hearing to light. For example, in coastal areas that were often bombed during World War II, the seagulls would after a while fly away with loud squawking long before people would become aware of the droning of airplane engines. The seagulls had learned to associate aircraft noise with falling bombs. Between the weak low-frequency vibrations that signal to a spider exactly what sort of victim has been caught in its web and the ultrasound signals with which hunting bats find their way in flight, there lies a whole sensory world. Animals, through highly specialized sound receptors, have unlocked the entire frequency range from less than 1 to more than 100,000 Hz. Do their high-performance sound receptors also enable them to sense earthquakes ahead of time? Only sound that people cannot hear could be acceptable as a possible earthquake sign and as an explanation for the mysterious behavior of animals. People hear within a broad frequency range, between 16 and 20,000 Hz, and are very sensitive in the middle part of this frequency range. Birds perceive sound in the same frequency range and do not react any more sensitively than humans. Finches and doves, in fact, hear far worse at all frequencies. Neither hedgehogs, nor cats, nor sheep, nor mice, nor rats hear significantly better than humans in the middle and lower frequencies. Insects are far less sensitive to low-frequency sound. Only fish hear low-frequency infrasound better than humans, but like reptiles, amphibians, and birds they don't seem to perceive ultrasound at all.

The picture of the ultrasound sensitivity of mammals is altogether different. Dogs, cats, foxes, and other four-legged carnivores hear at least up to 60,000 Hz. Even sheep are sensitive up to 40,000 Hz, and they probably hear as well as horses, deer, or antelopes. Good ultrasound ears that function above 100,000 Hz are possessed by dolphins, the smaller whales, and numerous moths and crickets, as well as bats. Most small mammals, especially rats and mice but also a number of insect species, hear equally well in the frequency range between 50,000 and 100,000 Hz.[117] Also widespread among animals is the use of ultrasound signals for communication, orientation, enemy identification, or hunting. In the larger mammals, such as sheep, dogs, and deer, ultrasound hearing probably evolved because breaking twigs, snapping grass, or rustling leaves can be easily detected with it. This ability once was vital to life in the wild, and at times still is.

Does this brief outline of the hearing sensitivities of animals provide a key to their earthquake premonition? Unfortunately, the balance of pro and con is not positive. Since pigeons and songbirds hear less well than humans, or at best only as well, their unusual deportment before earthquakes cannot be traced to sound signals that are transferred from the ground to the air. If the origin of a given earthquake lies (as is the case with most quakes) many kilometers deep within the earth's crust, then only very-low-frequency sound penetrates to the surface because of ultrasound absorption by rock. If cats, rats, mice, or sheep were frightened by that sound, people would be able to hear it just as well. But this is not the case. Conversely, if as a consequence of hairline cracks and rock fracturing within 10–100 meters (32.8–328 feet) beneath the surface there were still some ultrasound being radiated into the atmosphere, then reptiles, snakes, and birds would not sense it; they perceive no ultrasound. Cats and dogs, however, can perceive these signals. Why they should get so excited over them before earthquakes, although they are often bombarded with them in a technological environment, must be left unexplained.

Ground noises, then, offer no adequate explanation for the unusual behavior of animals before earthquakes. It is, however, possible that under certain circumstances single anomalies in animal behavior may have been started by ground noises, or at least influenced by them. Fish may have heard infrasound before earthquakes that was too weak for human ears. Cats could have received a warning of the above-mentioned rockslide in Switzerland because it happened on the earth's surface. Also, snakes (as well as pheasants and pigeons) are capable of reacting sensitively to vibrations in the ground. This plays a significant role in their detection of enemies, but it does not explain why snakes should flee from their burrows before an earthquake when normally, under the influence of different ground vibrations, they will quickly scurry back into them. Also, vibrations of this kind should not go unrecorded by sensitive seismographs. We have no choice but to extend the selection process to other possible physical earthquake precursors.

Animals and electrical fields

When a man stands upright on the ground, the average difference in potential between the top of his head and the soles of his feet is 300 volts. Nothing indicates any physical reactions from this natural electrical field of the atmosphere. Were he lying in a bathtub, such a high voltage would be deadly for him. This comparison points up how crucial the physical environment is to the way living beings perceive electrical fields. For a fish in the water, electrical potentials mean different sensory impressions than they do for a snake or a cat on the earth's surface. Because of the high resistance of the air above the earth's surface, the electrical field pushes only about 10^{-14} amperes of current through a person standing on the surface. That is far too low to disturb the nervous system. Moreover, the human body is such a good conductor of electricity that its surface assumes the potential of the ground and the electrical field is displaced from within the body. The current that would be generated by the same potential in water, on the other hand, would be so great that it would influence the function of nerves and cause physiological damage. Proportionate electrical fields, even when they are intense, are relatively harmless above ground. When people are walking along ridges in high mountains or sailing on the high seas, electrical discharges (called Saint Elmo's fire) can radiate from them without their suffering any outright pain. The impressions made by their hair standing on end, by crackling noises, and by the overall condition are of course quite unsettling. It is very likely that animals, with their delicate sensory hairs, react more sensitively to such discharges than humans. But atmospheric electrical fields become really effective physiologically when they vary their intensity rapidly. Then they generate in a conducting body, in accordance with the classic laws of electrodynamics, displacement currents—real, temporally limited current pulses. The greater the speed of alternation of the electrical field's strength, the stronger the current pulses.

The energy thus imparted to a body is enough to evoke physiological reactions.[118] With humans they are, as a rule, not especially intense, but they do contribute—not insignificantly—to the weather sensitivity from which numerous people suffer. Animals react to electrical-field changes very sensitively, as experiments have shown. This was demonstrated very elegantly in Schua's experiments with golden hamsters.[119] Several hamsters were kept, each separately, in glass terrariums until they had settled in and until feeding and nesting places had been firmly established. Then flat antennas were positioned above the nests. At irregular intervals, alternating electrical fields from 100 to 900 volts per meter and at frequencies ranging from a few to 10,000 Hz were applied for hours at a time. These are conditions found in ordinary thunderstorms. Within 48 hours all the hamsters had moved their nests into areas of their terraria that had remained free of the electrical fields. When an entire terrarium was put under the influence of a field, the hamster led a veritable gypsy life, wandering around aimlessly with its nest. Especially sensitive were mothers with young. Field changes of 10 V/m over the nesting place were enough to make the mother drag the young from the nest and into the most remote corner of the terrarium; then she would also move the nesting and feeding places.

Bees, too, react with astonishing sensitivity to alternating electrical fields. It has been shown that the proportion of pollen lost in collection flights is especially high when atmospheric field disturbances are intense. The exact physiological reasons behind all these phenomena are not known, but a series of biochemical changes have been detected that might be connected with them.[118]

Just how sensitive aquatic animals are to electrical fields and currents is shown by a discovery that puzzled scientists at first: Sharks, those quick, energetic robbers of the sea, do not only hunt for prey that swims free in the water, but also for flounder that might have burrowed up to 30 centimeters (12 inches) into the sand. The sharks will swim slowly over the bottom and then suddenly dive with sure aim for the invisible victim. If the flounder in the sand is surrounded by a plastic hull, the tracking sense of the shark fails. It is the odor of the flounder, one might hastily conclude. Far from it! If the flounder is surrounded with a housing made of gelatin, which lets no odor molecule escape but conducts electricity, the shark is again able to home in on its prey. What the shark actually detects is a tiny electrical field that the flounder radiates. If instead of a flounder two electrodes are buried in the sand and a small voltage is generated between them, the shark mistakes them for a flounder and attacks. The sensitivity with which electrical fields can be detected is extremely high. One millionth of a volt per meter is enough to excite the shark's highly developed search organ, the Lorenzinian ampulla.

Besides sharks, many other species of fish have been shown to possess remarkable sensitivity to electrical fields. Among them are catfish, rays, and eels. Seven families of fish also possess electrical organs that enable them to produce their own electrical fields for hunting, navigation, or communication. A sensitive detection system for electrical fields is a must if they are to make optimal use of their remarkable sensory capacities. Since more intense currents can have lethal consequences for all aquatic animals, their sensitivity to them is merely a question of load.

Electrical signals, then, are interesting as possible influences on the behavior of animals. Water dwellers might be able to react to them particularly sensitively, and the above-described Japanese investigations into the earthquake behavior of catfish[45] support this conclusion rather convincingly. Above the earth's surface, to judge by the capacity of animal senses, rapidly alternating electrical fields would be, theoretically, important earthquake precursors. Slowly changing electrical fields, on the other hand, would have considerable effects only if they departed from the normal value of the atmospheric field by comparatively large amounts.

Animals and the earth's magnetic field

No scientist can imagine how a "compass installation" that would enable animals to navigate by means of the earth's magnetic field would function. Nonetheless, researchers have searched for a century for a magnetic sense in animals, in complete trust in nature's inventiveness. Only in the last decade have experiments become so subtle and persuasive that there is no longer any doubt of the existence of such a magnetic sense in a number of living beings.

Untold numbers of orientation flights by carrier pigeons carrying small interfering magnets revealed no deviant behavior by the birds until the American scientist W. T. Keeton made a sensational discovery:[120] In sunny weather, which is when carrier pigeons are usually sent aloft, they had no interest in the magnetic field of the earth because they had a much more convenient navigational aid in the sun. But experienced pigeons find their way even under completely covered skies, and it was this ability that was impaired to a great degree by interference magnets. Interestingly, completely inexperienced pigeons are confused in their orientation by extraneous magnetic fields even in sunny weather. At the same time, it was shown that even natural magnetic storms in the ionosphere influenced the navigational behavior of carrier pigeons, and that the birds were able to register magnetic-field changes of 30–70 gamma.[121] Meanwhile, researchers succeeded in setting up controlled interference fields around the heads of carrier pigeons by surrounding the heads with magnetic coils in a hoodlike device. It now became possible to simulate repeatable errors in navigation.[122] The ability to orient according to the magnetic field of the earth, meanwhile, has also been shown to exist among some migratory birds.[123]

Similarly exciting discoveries were made by Lindauer and Martin with bees.[124] The object of their study was the orientation dance, discovered by Karl von Frisch, by which pathfinder bees convey the direction and the distance of newly discovered nectar supplies to their fellow bees. When they show the direction with dance motions on a vertical honeycomb section, they describe it as flight angle relative to the sun (azimuth). The direction of the force of gravity stands for the direction of the sun. Lindauer and Martin discovered that the navigational information of the pathfinder bees showed systematic errors that varied with the direction of the earth's magnetic field and could be influenced by artificial fields. Despite that, the signals were read correctly by the other bees. If the orientation dances had to be, perforce, done on horizontal surfaces, the dancing bees would preferably choose one of the four cardinal points of the compass as the "solar direction." These preferred directions disappeared when the earth field was artificially reduced to zero. It is possible to adduce proof that magnetic storms influence the dances. Thus, bees react to magnetic-field changes of less than 100 gamma or even less than 10 gamma.

Unmistakable reactions to weak magnetic fields have also been shown to exist in termites, bacteria,[125] various species of beetles, and even fish. Consequently, the possibility cannot be dismissed that living beings can occasionally recognize the magnetic-field changes of 1–100 gamma that may appear before earthquakes. Even so, these signals cannot be considered as the cause of the earthquake dread of animals. In the first place, as the experiments have shown, magnetic fields as orientation aids can cause confusion at worst, but no panic. In the second place, these magnetic-field changes appear much too early (months, sometimes) before an earthquake. And third, the magnetic-field variations to which animals are exposed in their daily wanderings on the earth's surface, because of day-to-night variations and because of rather frequent magnetic storms in the ionosphere, are at least as great as and usually considerably greater than the earthquake-associated variations.

Can animals smell earth gases?

The nose of a dog works about a million times more sensitively than that of man. The feats of smelling of which dogs are capable are familiar to everyone from some amazing reports of actual incidents. But there are limits even for the best canine nose. For example, dogs are not especially well equipped to smell out truffles, a tasty species of mushroom that flourishes in the ground to depths of 30 centimeters (12 inches). Even when trained for it laboriously they often fail, because earth, on account of its porous nature, binds odor substances very effectively. Pigs are favored for truffle hunting because they can smell this delicacy within a radius of 40 meters (131 feet) and steer for it unerringly. Possibly this tracking sense for truffles is so well evolved in pigs because truffles had been the favored food of the pigs' ancestors in the forests. Many animals living in the wild search for truffles, but the achievement of a small insect is truly remarkable. It lays its eggs in these mushrooms, and to do that it drives a narrow shaft toward them through the soil.

With insects nature has reached the natural limit of the sense of smell. This has been shown persuasively by the experiments with silk moths that made Adolf Butenandt famous. At mating time the female moth produces less than a millionth of a gram of a sex attractant, which is distributed by the wind. As far as 11 kilometers (7 miles) away, a male receives the signal and sets out to find the female. A single attractant molecule, which fits into the much-ramified antenna of the male like a key into a lock, seems enough to arouse attention, and a few are enough to move the insect to purposeful action.

Sensitive smell organs for finding nourishment and partners, as well as for the recognition of enemies, are widespread in the animal world. Ants, when they take an obstructed path to their hills, follow well-marked odor roads, and with their sense of smell they distinguish members of their colony from interlopers. Snakes use their forked tongues to catch odor molecules and then strip them off for identification in a smelling groove in their throat (Jacobson's organ).

The relative smelling abilities of higher animals can be readily compared by examining their odor lobes, which are distinguishable parts of the brain. In fish they are comparatively large; the example of the salmon, which can smell the creek in which it was spawned after migrating thousands of kilometers, is impressive testimony for the tracking sense of fish. Eels and morays, which look for carrion in murky depths and mostly at night, also depend mainly on their sense of smell. Eels, in fact, have developed this sense further than dogs. Sharks have giant smelling lobes, and experience has shown that the world in which they live is predominantly one of smells. Judging by the development of the smelling center in their brains, birds don't think much of fragrances. This agrees with the opinion of behavior researchers. But bird species that must rely on smell to find food have developed a remarkable ability. The fulmar, a North Atlantic pelagic bird, apparently smells the fat of marine mammals over long distances. When such fat is laid out, the fulmar steers for it without much deviation. Turkey vultures of the New World seem to have similar smelling abilities. This was discovered, not by scientists, but by construction workers who used to have to look laboriously for leaks along the oil pipelines in the North American deserts. Now they don't direct their eyes to the ground anymore, but to the sky—circling vultures pinpoint the spot where the malodorous oil is seeping out.

If we wish to examine the question of whether animals smell gases that leak out of the ground before earthquakes and are alarmed by them, we must start with the fact that all living things except apes and most birds have a keener sense of smell than man.

It is well known that in the rhythm of the lunar tides and under certain geological conditions the above-ground concentration of swamp gases, such as methane, can change slightly. The gases are also exhaled from the ground during earth tremors. But animals, especially those that dig holes in the ground, should not react with fear and panic to gas molecules that can be found in the ground under normal circumstances. If the argument were made that before an earthquake gases unpleasant to animals are emitted from newly created hairline cracks, we would have to ask why this does not happen when animals burrow in the ground or when they stumble on gas-filled cavities. Moreover, why do songbirds become so excited before an earthquake when they are so indifferent to odors? Why should dogs be able to tolerate outgassing in cities without panicking when they often are beside themselves before earthquakes?

As can be seen, the attempt to trace the unusual animal behavior before earthquakes to aromatic stimuli in general leads to contradictions. But it cannot be denied that these stimuli are occasionally responsible for observed anomalies. In fact, this is very likely. It would be very enlightening to see a flight or panic reaction caused by odor perceptions if the gas causing it were one that does not normally appear in the ground and if that gas had unpleasant effects on living organisms. Can geophysical processes synthesize new molecule combinations before an earthquake? As incredible as this question sounds, there is a very simple possibility: Electric tensions of only 2 volts would theoretically be enough to electrolyze groundwater. For example, an acrid, evil-smelling chlorine gas could be liberated from dissolved salt (sodium chloride) if strong enough earth currents were to flow. People have reported now and then that during an earthquake they had perceived a "sulfur smell" in isolated spots. Thus, the idea is not all that farfetched.

Electromagnetic radiation and life

From among the electromagnetic waves that constitute the vast energy range between the "hard" cosmic rays and the longest radio waves, life has selected only the relatively energy-poor radiation below the near-ultraviolet range as a means of carrying information from the environment. Rays with higher energy destroy the sensitive tissue of biological structures. What is highly interesting (and therefore worth a close look) is the emission range of the electromagnetic radio waves, and especially the extremely long waves. Waves of this kind are also emitted during thunderstorms, and several electrical phenomena in rock could generate them too.

The body of information about the biological effects of this long-wave electromagnetic radiation is still full of gaps. Nevertheless, we can assume with some certainty that the long waves can have effects on living creatures that are at least as great as those caused by the much weaker rapidly alternating electric fields. Accidental experiments provide a rough description of the symptoms evoked: For example, people servicing powerful but poorly shielded transmitters have complained of depression, fatigue, insomnia, and general malaise after spending several hours daily in the radiation field. A long-wave radiation diathermy treatment, long since replaced by ultrasound, induced "short-wave hangover." In patients who had temporarily been exposed to an alternating electric field instead of a direct-current field in a defective inhalation chamber, heart pains, rapid pulse, increased blood pressure, insomnia, nausea, and a severe coronary collapse were observed. Extensive and conclusive investigations have been made concerning the influence of atmospheric electromagnetic long waves on human weather sensitivity, on the appearance of such severe weather-related bodily failures as embolisms and coronary infarctions, and on the frequency of traffic accidents.[118] It is considered certain that there is more than an accidental connection between these events and an increased incidence of the waves.

Animals probably suffer still more under the influence of electromagnetic radiation of low energy. It has become known, for example, that the electromagnetic disturbances caused by a test antenna of the U.S. Navy's Project Seafarer [the controversial proposal to build an underground antenna in Wisconsin for communicating with submerged submarines over extremely-low-frequency radio waves—Tr.] influenced the flyways of migratory birds considerably. The reasons no well-controlled experiments have been carried out in this area must be ascribed mainly to the experimental problems encountered in the work with meter-long to kilometer-long waves. But their biological effect cannot be doubted. Therefore, long-wave electromagnetic radiation from the ground must be considered as a possible precursor of earthquakes that sets off unusual animal behavior.

Not all signals arouse fear

Identified above have been a number of signals, possibly generated by geophysical processes preceding earthquakes, that could theoretically be perceived by animals. However, there has been no enlightening explanation for the animals' fear. The individual physical signals might occasionally be responsible for abnormal animal behavior before earthquakes, or at least share the responsibility. But if we compare many different observations and try to reduce them to a common denominator, we get caught up again and again in contradictions.

Changes in air pressure, in the local acceleration of gravity, or in the earth's magnetic field, or minor ground deformations, can hardly be considered, because animals experience far greater variations in their daily wanderings than an approaching earthquake can produce.

Acoustical warning signals would have to lie in the ultrasound or infrasound ranges to be perceived by animals but not by humans. Many animals are remarkably sensitive to ultrasound, but this capability of their hearing organs would help them little before an earthquake. Ultrasound cannot penetrate rock more than 10–100 meters (32.8–328 feet), whereas the sources of most earthquakes lie several kilometers down. Then, too, snakes are deaf to ultrasound. On the other hand, dogs, cats, rats, and mice are by no means more sensitive to low-frequency tones than humans. Their panic reactions, then, could not be produced by infrasound. And if animals were to react especially sensitively to microquakes, they would seldom get any rest; these smallest quakes often occur in bunches before great quakes, but they also happen without being followed by a big quake far too often to be considered as reliable alarm signals. Also, if animals were that sensitive to vibrations, it would surely be impossible to carry them in vehicles.

Why would birds in the branches of trees get excited? And do mice and snakes flee from their burrows when a truck rolls past nearby? Changes in the groundwater table could occasionally drive snakes, mice, and other burrow dwellers from their holes, but the animals that populate the air and the surface would take no notice of them. Perhaps gases with unpleasant effects come out of the ground now and then, produced by electrochemical processes in the earth. But why, then, do birds become excited when they have such a poor sense of smell?

The only possible physical earthquake signals so far discussed that at least could explain the wide distribution of alarm behavior among animal species are electrical in nature. Electrical fields (particularly rapidly alternating fields) and long-wave electromagnetic radiation would be disturbing to many living beings, and electrical currents have been shown to have lasting effects on aquatic animals. Unfortunately, there have been practically no serious geophysical investigations into this group of possible earthquake precursors. It is certain, however, that these phenomena alone cannot explain earthquake fear satisfactorily. These electrical phenomena also appear in connection with thunderstorms, and on such occasions dogs do not howl, snakes and rats do not flee from their burrows, and domestic animals do not try to break out of their pens.

Only a process that interferes dramatically with the hormone balances and the nerve functions of animals could produce the dramatic changes in behavior that have occasionally been observed before severe earthquakes. But what sort of signals produce these interferences? Are there any physical processes at all that can affect the threshold of excitability of animals so effectively?

6

Circumstantial Evidence for Charged Particles

More experiences in Friuli

After the earthquake in Friuli I tried hard to see some scientific meaning, some connection with an understandable geophysical process, behind the animal behavior the villagers had told me about. At that point I did not know that other people had had similar experiences and that, in fact, some of this knowledge had been written down. Later I would collect many documents by laboriously searching through libraries and by following up hints from other scientists. Some of the documents were hard to get access to because they were ancient, because of the language they were written in, or because of the unusual script in which they had been composed.

What made me stick with this inquiry was, above all, my trust in the words and observations of people I treasured. When I learned that the phenomenon was typical and had been observed all over the world, I felt vindicated. Still, I had to find a scientific meaning in this mysterious animal panic. Was it not strange that dogs, cats, and other domestic animals tried to leave houses and towns even though they had no idea of how dangerous man-made structures are in an earth-quake? Why do birds get so excited when they have no reason to fear anything up in the branches or in the air? Why did nature equip animals with an ability to sense earthquakes? Quakes don't happen often enough to apply strong evolutionary pressure on animal species. After all, what would it matter to the propagation of the species if a few individuals in one generation were to die in an earthquake? What would justify the evolution of acute sensitivity when it might not be put to use for centuries?

This riddle would not be the only one confronting me in the months ahead. In my search for some physical reasons for the earthquake premonition of animals, I stumbled on an eyewitness report that riveted my attention: A train loaded with cattle and horses had been parked in the freight yard of Pontebba, the town next to my village, on the evening of May 6, 1976, the day of the earthquake. The train had arrived in late afternoon, and the customs formalities could not be finished that day. As usual in such cases, the animals were fed and watered. Normally, animals in transit stay fairly quiet all night after they have been cared for, but on this evening they were showing a high state of nervousness. The workers who had been caring for the animals that night said later that, shortly before the earthquake, they had noticed a great deal of mooing, whinnying, and crashing of hooves against the sides of the freight cars. This excitement started about 15–20 minutes before the quake and kept getting worse until the quake struck. The caretakers found this behavior so unusual that they began to wonder whether the animals might have been poisoned or whether an epidemic had broken out, and they notified their supervisor.

What fascinated me about this whole episode was not that it was still another clear example of earthquake premonition by animals; many such observations had been made in that area. The thing that struck me was that here I was dealing with a genuine (if accidental) scientific experiment, run within strict limits. The roofed railway cars in which the animals were being shipped were built of sheet iron and had only a few slits and rectangular openings for ventilation. The cars were nearly perfect Faraday cages—that is to say, metal containers into which neither electrical nor magnetic fields could penetrate and whose interiors were largely screened from electromagnetic waves.

The Faraday-cage effect (which is what causes a car radio to stop playing when the car passes under a bridge built of reinforced concrete) eliminated with one stroke several possible geophysical phenomena as factors in the animals' behavior. No change in the earth's electrical field, no change in the magnetic field, and no rise or fall in the intensity of electromagnetic radiation could have affected the animals in the railroad cars. As a bonus, this coincidental experiment also excluded small prequakes or low-frequency sounds; the only preshock had been one isolated, strong, clearly perceptible tremor, which happened less than a minute before the main quake.

What else could explain the animals' strong reaction to imperceptible vibrations after they had been traveling in a train for several days from Poland and had suffered a numbing concert of noise and rattling with comparative equanimity? The riddle seemed complete!

I must confess that when I looked into this case, the whole phe-nomenon of abnormal animal behavior before earthquakes suddenly became frightening. That was the only time in this whole research project that I seriously thought of dropping it. Either this mysterious earthquake premonition had nothing to do with natural science or the many observers had imagined a phenomenon that did not exist. At this point I took a hike into the mountains, as I had done before when I had important things to think about. I know a remote spot there where there are petrified impressions in the rock dating from another epoch of the earth's history, impressions that have preserved prehistoric ferns in youthful beauty. I know of no better place in which to brood over nature and the fate of man. But everything seemed changed, somehow. The mountains had moved! Their familiar faces showed new lines. Everywhere in the masses of rock I could see wounds struck by the earthquake. I was shaken and fascinated by the violence of nature, and I suddenly became convinced that it would be worth any effort to wrest even a trace of her secrets from her.

The effort was not wasted. Back in my home village I looked up an old man named Rudi Zuder whom I knew well. I found him living in the little woodshed he had moved into after the earthquake. Here I stumbled on my first important scientific proof. After Zuder told me how the catastrophe had run its course and what damages it had caused, I asked him whether he had noticed anything unusual just before the quake. I could tell right away from his face that he had something important to tell me. His story sounded like the description of an experiment in physics. Before the disastrous earthquake, Zuder, a retired *Feinmechaniker* (precision mechanic), had been putting a small wristwatch together. The job required him to put a thin stainless-steel plate into place. It had a relatively large surface area for its weight, which Zuder guessed to be a few tenths of a gram. The little plate kept repelling itself from its intended place and jumping off. The old mechanic tried several times to put the plate into place, with the same result. Bewildered, he went outside to look at the weather. It was a clear night. After a brief stroll he tried again to finish assembling the watch, but the strange electrostatic load on the plate kept interfering. He thought he was feeling electricity running through his body when the first quake put a violent end to his careful observations.

Does the ground emit electrostatic charges?

How could the works of a watch and a thin metal plate sitting on a wooden table charge themselves up so strongly as to repel each other? The only possible explanation is that charges of equal sign had been transferred from the air to the metal parts. Since oxygen, nitrogen, and the noble gases cannot carry electric charges, they must have been carried by particles suspended in the air—aerosol particles.

It is common knowledge that aerosol particles produce the "haze dome" over big cities. But the study of aerosol particles leads into a complicated, much-ramified area comprising not only environmental pollution but also meteorology and medicine. The reason this branch of knowledge is so difficult (nearly incomprehensible, actually) is that there are so many kinds of aerosol particles. The smallest are no bigger than a few molecules and are called *small ions*, because mostly they are stabilized by one, more rarely by two, unit electrical charges. Their life spans are usually only a few minutes, after which they decay and form again. Next in size after small ions is a group of larger particles, with diameters up to 1×10^{-7} meter (0.1 micrometer), called *nuclei*. These are the particles around which water vapor condenses to form fog droplets. The average life span of nuclei is around several days, and they carry many electrical unit charges. The larger nuclei, in general, carry more charges than the small ones, but between 10 and 60 percent are not charged. Next come the *ultralarge ions*, which measure up to 1 micrometer. Only 10 percent of them are not charged. Beyond this group we find *giant nuclei* with diameters reaching 10 micrometers; these particles settle in still air and thus are not genuine aerosol particles.

Just as diverse as their sizes and charges are the compositions of these suspended particles. Traces of every possible solid, ground dust, the finest of water droplets, salt crystals, pollen viruses, and bacteria can be found among them. Knowing the various kinds of aerosol particles is only the beginning. A host of environmental influences can affect their concentration, their structure, and their electrical charges within wide limits. The effects of industrial and automotive exhaust gases are well known, as are the effects of many chemical processes; these sources contribute significantly to the enrichment of the air with nuclei of all kinds, from 0.001 to 1 micrometer in diameter. The nearness of the sea, too, affects the aerosol content of the air considerably because of the surf. The charges of aerosol particles are affected to a large extent by such processes as fire, the effects of friction, natural radioactivity, high-energy solar radiation, and electrical discharges from sharp points. Different mean values have to be given for the concentration, distribution, and charge of aerosol particles depending on whether the location is urban, rural, or near the sea. For obvious reasons, the total concentration of aerosol particles is significantly higher in settled areas than it is in open spaces. Also, a multitude of technological activities emit especially large aerosol nuclei.

But the situation is different for charged nuclei. In the streets of big cities or in industrial areas the concentration of small ions can amount to fewer than 100 per cubic centimeter, while the same kinds of ions can be ten times as concentrated in a clean residential area. This difference is accounted for by the fact that few human activities increase the number of small ions in the air, but many activities reduce it. For example, small ions in the air attach themselves easily to the larger suspended particles, and these can thus accumulate many positive and negative charges.

There was only one possible explanation for the electrostatic charging of Zuder's watch housing and the little metal plate: They had come in contact with highly charged suspended particles. Since the weather was fair at the time of the earthquake and remained unchanged for two days, the electrical charge must have gotten into the atmosphere from the ground by way of aerosol particles.

It was immediately clear to me that the accidental experiment with the watch had given me a line of scientific inquiry that I would be well advised to follow. That mysterious episode with the agitated cattle in the iron freight cars was suddenly no dead end anymore. Electrostatically charged particles could easily have drifted into the cars through the ventilation openings. The Faraday cage offered no protection against aerial electricity. The animals had inhaled it, and because their bodies had been isolated from the metal walls by their horny hooves and the wooden floors, they had become charged up. What had happened to them was the same thing that happens to the small plates of an electroscope, a simple device to measure charges. The plates are screened by a metal housing. When an electric charge is transferred to these plates from outside through an opening in the housing, the two plates repel each other.

Now it became possible to understand the strange bathing mania of a canary one woman had told me about: As can be easily seen when hair is standing on end because of friction-generated electricity, moisture conducts electricity away. Perhaps the canary had found out that it could get rid of the bothersome or painful static electricity by moistening its dry feathers and shaking off the water droplets.

The hypothesis that the ground gives off static electricity before an earthquake was given strong support by observations made by people who had been outdoors during the Friuli quake. They had noticed strange lights on the mountains, but only during the strong tremors. The glowing light that had briefly illuminated the rocky crags of Gleries mountain, visible from the village of Apua, was described as "like in a thunderstorm, but more intense and without clouds." On the wooded

Velica Rauna near San Leopoldo, people had noticed irregularly shaped glowing patches flitting over the mountain flanks in quick succession. Elsewhere, people were talking of "fiery tongues" that had spurted out of the ground. Peasants asked me, more than once, what sort of "flammable gas" we were dealing with here. There was no doubt in my mind that these earthquake lights were appearances of Saint Elmo's fire—electrical discharges such as can be observed at the tips of masts, on lightning rods, or on sharp corners of buildings when the atmosphere is strongly charged.

Finding a possible scientific explanation in the charged aerosol particles allayed most of the doubts that had made me think of mass pyschosis, preconceived notions, and shock-disoriented memories whenever I had heard reports of earthquake premonition by animals.

Mysterious demagnetization

In the middle of the nineteenth century, an optician kept a small shop in the center of Edo (now Tokyo). In his show window, to which he always devoted exceptional care, he displayed a large horseshoe magnet of which he was exceedingly proud. It is said to have measured 90 centimeters (35 inches) across. Nails and various other iron parts were kept sticking to it, demonstrating its magnetic power. On November 11, 1855, however, the magnet suddenly let go of all its clinging iron parts. The optician was very disappointed, because this showpiece had been attracting the curious. He thought the magnet had lost its power because it had become old and weak. A severe earthquake devastated the city 2 hours later. What made the episode doubly baffling was that the magnet regained its attractive power after the earthquake.[39,42]

The optician is said to have tried to build an earthquake warning station using the effect observed on his magnet, but it is not known whether he did. The incident drew a great deal of attention at the time because it was believed that a change in the earth's magnetic field associated with the earthquake had caused the magnet to lose its magnetism. This explanation is highly improbable in light of current geophysical knowledge. The changes in the magnetic field that can be expected in an earthquake are thousands to tens of thousands times smaller than the earth's magnetic field. Even if the polarity of the earth's magnetic field were reversed, the small magnetic domain of the permanent iron magnet would not have become disordered because of it. Opposing fields must be hundreds of times greater than that of a magnet they are supposed to demagnetize. In addition, it takes very curious windings to remove the magnetism from a horseshoe magnet.

It would be pointless to waste any more words on something that is impossible if it weren't for the fact that similar stories of demagnetized magnets have been reported in connection with European earthquakes. These reports attracted much attention. Immanuel Kant mentions them in a work about the earthquake of Lisbon of November 1, 1755: "I cannot pass in silence over the fact that on that terrible All Saints Day the magnets in Augsburg threw off their load and that magnetic needles were brought into disorder. Boyle [the great seventeenth-century physicist] reports that the same thing occurred after an earthquake in Naples. We know too little of the concealed nature of magnets to be able to give a reason for this phenomenon."[11b] According to reports by the earthquake researcher Milne dating from the end of the nineteenth century, iron objects fell off many horseshoe magnets during an earthquake in Rome.[42] This phenomenon was taken seriously enough to prompt Count Malvasia, a scientific amateur, to spend some time in the 1870s observing a magnet with a small piece of iron sticking to it. The piece is said to have fallen off occasionally during an earthquake, but not at every earthquake. It seems that this phenomenon has never been disproved.

If the earth's surface became enriched with charged particles before an earthquake, objects would become electrostatically charged and metallic parts would repel each other the way they did in Rudi Zuder's accidental experiment with the watch. Since an iron part sticks to a magnet when the magnetic attraction overcomes the weight of the part, a small repellant force might be enough in some situations to make the part fall. We don't know how strong Count Malvasia's magnet was or how heavy the load of iron pieces, so it is at least possible to advance an electrostatic explanation for this "demagnetization phenomenon." The charged-particle hypothesis also explains why the magnet regained its power later and why the experiment would occasionally fail.

Charged aerosols and the serotonin syndrome

A scientist's mood can fluctuate wildly with the ups and downs of his research project, but the mood swings experienced by a colleague of the American physicist C. W. Hansell were extreme.[126] On some days while working on his electrostatic generator (a device for producing ions), he would be relaxed, friendly, and chipper; on other days he would scowl and be exceedingly irritable. No one would have minded these fluctuations if they had been due to the degree of success of the researcher's work, but why did he sometimes look disconsolate when his work was going well, or cheerful when nothing was going right? The moody researcher finally noticed this contradiction himself and became curious. He kept a log of his activities and solved the riddle: Whenever he was producing negative ions with his generator he was happy, and whenever he worked with positive ions he was glum.

This discovery, made in 1932, did not surprise some European researchers. By 1928 G. Schorer had concluded, after a series of experiments with weather-sensitive patients, that the ion content of the air had a direct influence on the well-being of humans, and in 1931 the biophysicist Friedrich Dessauer carried out the first systematic clinical examination with an ion machine developed for the purpose.[127] In the beginning, Dessauer allowed all different kinds of patients to inhale positive ions. The effects were disquieting. Generally, the positive ions brought on a radical deterioration in the patients' sense of well-being and, what is more, caused highly uncomfortable sensations. After a while, two of the patients had to be given intensive clinical care because of pronounced symptoms of coronary weakness, and the researchers were forced to abandon treatment with positive ions altogether. Fortunately, negative ions had the opposite effect. Patients who had been suffering from headaches and migraines for years lost them after a few inhalation sessions. Dizziness and ringing in the ears suffered by people with high blood pressure were also affected favorably. Fatigue and listlessness were gone as if blown away, but about 75 percent of rheumatism patients who were treated with negative ions showed distinct signs of pain in the usual parts of the body.

Dessauer and his colleagues pointed out that the *Föhn* [a warm, dry wind that blows down the leeward slopes of mountains, especially the Alps—Tr.], because it is rich in positive small ions, tended to depress people, and that altitude sickness was caused in equal measure by the high ion content of the air and by an excess of positive ions. There is also an interesting speculation that, as atmospheric pressure falls, air rich in ions is drawn out of the ground and onto the surface.

In the ensuing decades scientists tried to follow up on the effects of airborne ions on biological processes. By 1958 more than 300 works dealing with this topic had appeared.[118] Most prominent among them are the investigations by Hicks and Beckett[128] and those by Besa.[129] The physiological effects of airborne ions were confirmed unanimously. Negative ions usually were given credit for promoting well-being; positive ions were said to be hard to tolerate. As a rule, the opposite effects of the positive and negative ions were accepted. However, despite strenuous efforts, this line of research did not get full recognition. It was criticized (deservedly, to some extent) for experiments that were poorly controlled, unrealistic, or prone to too many errors. For example, experimenters frequently failed to control the quantities of ozone or nitrogen oxides produced by certain ion generators, or else the ions attached themselves to larger aerosol particles and thus had their effect modified or lost. Often, too, the patients were not properly grounded, and so they would become electrically charged enough to repel the ions. Moreover, many researchers drew their conclusions from experiments that had been done with ion concentrations seldom found in nature. Only in the last decade or two did the study of the effects of ions on living beings take a few decisive steps ahead. These successes were achieved when the work was limited to simple, manageable portions of the total problem. The experimental conditions were improved, and clear and definite study objects were picked. The work was concentrated on small ions and on bacteria.

Small ions in the atmosphere are, after all, pretty important in nature. The *Föhn* and similar warm dry winds, such as the *Sharav* in the Near East, the *Chinook* of the Rocky Mountains, and the *Zonda* of Argentina, pick up vast quantities of these ions on the tops of mountains, where they are produced by natural radioactivity and by friction. Cosmic rays, short-wave light, and atomizing water also lead to the formation of small ions. The small ions generally possess a single electric charge to which are attached one to eight molecules, mostly water. Pure country or mountain air rarely contains more than 20,000 ions per cubic centimeter, and usually the concentration of small ions is significantly lower.

By now there is a body of convincing findings about the effects of small ions on microorganisms.[130] Many researchers have agreed that when these ions are applied to bacteria, they reduce their vitality dramatically. Within a short time, ions reduce the number of bacteria still able to function to a fraction of the original number. The lethal effect of small ions, of course, depends very much on their concentration as well as on the kinds of microorganisms. In a typical experiment with ion concentrations ranging from 20,000 to 250,000 per cubic centimeter, the proliferation of bacteria (*Neurospora*) was reduced to 50 percent by negative ions and to 10 percent by positive ones.[128] In other series of experiments, negative ions proved more effective.[130] But the most significant impulse given to research on airborne ions came from the work of the American scientist A. P. Krueger and his co-workers. Under painstakingly controlled experimental conditions, guinea pigs, rabbits, and especially mice were exposed to positive and negative ions over 16 years. More than 12,000 brain samples and 36,000 blood samples were examined in an effort to learn just how ions affected the biochemical functions. These careful, patient experiments showed unmistakably that small ions in the air have a pervasive effect on the concentration of serotonin (5-hydroxytryptamine), a nerve hormone that abounds in the lower middle brain. Serotonin can cause far-reaching changes in the body's metabolic processes, and also affects the transmission of nerve impulses, sleep, and the development of moods. When Krueger's animals inhaled negative small ions, the concentration of serotonin in blood and brain dropped; when positive ions were inhaled, it rose markedly.[131]

These findings have since been confirmed by other researchers. Gilbert showed that negative small ions not only reduced the concentration of serotonin in the brains of rats, but slowed down their temperaments, too.[132] Olivereau devoted his doctoral dissertation to the same set of problems.[133] His biochemical investigations showed that changes in the serotonin concentration in rats brought on by small ions had dramatic effects on the processes in the central nervous system, followed by significant physiological changes. One thing these studies showed was that negative ions noticeably reduced the anxiety of rats and mice in stress situations. They had the same effect as the sedative Reserpin, which also reduces the serotonin concentration in the middle brain. The similarity of these effects was confirmed in experiments with rats that were taught a stressful game: When they pressed a key, food would fall into their cages, but if a humming tone was sounded they had to stop pressing the key quickly lest they receive an electric jolt. It turned out that negative ions, as well as Reserpin, reduced their fear of punishment noticeably.[130]

Airborne ions even have a powerful effect on the course of disease in mice, as Krueger and his colleagues showed. Positive ions worsened significantly the illnesses of animals that had been injected with influenza viruses, and lowered their life expectancies; negative ions ameliorated the course of the disease and prolonged the animals' life spans.

The serotonin hypothesis can be used just as well to explain the sensitivity of humans to airborne ions. This was shown by Robinson and Dirnfeld[134] and by Sulman et al.,[135] who studied people suffering from the *Föhn*-like weather condition of the *Sharav* in the Near East. About 30 percent of the total population there were affected by the *Sharav*. Their symptoms, such as migraines, nausea, vomiting, and high nervousness, would show up with the rapid rise in the concentration of positive small ions in the air 1–2 days before any other meteorological changes could be clearly recognized. These symptoms are now summarized by the term *serotonin-stimulation syndrome*. This diagnosis is based on the hyperactivity of serotonin in the middle brain, and it has been shown that patients excrete abnormally large amounts of serotonin in the urine. Negative airborne ions, as well as serotonin-blocking drugs, are effective against the symptoms of the disease.

These experiments opened a window on a large field of research that still lies almost completely fallow. It is not only small ions that can be found in nature, but a multitude of suspended particles of various sizes and charges. Also, in nature the positive and negative airborne ions are usually intermingled. What their combined effect is we can only suspect, but it seems certain that life in nature has adapted to a certain minimum concentration of ions.

The aerosol hypothesis as explanation for strange behavior

The severe nervous and health disorders of the serotonin stimulation syndrome that are evoked in humans and animals by small airborne ions, and the persistent effect they have on microorganisms, are quite enough to explain the intense reactions of animals before earthquakes. Only a physicochemical process that affects the hormone balance of the nervous system directly could evoke such intensive reactions from so many different species. Most of all, such a process would explain the unbridled way in which the animals give vent to their feelings.

We have no clues as to what kinds of charged aerosol particles can appear before an earthquake, and even if we knew it would be difficult to draw conclusions about the behavior of animals. Neither the psychological effect of the larger charged aerosol particles nor the effect of more highly charged airborne ions has been studied sufficiently. We also do not know what effect positive and negative ions have on an organism when they work in combination. However, the following general outlines seem to be apparent.

Under certain geological and atmospheric conditions, positive airborne ions—which have a powerful effect on living beings—seem to appear in abundance before an earthquake. There are other circumstances in which this does not happen; for example, when it is raining, the charged aerosols are precipitated back into the ground. There may be geological conditions that favor the proliferation of negatively charged airborne ions, which do not agitate living beings but instead soothe them and reduce stress. Certain kinds of unusual animal behavior could have been caused by this soothing effect. The irregular distribution of reported cases of nervous animals before the Haicheng earthquake (figure 2) and the fact that these reports were limited to isolated areas could thus be accounted for.

Some typical individual behavior patterns can simply be interpreted as the animals' flight responses before charged clouds of particles streaming out of the ground. It seems to make sense that suspended charged particles penetrating the burrows of snakes, mice, and other small animals would drive the animals to flee, and the idea of charged clouds rising from the ground seems to explain the flight of chickens into treetops, the continuous fluttering around of pigeons, and the high circling of large flocks of other birds.

Surely the clearest proof for the existence of electrostatic charges before earthquakes is the aforementioned folk wisdom, current in the Isola delle Femine and in Capacci, Sicily, that an earthquake is about to happen when cats start screaming and raising their hairs and when sparks jump from their backs.[87] Observations related to the author by peasants in Friuli also point to electrostatic charge. When a cat ran around nervously inside a house and jerked its ears vigorously, and when cows wagged their ears and tails violently, they must have been feeling discomfort in their body surfaces. A cat will also jerk its ears when tickled with a blade of grass, and cows flap their ears and tails when flies bother them.

The land animals popularly believed to be typical earthquake prophets—cats, birds, dogs, snakes—have dry body surfaces. (Human skin, comparatively moist and conductive, is less sensitive to electrostatic charges.) The Chinese experience that smaller animals are more sensitive than larger ones also indicates that alarm signals are caused by a stimulus that works on the body surface; the ratio of body surface to body volume is significantly greater for small animals.

The reason for the frequently reported observation that horses and donkeys halt shortly before the start of an earthquake and cannot be persuaded to continue may have a perfect explanation: Since the electrostatic charge increases as the earthquake approaches, the animals must think they are entering a danger zone.

Probably the most often noticed and hardest to understand behavior of animals before an earthquake is their apparent urge to leave roofed dwellings, houses, apartments, stables, nests, corrals, and villages for the open country. The aerosol hypothesis also offers a possible explanation: Enclosed spaces with much human activity have suspended particles in concentrations hundreds to thousands of times higher than in nature. These are very large particles put in the air by the activities of man. It thus makes sense to look for the connections between animal behavior and aerosol-particle concentration. Two principal possibilities suggest themselves. One is that suspended particles, when they are numerous and large, can take up significantly more charges through contact with the ground than when they are fewer and smaller. The other is that the short life span of small mobile ions in aerosol-laden air leads to the accumulation of charges on heavy particles. These charges can only be transferred very slowly to the overlying atmosphere, and thus electrostatic charges would be felt more clearly in dust-laden air than out where the air is pure. Who has not known the claustrophobic feeling that comes when body hairs are standing on end? How much more sensitively must cats and dogs react when their nerve-loaded whiskers are stimulated by electrostatic charges? It is not the danger of the collapse of buildings that sends domestic animals fleeing from stables, houses, and villages, but the desperate attempt to find relief for the bodily discomfort in the moist, aerosol-poor outdoors.

Electrostatic processes similar to those that lead to the charging up of aerosol particles above land would have the effect of building up electric tension at the bottoms of bodies of water—tensions that would be equalized by flowing currents. When the electric eel of the Amazon River hunts by means of electrical discharges, its prey jump from the water in terror; fish that do the same thing before earthquakes may be trying to escape from similar electric discharges. Fish breeders know of a strange and sometimes fatal disease of fish that is caused by thunderstorms and can be traced to electrical discharges.[20]

It has been suggested that when fish migrate far across the open sea they orient themselves by electric currents in the ocean that are caused by geophysical processes. Schools of fish in Japan have been observed to deviate from their migratory tracks before earthquakes, behavior that might be connected with unusual electric currents in the ocean. Experiments on the earthquake premonition of catfish also indicate the possibility of electric alarm signals.[44]

Many other arguments and examples could be marshaled to build a foundation under the charged-aerosol thesis. For example, bees occasionally swarm in the electricity-laden air before thunderstorms just as they do before or during an earthquake;[20,21] but whereas they seek shelter in a thunderstorm, earthquakes sometimes seem to drive them into a frenzy. The difference may be accounted for by the fact that the ground normally is negatively charged and that it apparently changes its polarity as a consequence of an earthquake. In either case—thunderstorm or earthquake—electrical discharges are dangerous to bees, but the effect of ions on the bees' nervous systems would be totally different depending on whether the ground were positively or negatively charged.

Many baffling individual observations of a mysterious, often questioned phenomenon now seem to fit into a scientific frame like the pieces of a puzzle. But we should be clear in our minds that with the biological effect of charged particles we are only drawing a caricature of earthquake fear. Just as a musically gifted listener at a concert in which the orchestra has slipped from the rhythm of the conductor can detect dissonance through many subtle auditory impressions, so animals can probably recognize the smallest changes in the rhythm of nature by many subtle signs. Our search can be devoted only to the most dissonant disruptions of the environment that precede an earthquake.

7

Searching for the Causes of Electrostatic Phenomena

The piezoelectric effect

The question of how charged aerosols get into the air before and during an earthquake is fundamental. Among the things that must be considered is the energy involved. It takes considerable energy to liberate electrical charges from atoms or crystals, and it is no coincidence that radioactivity, short-wave ultraviolet light, and intense friction are the typical processes that accomplish it. However, not very much energy is needed to produce the small ion concentrations that can have physiological effects. Raising the ion concentration in the air over a village about one kilometer square to values that clearly exceed the weather-dependent average and might produce light phenomena under some conditions would require energies of 100–10,000 watt-seconds — the equivalent of a 100-watt bulb glowing for 1–100 seconds. Thus, the phenomenon that produces charges might be confined to a few isolated — and physically and chemically well-suited — places in the ground, but it requires a high concentration of energy.

Pressure electricity, or piezoelectricity as it is sometimes called, is the physical agent nearest at hand that could be considered as the cause. Certain crystals (quartz crystals, for example) are arranged in such a way that when pressure is applied along certain of the crystal's axes, the distribution of positive and negative charges can shift slightly. In this way pressure changes produce electrical charging of the crystal's surfaces, and when voltage changes are applied to the crystal it starts to vibrate mechanically. This property of crystals is what governs the rate of quartz watches.

The geological conditions that would let piezoelectricity of quartz play an important role in generating electric charges before an earthquake are quite favorable. On the average, the earth's crust consists of 15 percent quartz. In granite formations the quartz content reaches 30 percent, and in volcanic rocks it can reach 55 percent. But by itself a high proportion of quartz is not enough to create intense electric fields through pressure changes in the ground. Another requirement is that the quartz microcrystals not be totally randomly arranged, but that their crystal axes have a certain alignment so that the charges produced by the individual crystals do not cancel each other out. It is known from some geological investigations that unidirectional orientations of quartz microcrystals do occur.[136,137] These orientations apparently came about when the crystals formed under pressure in the cooling rock masses and aligned themselves in obedience to that pressure. The piezoelectric efficiency of natural microcrystalline quartz rocks is, of course, less than that of a single, well-grown large quartz crystal. Still, investigations by the Soviet geophysicist Parkhomenko have shown that it will amount to 0.8–10 percent in quartz veins, 0.07–15 percent in quartzites, 0.1–0.5 percent in granite, and 0.07–0.2 percent in gneiss.[137] Zones containing quartz crystals partially aligned in the same direction may extend for distances of between 10 meters (32.8 feet) and 1 kilometer (0.62 miles).

These conditions are sufficient for the generation of strong electrical fields in suitable geologic strata, provided that the pressures applied are great enough. Some earthquakes can burst rock formations, which requires pressures of 1,000 kilograms per square centimeter (14,233 pounds per square inch). A typical, moderately severe earthquake can be expected to produce subterranean pressure changes on the order of 25–250 kg/cm^2 (355–3,556 lb/in.^{2}).[138] We shall assume pressure variations of only 25 kg/cm^2, which are apt to be found when hairline cracks appear in compressed rock before an earthquake. Under such pressures, a rock ledge with a piezoelectric efficiency only 1 percent of that of an aligned quartz crystal could still generate an electrical field of 10,000 volts per meter. Along quartz veins with 10-percent piezoelectric efficiency it would generate 100,000 V/m. Such strong fields might appear even in ordinary granite formations if pressures in them would fluctuate around several hundred kg/cm^2 during an earthquake.

There is no doubt that the piezoelectric effect of quartz is capable of generating enough electrical energy to account for the creation of airborne ions before and during an earthquake. These energies would even be enough to cause lightninglike phenomena in the air.

When I presented my hypothesis about the electrostatic charging of aerosol particles to earthquake researchers and geophysicists at the Massachusetts Institute of Technology and when I suggested the piezoelectric effect as a possible cause, I ran into unexpected criticism from Professors William Brace and Theodore Madden of the earth and planetary sciences department. Other researchers had already considered the piezoelectric effect in order to explain popular reports of light phenomena during earthquakes,[139-142] but a piezoelectric hypothesis worked out in extensive detail by D. Finkelstein and J. R. Powell had received a mortal dagger thrust during a discussion at an international congress of geophysicists in Moscow in 1971. There it was pointed out that the electrical conductivity of the ground, because of the water in it, was too great, generally speaking, to sustain electric fields of the magnitude suggested.

Madden made an alternative suggestion for a mechanism that would set electrostatically charged aerosols free. He suggested that, because of natural charge-separation processes on rock surfaces, ions might already be present in the fine pores of the ground, and that they might merely be exhaled as a consequence of pressure changes or variations in the groundwater level. My view is that, although there is no doubt that charge-separation processes do occur along border surfaces, there is far too little energy in simple exhalation processes, in contrast to atmospheric and sand storms, to account for the buildup of concentrated clouds of charged particles.

The objections raised against the piezoelectric effect of quartz as a cause of electrostatic charges became clear to me only after I looked more closely into the ideas Finkelstein and Powell had advanced. They had assumed that earthquake waves, through pressure changes that they generate in quartz-containing ground, lead to opposite electrostatic charges at spatially separated places—charges that are then discharged into the air across distances ranging from 10 to 100 meters, accompanied by light phenomena. Finkelstein and Powell were able to adduce proof that this mechanism could, without difficulty, produce light phenomena, but they had to admit that this worked only when the electrical resistance of the ground was unusually high (10^9 ohm-meter). However, under normal circumstances (10^3 ohm-meter), the accumulated difference in potential would equalize itself effectively through the ground without giving off any detectable energy to the atmosphere. One would have to assume pressure and charging waves of very high frequency to save this theory, which is what Finkelstein and Powell finally did.[142,143]

I did not even consider piezoelectrically produced discharges through the atmosphere as a means for the production of air ions during earthquakes. I had my eye on a mechanism far more subtle and less wasteful of energy. This mechanism depends on the piezoelectric liberation of energy, but it is, essentially, created by earth currents that would equalize the piezoelectrically generated differences in potential in the ground. With this theory, arguments marshaled against the ideas described earlier fall apart, and all signs point to the fact that the phenomenon can start even during the runup phase of an earthquake, before the earthquake waves proper whip through the masses of rock.

Electrochemical glow discharge

From a physicochemical point of view, rocks are very complicated systems. This is not just because they are, as a rule, composed of a multitude of differently constructed and polluted microcrystals whose contact zones are very disordered. They are also shot through with many fine pores and cracks, which often contain water, and even in times of very little air moisture very thin films of water remain on their surfaces. When a network of the finest hairline cracks eats its way through rocks under the pressures of an earthquake and when the pressures on piezoelectric quartz crystals change markedly, then electric currents, following the paths of least resistance, will flit through the ground. There is ample proof for the proposition that earth currents appear in connection with earthquakes and volcanic eruptions, even though their causes could not be explained until now.[144,42] Geophysicists have repeatedly reported abnormal earth currents as earthquake precursors, as far back as the nineteenth century. The measured potentials or currents were, of course, quite small. Studies carried out in Kamchatka gave typical potential changes of 30–300 millivolts, which usually preceded an earthquake by hours or by several days. Some measurements taken in China several minutes before the Haicheng earthquake also showed changes. The method of measuring consisted of registering the current or the voltage between copper and lead electrodes that had been stuck into the ground at distances of 30–70 meters (98–230 feet). The measured electrochemical differences in potential occasionally varied by more than a volt,[2] and the currents by between 50 and several hundred microamperes. Since the electrodes had been buried in clay soil, only the remnants of piezoelectric currents generated far away would have been detected. But they turned out to be related to the approaching earthquake just the same. For example, at the beginning of February 1975, the Chinese amateur group no. 2 in Pan Shan observed a marked change in the measured ground current. At the same time, a drop in the groundwater table of 3.8 centimeters (1.5 inches) was observed nearby, and reports of unusual animal behavior began to crop up. On the morning of February 4 the group predicted that a destructive earthquake was about to happen, and it came that same day.

When currents flow through moist, cleft bedrock, they must overcome border surfaces where water touches rock or air. When this happens, two kinds of electrochemical processes must take place that might play a part in initiating excitement among animals before earthquakes. If a current passes through a water-filled crack in conducting rock, and if the voltage behind it is about 2 volts, then electrolysis of water into hydrogen and oxygen—that is, an explosive gas—is unavoidable. If the voltage is somewhat higher, then it begins to precipitate the salts dissolved in water. The liberation of a pungent gas (such as chlorine, which smells like sulfur dioxide) would be the natural consequence. Since the piezoelectric effect can, theoretically, produce 10,000–100,000 volts per meter, the amount of gas generated electrolytically from the ground could be very large. A communication from the Chinese seismologist Deng Qi-dung in which he refers to precursors of the Haicheng earthquake proves that we are on the right track: "The rising groundwater contained gases which broke through the ice only to disperse, and in some places they had a pungent smell."[145] The possibility cannot be excluded that hydrogen liberated by electrolysis might now and then cause local explosions or fires, which have on occasion been observed in association with earthquakes. Electrochemically produced gases may also have been responsible for the evil smell of spring water which Pliny described as a typical sign of a coming earthquake.

The second electrochemical process that may be expected to occur in rock has to do with the passage of current from the water through a thin layer of air. We must assume that when hairline cracks spread through rock and cause it to swell, especially immediately before an earthquake, the current must bridge many fine air gaps which might even be in partial vacuum shortly after they are formed. What happens when an electric current passes from a comparatively conductive solid through a thin film of air into equally conductive water?

This probing question leads us to the electrochemical glow discharge, a poorly known phenomenon that seems to have all the qualifications necessary to produce airborne ions before and during an earthquake. It was discovered 90 years ago, and since then several dozen detailed studies have been done about it.[146,147] An electrochemical glow discharge is produced simply by pulling one of the two electrodes in an electrochemical cell a few millimeters above the aqueous solution. If the applied voltage is increased to 500–800 volts at the same time, a perceptible current continues to flow through the air gap. This glow discharge is usually studied under low pressure (around 10–30 percent of atmospheric pressure). But if the film of air is made thin enough, it will work under normal atmospheric pressure. This condition is attained, for example, in the so-called contact glow electrolysis.[148] In this case the film of gas is formed by heat, as in a drop of water that dances around on a hot plate. This heat is caused by the current passing through the electrode, which is simply immersed in water. Here 500 volts is more than enough to maintain the glow discharge. The evolution of this phenomenon in the ground, then, would not fail for lack of energy. What is interesting about glow electrolysis is that the reactions caused by it no longer resemble electrochemical processes but instead resemble those caused by ionizing cosmic radiation, by x rays, and above all by low-energy alpha radiation. This is because the flow of current through the film of air is being maintained by ions, (mostly by positive water ions). These ions, which are near the water surface when that surface is negatively charged, are accelerated toward it by a difference in potential of about 100 volts and strike it with considerable energy. This bombardment shatters water molecules, whose highly reactive fragments are capable of setting off numerous reactions in turn. Accelerating water ions with a difference in potential of only about 500 volts across a film of air produces about the same reaction products that would normally take ionizing radiation of energies 100–10,000 times as great. Compared with this, the freeing of the most reactive products of split molecules in the electrochemical glow discharge is considerably more efficient.[147] The production rate of reactive products is also considerably higher. In a glow-discharge current of only 1 milliampere, 3.8×10^{17} water-vapor ions per minute are accelerated from the film of air toward the water surface. After passing through at 100 volts, each one could split at least one water molecule with its impact. The products of such a splitting are chemically so reactive that they would immediately start other reactions. Just as with ionizing radiation, the consequence would be the freeing of a lot of charged particles. If we remember that normally only about 10^9 ions are available in a cubic meter of air, we can begin to comprehend how effectively a few isolated electrochemical glow discharges in the ground can affect the ion content of the air above it.

In connection with these reflections, it is interesting to point out that during volcanic eruptions changes in the ground current are also observed, lightning frequently can be seen in the rising smoke, and highly electrostatically charged clouds leave the crater.[144,149]

A step-by-step analysis of possible electrical phenonena in the earth's crust has led unerringly to a simple, effective mechanism of just the kind that would have to be postulated for the liberation of charged aerosols. Since positive water ions are in essence responsible for the current flow through a film of air and for impact reactions, the process ought to favor the enrichment of the air with positive ions, which lead to the serotonin syndrome. But many complicated molecular reactions can be imagined that could interfere in this process.

The piezoelectric effect of quartz, the electrochemical glow discharges with their powerful ionizing effect, and the serotonin syndrome produced in humans and animals by air ions have been confirmed by many scientific experiments. Let us consider these interconnected processes as a basis for the premonition of earthquakes.

Earthquakes and long waves

It was Februaray 23, 1887, and in the traffic office of the railroad station of Santa Vittoria d'Alba in Liguria men were staring transfixed at the writing telegraph. There it was again, that strong, unmistakable Morse signal! The onlookers hurried outside. Moments later a new earth tremor shook the building. It was uncanny. It was the third time that the heavy tremors had telegraphed their coming.

This story, told to the earthquake scientist Mercalli,[14] is reminiscent of witchcraft but is completely within the realm of the possible. Wherever electrical charges are generated or neutralized, electromagnetic waves are produced. Everybody knows them from interference in broadcast reception during thunderstorms. Also, when earthquake waves course through quartz-containing rock formations and separate positive from negative charges within the rock in the rhythm of their oscillations, they are bound to produce electromagnetic radiation. Since the basic frequency of earthquake waves lies between 0.1 and 10 hertz, these radio signals from earthquakes must contain some very long waves.[141] But since crystals can also break, yield, or suddenly deflect, there is also bound to be electromagnetic radiation of much higher frequencies. Since radio waves move at the speed of light, they would race ahead of an earthquake front, and a suitable antenna could pick them up and convert them into electric signals. Did the long telegraph wires in Liguria fulfill this function?

It has been shown that certain animals react to long-wave electromagnetic radiation, so it would not seem too farfetched to think that these animals' attention could be attracted by such electromagnetic interference signals. When frogs cease their croaking as if on cue moments before an earthquake, or when pheasants emit shrill screams, it is not necessarily the tremor-poor P waves that are responsible. The warning could have come in over the ether. Thus far no one seems to have looked with suitable instruments for the long-wave electromagnetic noise before and during an earthquake.

Forgotten experiments in electrostatics

There are practical reasons why there are almost no representative measurements concerning the phenomena of electricity in the air before or during earthquakes despite exceedingly refined measuring techniques and intense research activity in all areas of natural science. First, only a scientist already specialized in this line of research would dare to think of measuring charged aerosols; second, he would choose the most sensitive, most complex instrument possible; and third, he would figure to himself that his career might be over before the next big earthquake. In short, the chances of someone going after such measurements voluntarily are extremely small. Back in 1800 a different wind was blowing in science. In those days it wasn't specialists who were on the front lines of research, but highly educated, polymathic amateur scientists. They practiced science, basically, to satisfy their intellectual curiosity, not to prove themselves before others. Alexander von Humboldt was one of these men.

Von Humboldt was surprised by earthquakes on several occasions while traveling in South America. While he was staying in Cumana, Venezuela, in 1799, he became curious about some strange atmospheric events and reached for his instruments a short time before the quake — the first one he had ever experienced. The simplicity of the experiments, the precision of the observations, and von Humboldt's *sang-froid* should make modern scientists stop and think: "Several minutes before the first shock, an intense storm blew up, followed by an electric rain with large drops. I immediately observed the electricity in the air with the Volta electrometer. The little balls deflected from one another by four lines, the electricity often alternated between positive and negative. . . . Presently, as the most powerful electric discharge was taking place, at 4:12, two earth tremors occurred, 15 seconds apart. The people cried loudly in the street."

With his small pocket electrometer, a barometer, and other instruments, von Humboldt was eventually able to show that earthquakes did not cause pressure changes in the air but that they did cause changes in the amount of electricity it contained: "It cannot be gainsaid that often, when strong tremors follow one another over the course of several hours, the electric tension in the air rises markedly at the moment of the strongest trembling of the ground."[54d]

A thunderstorm and an earthquake happening exactly at the same time may have been a rare coincidence, but von Humboldt's observations of the increase in airborne electricity during the tremors of a series of aftershocks have found corroboration. During the swarm of earthquakes that ravaged the Italian province of Piedmont in 1808, an Italian scientist named Vassalli-Eandi had made preparations to carry out electrostatic experiments.[150,14] His observations showed that electricity in the air was always weak and positive when several hours elapsed between tremors. But at the moment of a quake, the electricity of the same sign would increase so much that it could no longer be measured with the electrometer. In Torre Pelice the leaflets of the electrometer still showed 30 degrees of deflection toward the positive sign 20 minutes after a rather strong tremor. In connection with those quakes in which rises in positive air electricity were observed, Vassalli-Eandi noted the following physiological effects: "The more nervous people were seized, for some time before the tremors, by a certain indefinable restlessness, by a kind of trembling and pounding of the heart. Besides that, the inhabitants were given a 10-minute warning by the animals. Dogs, cats, sheep, and goats gave no particularly distinct sign. Horses seemed to be more sensitive. Several minutes before the tremors they exhibited restlessness, became excited, rolled on the ground, kicked and stamped the ground with their hooves."

Nineteenth-century railroad stationmasters and telegraph operators contributed significantly to the study of earthquake phenomena. They were highly regarded, had advanced technical training, and dealt in precise terms. Some of their other observations in connection with the Ligurian earthquake of 1887 (in addition to the one mentioned above) made it possible to look more closely at earthquake-related electrostatic phenomena. In Diana Marina, for example, direct currents were observed in the telegraph apparatus during the period of earthquake noise before the quake itself became perceptible. These currents did not stop until the earthquake had passed. In Oneglia and untold other communities in Liguria the railroad superintendants also noticed that the galvanometers deflected and that the magnetic armatures were set in motion by fluctuating direct currents, or deflected completely. A strong direct current flowed continuously for 7 minutes in the telegraphic office at Bra during a severe aftershock. The most remarkable incident, however, happened beyond the Italian border in a military fortress near Nice. It attracted so much attention that it was reported to the minister of war, and afterwards it was published in the famous periodical *Comptes Rendus:*[151] Two strong earth tremors had already shaken the fortress in the morning when at 8:50 A.M. a member of the battery decided to send a message by telegraph describing the effects of the tremors. He was in the middle of communicating with the operator at the other end of the line when he was interrupted by crackling signals. When he tried again to establish communication, a strong earth tremor was felt and at the same time such a strong electric shock struck his right hand that he fell back into his chair unable to move for several minutes. Not until 4 P.M. was he able to resume his telegraphic duties, still suffering from headaches and nervous complaints. It is hard to imagine where these direct currents came from unless airborne ions from the earthquake had charged up the insulated telegraph wires, which then functioned as electricity deflectors. This would also explain why these wayward currents arrived in the telegraphic office in Milan from the earthquake region in the south, but not from a conductor that ran at right angles to the latter. (This was the quake from which Taramelli and Mercalli collected reports of unusual animal behavior from more than 130 communities.[22])

With the twentieth century came the seismograph, and with it the age of exact earthquake research. Stationmasters were no longer asked about their observations, and the uneducated people also lost their opportunity to pass on their observations to enlightened scholars. Today even small quakes are registered by a dense network of earthquake stations that covers the world. Storing that profusion of data is a basic problem for seismologists, but when you ask them whether the air above the trembling ground does indeed become electrostatically charged, whether von Humboldt's observations are correct, they can only shrug.

It is the Chinese earthquake researchers who are working more in the open-minded spirit of von Humboldt. "Hard data" (that is, reliable automatic recordings) are scarce goods for them, but the phenomena themselves do not escape their watchful eyes. The earthquake scientist Deng Qi-dung of the Geological Institute of Peking, taking a position on my air-ion hypothesis, writes the following concerning the observations during the Haicheng earthquake: "There was an obviously strong change in the electric field of the earth which preceded the earthquake. This leads us to the conclusion that a great difference in potential ionized the air, which is in itself an important earthquake precursor and perhaps one of the important causes of the anomalies."[145]

8

Earthquake Fogs

When the sun wears a halo

Fog droplets, raindrops, and ice crystals are formed by a well-known physical process, the coalescing of water around condensation nuclei. These nuclei are suspended particles that, because of the condition of their surfaces, make it easy for individual water molecules to coalesce into groups. Aerosol particles tht can bind water molecules easily to their surfaces assist this process. Modern rainmakers exploit this when they spray tiny silver iodide crystals into clouds. Electrostatically charged aerosol particles are also good condensation nuclei, since the electrical charge lowers the water droplets' surface tension, and this tends to stabilize them.

Usually, enough condensation nuclei are available in the air near the ground to allow fog droplets to form. In such cases an electrostatic charging of suspended particles can lead to the formation of fog even if the air is not saturated with water vapor. As has been shown, electric charges lower the water vapor pressure above the surface of the droplets and allow them to persist in unsaturated air.[152] The charging up of suspended particles in the air should theoretically make possible the formation of fogs at significantly less than the normally required 100 percent humidity—for example, at 80 percent. These theoretical principles subject the aerosol hypothesis to a stern test. If suspended particles do indeed get charged up in the air before an earthquake and if additional particles are repelled by the ground, then strange fog or cloud formations should be observed under proper atmospheric conditions. Of course, such an earthquake fog could appear only when the concentration of nuclei controlled its formation or when it was formed below the saturation limit of the air because of electrostatic charging. The latter phenomenon is well known to practical meteorology. Because of the effect of air ions—from outgassing, for example—fog phenomena (smog) are seen that would normally be observed only in air with a higher water content.

Among the many earthquake reports we have, there should be a number of cases where the meteorological conditions happened to be favorable to the formation of fogs as earthquake precursors. A survey of descriptions of earthquakes and of the phenomena that accompanied them has indeed yielded an astonishing number of independent observations of such earthquake fogs.

Reports of atmospheric changes associated with earthquakes go back to Egyptian mythology. Apparently they were easily noticed in Egypt because the sky there is usually clear. The "cannibal hymm" of the pyramid texts, for example, says that the bones of Akeru (the earth god who makes earthquakes) trembled simultaneously with the clouding of the sky and the darkening of stars after the dead ruler appeared as a god.[153]

The oldest detailed description of earthquake fogs is found in the earthquake theory of Aristotle (384–322 B.C.): ". . . the earthquake is sometimes preceded during the day or after sundown in clear weather by a sign, a thin cloud layer that spreads out into space. . . ."[154a] The consequent discoloration and darkening of the sun was to Aristotle, as it would later be to the writer Pausanias (second century A.D.), a reliable earthquake precursor.[78] Aristotle also describes some of the fog's properties in greater detail: "Besides the weakening of the sun and the [relative] darkness that comes about without clouds [being formed], the calmness and great cold that occasionally occur before earthquakes that happen in the morning, confirm the above-named cause" [the gas, *pneuma*, that in his view produced the earthquake].

Pliny the Elder made essentially the same observation about earthquake fogs in his *Natural History*:[8j,154b] "There is also a sign in the sky: When an earthquake is impending, either in the daytime or a little after sunset, in fine weather, it is preceded by a thin streak of cloud stretching over a wide space." Reginaldo de Lizarraga, a Spanish traveler, tells of a similar popular lore from early-seventeenth-century Chile:[155,154] "It is easy to find out when an earthquake is going to come. When at sundown or two hours before there is in the direction of the sea a *barda de nubes* (that is what the sailors call it), a kind of cloud bank that tends north-south, then an earthquake will occur the same night or on the following day with certainty."

A Chilean proverb still widespread today[77,90] is "Circulo en el sol, aguacero o temblor." This means, roughly, "If the sun has a ring, there will be rain showers or an earthquake." It makes sense, no doubt, to interpret a ring around the sun as a sign of coming rain. The Zuni, a tribe of the Pueblo Indians in the American southwest, know this weather rule.[156] They say, "When the sun is in his house [the court or ring] it will rain soon." A ring that is created by a diffusion of sunlight in "frozen fog," a thin layer of tiny ice crystals, announces an approaching warm front. Warm fronts normally bring rain. If there is indeed a connection between the ring or halo around the sun and an impending earthquake, then that means that before an earthquake a thin ice fog places itself between sun and earth.

Many of the reports of unusual fog or cloud formations before earthquakes have come from Italy. Chronicles mention an unusually dense ground fog in Reggio Calabria in connection with the earthquake of 1706.[23] Giovanni Vivenzio, the chief physician of the kingdom of Naples, who with the help of some army officers made a statistical evaluation of the earthquake period of 1783 in Calabria, asserts that the earth tremors announced themselves with dense fogs.[112,23] This would be followed by rain until only a few dispersed clouds were left, which again bunched up into a dense pile that remained completely immobile during the ensuing quake. The Italian philosophy and mathematics professor Andrea Gallo, who recorded highly valuable data about the earthquakes of 1783 in letters from the destroyed city of Messina to the scientific academies of London, Bordeaux, and Uppsala, confirmed these observations. He swears to having foreseen several earth tremors by several hours only because of the familiar ash-gray clouds he could see coming from the north as if pulled by a magic hand. An observer named Scina, who had studied the earthquakes of 1818 and 1819 in Madonia, maintained that "with each quake the air turned to fog for a few minutes only to become completely clear immediately afterwards."[23] On the morning of July 26, 1855, an unusual fog was seen in the vicinity of Turin, and perceptible quakes occurred the same day.[23]

Similar reports surface in the painstakingly conducted inquiries that Mercalli made after the earthquakes of Calabria and Liguria.[23] Among them is the account of a resident of Villa San Giovanni that after the earthquake of November 16, 1894, he had noticed isolated clouds before almost every earth tremor and that they had disappeared immediately after each tremor. The priest of Delianova reported a similar observation. During the night of November 16–17 he saw some clouds forming of the ridge of a hill which dissolved into fine rain. An intense earthquake followed immediately. In the following months he observed the forming of the same cloud layer before each earthquake except that of January 20, which was immediately followed by cloud formation.

Among eyewitnesses' reports of special phenomena that preceded the great Ligurian earthquake of February 23, 1887, collected by Taramelli and Mercalli, are many such reports of fog formations.[22] At sunset on the eve of the quake, the residents of Alfiano-Natta noticed a "kind of dense fog" that swallowed the rays of the sun. From other places, such as Cervo, it was reported that on the eve of the earthquake the sunlight had appeared strangely misted and pale.

The most impressive and precise description of such an earthquake fog is to be found in the writings of Alexander von Humboldt.[54d] While staying in Cumana, Venezuela, in 1799, he became preoccupied by an unusual phenomenon of nature. Several days in a row a red fog would rise on the horizon at nightfall and in a few minutes would draw a dense veil across the blue vault of the sky. What was especially baffling was that the hygrometer which von Humboldt, always avid for knowledge, would consult immediately showed no increased moisture but a distinct drop from 90 to 83 percent. He also noticed that stars of first magnitude, which ordinarily barely flickered 20°–25° above the horizon in Cumana, would not even glow steadily in the zenith. They flickered at all altitudes as if after a severe thundershower. The fog appeared so unusual to von Humboldt that he spent part of a night sitting on a balcony, the better to follow the course of things. As the fog became denser and the only thing visible of the moon was a halo of 12° diameter, the air felt hot. Even so, the thermometer climbed only to 26° C (79° F). Black clouds were forming, and at the moment of an intense electrical discharge (which von Humboldt followed on his electroscope) two powerful earth tremors were felt. The day of the earthquake ended with an unusual sunset: "The sun, which appeared 12 degrees high against an indigo blue background, was spread wide to an unusual degree, distorted and flared out on its rim. The clouds were gilded and bundles of rays in the most beautiful colors of the rainbow spread up to the middle of the sky," von Humboldt wrote. Three days later every trace of the reddish fog had disappeared. Von Humboldt observed that "the people view the fogs that ring the horizon (ground fogs) and the absence of the sea breeze at night as sure evil omens,"[54e] and also noted the following: "According to an ancient view held widely in Cumana, Acapulco, and Lima [which also appears as early as Aristotle[157] and Seneca[158]] earthquakes and the condition of the air before the beginning of the latter are visibly connected. On the coast of New Andalusia people become anxious when amid great heat and after a long drought the sea breeze suddenly stops and the sky, which is clear and cloudless in the zenith, becomes covered with a reddish haze for up to six, eight degrees above the horizon."

Chiki—*Air from the earth*

From Japan, too, there are many reports about unusual weather conditions that precede earthquakes. It is often asserted that immediately before an earthquake the air becomes muggy and that sometimes mysterious fogs appear.[42] Examples include the following reports.[51] Before the earthquake of 1802 (force M = 6.6), which ravaged Sado Island in the Sea of Japan, a businessman climbed a hill to assess the sailing weather. A seaman who accompanied him was amazed by the very strange weather. It was like no weather he had ever seen before. It was foggy, but in a very unusual way: Only the lower mountain slopes were covered by fog, while the upper ones could be seen quite clearly. The sailor, who could usually predict the weather by observing the sky, did not know what to make of this situation, but the businessman remembered something his father had told him several years earlier: "Before an earthquake a strange air called *chiki* [literally, air from the earth] comes out of the ground." Both got their baggage from their inn, and they had marched about 15 kilometers (9 miles) when an intense tremor shook the ground. Later when the businessman visited a gold mine he was surprised to learn that none of the miners had been hurt in the earthquake. The miners told him that they had known 3 days ahead of time that an earthquake was coming. As they had been doing for years, they had watched for the appearance of *chiki*, which in the mine can become so thick that you can barely see the man working next to you.

The appearance of *chiki* is also described in connection with the earthquake of Kyoto in 1830 (force M = 6.4).[51] Another interesting story is that of the gatekeeper of a high-ranking samurai who predicted the earthquake of 1855 in Edo.[39,42] One early evening, after he had scanned the landscape closely, he announced that an earthquake was imminent. He boiled some rice for himself for the emergency and sat waiting in the courtyard. Toward 10 P.M. it became foggy and clouds covered half the sky. But the stars, strangely, seemed bright as if they were very close. The earthquake struck immediately. Because the gatekeeper had been alert, a fire that started in the ruins was quickly extinguished. The gatekeeper told the samurai his secret: Before the earthquake of Echigo (force M = 6.9) in 1828 and before the one of Shinshu (force M = 7.4) in 1847 he had seen the stars shine brightly through the foggy sky as if they were nearby. Since he had noticed this same phenomenon for the past day or two, he had simply concluded that another earthquake was coming.

The Japanese reports of intensely glowing stars and von Humboldt's of stars flickering through a veil of fog are interesting in the context of yet another Chilean earthquake proverb: "When starlight is very lively as if flames are shooting forth, then there is no doubt that a strong earthquake will happen the same night."[77] Does this define an optical property of earthquake fog? This fog should differ from an ordinary fog because of the powerful electrostatic charge of its particles.

Earthquake fogs have also been observed in more recent times. Strange ground fogs were seen in several areas before the Haicheng earthquake of February 4, 1975.[159,2] Before the heavier tremors of the 1976 earthquake series in Friuli thin fogs may also have appeared. A peasant there told me that before the more powerful earthquakes the clear sky had regularly become whitish. He was so sure of this that afterward he would try to assess the earthquake danger by observing the sky.

It would, obviously, not be very practical to attempt earthquake prediction by observing fogs. Whether earthquake fogs will be even visible depends on many meteorological factors, such as humidity, temperature, wind, and precipitation conditions. But scientists could easily get a grip on the cause of occasional fog formation before earthquakes by keeping track of the suspended particles in the air with suitable measuring instruments.

Earthquakes and changes in the weather

In Immanuel Kant's report on the earthquake of Lisbon,[11b] which on November 1, 1755, shook the foundations of all of Europe, we find a juxtaposition of unusual meteorological phenomena that began to appear about two weeks before. This report is noteworthy not only because it tells of reddish fogs, which von Humboldt later also observed during the earthquake in Cumana, but because it mentions unusually strong precipitation:

I see the rehearsal of this subterranean conflagration which was so terrifying in its consequences in the air phenomenon that was perceived at Locarno in Switzerland on October 14 of the previous year (1755) at 8 o'clock in the morning. A warm steam, as if coming from an oven, spread out and in two hours changed into a red fog from which a blood-red rain came towards evening which when collected precipitated a ninth of a reddish claylike substance. The 6-foot-deep snow was also colored red. This purple rain was noticed 40 *Stunden* [about

120 miles] away . . . as far away as Schwaben. After these air phenomena, unnatural rain torrents came which in 3 days yielded 23
inches of water. This is more than falls in an entire year in a country
with average moisture conditions. This rain lasted 14 days, although
not always with the same intensity. The rivers of Lombardy which
rise in the Swiss mountains, as well as the Rhone swelled with water
and went over their banks. From this time on terrible storms reigned
in the air which raged gruesomely everywhere. Even in the middle
of November a similar purple rain fell in Ulm and the disorder in the
air, the twisting winds in Italy and the excessively moist weather
continued.

Kant also points out that the strongest of the aftershocks, which was
again felt in many countries of Europe (on February 18, 1756), was
also heralded by unusual weather conditions: ". . . in those days, especially from the 16th to the 18th, gales raged far and wide in Germany,
Poland and England. Lightning and thunderstorms appeared, in short,
the realm of the air was set into a kind of fermentation."

Two millenia, diverse cultures, different sources of information, and
many disparate ideas separate Kant from Aristotle. Still, their information and views about notable earthquake precursors are astonishingly
similar: Not only are the fogs that discolor the sun and darken it
earthquake precursors to Aristotle, but so are intense storms.[78] Are
these opinions supported by fact? Where are the suggestions and
proofs that some meteorological processes are initiated by earthquakes
and might actually be taken as their precursors?

It is only necessary to inquire what the weather was before another
great European earthquake, the one in Calabria in 1783, to start
pondering again. The earthquake pioneer Mercalli writes: "In the five
months that preceded the great Calabrian earthquake of 1783 there
were in Calabria intense and constant rainfalls which caused severe
damage, that is to say, they flooded land and eroded it. These rainfalls
probably had no causal connection with the earthquake phenomenon,
but they explain why they set off such strong earth motions in the
soaked ground."[23]

The aerosol hypothesis could, theoretically, accommodate the proposition that a coming earthquake influences the atmospheric processes
so powerfully that meteorological events are altered profoundly. The
many reports of strange fogs as earthquake precursors seem to confirm
this. That heavy precipitation might appear weeks before an earthquake
disaster cannot be proved easily, but that dramatic weather changes
can be brought about by processes associated with earthquakes is
shown by eyewitness accounts from all over the world. In Chile there
is even a popular saying that an earthquake changes the weather. The

weather observations are exemplified by the following description: The priest of Polistena in Calabria told Mercalli that many of the aftershocks of the earthquake of November 16, 1894, which happened under cloudy skies, were accompanied by strong gusts of wind and a roaring in the air. When the tremors came, the wind stopped and the sky cleared.[23] An observer named P. Macri from Scilla reported about the aftershock of December 9 of the same series as follows: "Before the earthquake it rained and the wind blew. Immediately after the earthquake the sky was without a single cloud and the wind stopped." A meteorological institute informed Mercalli that before almost every quake isolated clouds were noticed which disappeared shortly afterward. At times individual clouds would dissolve into fine rain before the earthquake.

Other observations on weather are contained in eyewitness reports of the Valparaiso, Chile, earthquake of August 16, 1906, collected by the earthquake researcher F. de Montessus de Ballore.[87] From the village of Lolol came this report: "Before the disaster, the sky was clouded over and many dark clouds could be seen. Afterwards the sky was completely clear and strewn with stars." From Limache Viejo it was reported: "During the quake the rain stopped, to continue falling afterward with full force."

It is possible to explain weather changes during an earthquake as phenomena related to changing elecrostatic charges in the atmosphere. The disappearance of clouds from the sky could as easily be the consequence of an excessive charging of cloud particles as the consequence of the neutralization of existing charges. In one case the droplets would grow and fall to the ground, and in the other case they would lose their stability.

"Earthquake time"

As a scientist I have always found it fascinating to talk with an old farmer about the weather, the plants, and the animals. In some of these conversations I have detected connections that have preoccupied me more than many an academic insight. Occasionally such conversations present to me views which at first blush I would like to see consigned to the realm of pure superstition, or to parapsychology.

For example, I have been told, on an unusually hot, dry, and oppressive day, "*Es tiempo de terremoto*" — "It is earthquake time." This assertion is the more surprising because everybody knows that earthquakes can happen during rain as well as in dry weather, in heat as well as in freezing cold. What is baffling is that identical assertions are made in widely separated countries. As far back as 1800, Alexander von Humboldt wrote that in southern Italy the *Scirocco*, the unique hot, dry wind that blows from northern Africa, is associated with earthquake danger.[54c] This wind, like the *Föhn*, has a stimulating effect on the nerves and saps the body's vitality. People feel its effects unmistakably. Its influence on behavior is even considered in modern Italian jurisprudence.

The eighteenth-century Italian earthquake scientist Benevelli reports that during the earthquake period in Liguria in 1786 the air was "very elastic."[160] This is obviously a description of "earthquake weather." References to this old and strange popular opinion also occasionally appear in Mercalli's records. After the Calabria earthquake of November 16, 1894, the priest of Polistena wrote: "The earthquake was preceded by a long drought and an unseasonable heat wave with east-southeasterly and easterly winds. Under these circumstances everybody was anticipating an earthquake."[23]

When I told the American seismologist R. A. Schweickert of this mysterious "earthquake weather," he surprised me by saying that in California people have come to believe the same thing. In March 1971 Schweickert and a correspondent for the *New York Times* had taken a trip along the San Andreas fault to interview the people living there. A resident of the city of San Juan Bautista had maintained that one could feel a "characteristic earthquake weather. . . .a dry, hot weather situation which is marked by peace and quiet." An older scientist at the University of California at Berkeley admitted that he had been quite familiar with the concept of "earthquake weather" since the days of his early youth. In those days, he said, the natives meant by that a weather condition with a peculiarly oppressive effect on people.

Using a little tracking sense, and assuming that the ancient Greek physicists departed from observed facts in forming their earthquake theories (there are many reasons for thinking so), we can trace references to changes in the atmosphere before an earthquake back to the fifth century B.C. The Greek physicist Anaxagoras assumed that earthquakes were set off by the effects of an airlike substance from above the earth. His pupil Archelaos tried to explain, with a slightly altered theory, the strange calmness that is supposed to have been observed immediately before earthquakes. Aristotle devotes some attention to this calmness, and references to it can be found again and again in eyewitness reports on earthquakes, such as the three independent reports from the Ligurian earthquake of 1887.[22] The idea of the *pneuma*, a gas that causes earthquakes and is held responsible for such earthquake precursors as the darkening of the sun or the appearance of a characteristic thin cloud layer, was worked out so persuasively by Aristotle that it shaped the earthquake ideas of all of Greek antiquity. Thenceforth seismological processes were always described in Greek literature as meteorologicac phenomena.

The riddle's solution is suggested in the words of the priest P. Ambrogio of Cornigliano Ligure, an attentive witness of the 1887 Liguria earthquake: "From midnight to the hour of the quake [6:20 A.M.] I felt strangely without strength and perceived a mysterious nausea so that it seemed to me as if I were exposed to the influence of a severe storm loaded with electricity."

Airborne electricity, an electrostatic charging of aerosol particles, can indeed set off sensations that have been popularly summarized in the concept of earthquake weather. Everybody knows of the oppressiveness that lies over the land before a heavy thunderstorm. The riddle of why *Föhn*-like or dry, warm weather reminds earthquake-experienced people most readily of the atmospheric conditions before an earthquake solves itself without contradictions: The concentration of charged particles in the atmosphere is especially high under just such weather conditions.

Thus, the *pneuma*, which the ancient Greek scholars occasionally regarded as compressed air because it seemed tough, was air electricity. It is not departing too far from scientific reality to describe electrostatically charged air as "heavy" or "elastic," or to imagine that it gives the impression of calmness. More than 2,000 years ago Aristotle made a logical deduction that the earthquake precursors in the atmosphere were caused by *pneuma*. Where he erred was in assuming that *pneuma* also caused the earthquake. Can one hold this conclusion against him scientifically, considering that first comes the *"pneuma"* and afterwards the quake?

Earthquake fogs: Scientific fact 150 years ago

Modern science does not discuss changes in the atmosphere before a substantial earthquake. No scientist of this century has observed them, studied them, or predicted them theoretically. Yet 150 years ago they were accepted as a natural phenomenon, and theories about their causes were developed as a matter of course. As proof and example I introduce a scientific dissertation which the Italian scholar Antonio Rutili Gentili presented to the Academy of Natural Sciences in Rome (the *Accademia dei Lincei*) on February 5, 1832.[212] It describes careful observations of nature in connection with an earthquake wave that shook central Italy (the valley of Umbria) in the fall and winter of

1831–32 and tries to explain these events scientifically. According to Gentili's report, in the days preceding the earthquake the air seemed saturated by hazes that would not leave the earth's surface. This phenomenon was particularly pronounced on the evening of October 26, 1831.

During the night the air cooled off, and in the hour before dawn these vapors condensed into a fog. Immediately the first strong tremor was felt, and weaker ones followed close behind. After that the sky cleared for two days. It remained covered by individual clouds that scudded before a strong wind. This was followed by complete clearing and then again by a clouding over with more wind. On the evening of November 6, the wind let up completely. The clouds sank to the ground and there were three powerful quakes within a few minutes. The sky remained cloudy and fogs continued to lie over the earth's surface, while earth tremors shook the land for several days and nights. The denser the ground fogs, the more numerous the tremors; and the rarer the tremors, the higher rose the fog. The clouds seemed to be motionless almost all the time during those days and they were arranged in several horizontal layers. Clear weather came and there was a pause in the quakes. On January 13, a cloud bank that remained totally motionless appeared on the hills that ring the valley. Toward 9 P.M. it moved out over the valley and rapidly sank to the ground. The air filled with "fear and terror," hail and rain fell, and the powerful main quake shook the earth for a long time. Immediately afterward, as Gentili observed himself, the cloud fled in the direction of the Appennines.

The conclusion Gentili reached was that earthquakes have appeared regularly after fogs or clouds had settled to the earth's surface. Today there is no longer any basis for his explanation that electrical discharges set off quakes within the ground, but his observations of nature are worth noting. They agree surprisingly well with the experiences of the ancient Greek philosophers.

9

Earthquakes and Light Phenomena

If it is true that the earth transmits electrostatic charges to the air during the development of an earthquake, then yet another, most impressive phenomenon ought to be observable: A powerful enough charge on the earth's surface should produce electrical discharges like lightning or Saint Elmo's fire. It turns out that there are indeed earthquake lights. The forms in which these lights become visible are varied, and until now no satisfactory explanation about their origin could be found. By far the greatest number of observations have been reported by untrained people, and because of that most earthquake researchers have doubted the existence of these earthquake lights until recently.[70] Not until the first creditable photographs by amateur photographers began to surface during the Matsushiro earthquake series in Japan in the years 1965 to 1967 did scientists begin to strain their heads over this problem.[139,161,70] Some researchers are now tackling this phenomenon, which has been passed down in folklore from time immemorial.

Earthquake lights are mentioned in the ancient Egyptian pyramid texts: "With mountain rifts, rain torrents, and lightning bolts an earthquake accompanies the rebirth of the king," says one such text.[162] In a country in which torrential rains and lightning bolts are as rare as they are in Egypt, the combination of these two phenomena must be a startling thing to see.

Greek mythology associates earthquakes, lightning, and other light phenomena with the gods. An appearance of a Greek sun god was said to be accompanied by an earthquake, lightning, and light phenomena. Pliny tells in arresting detail of a light phenomenon that accompanied an earthquake in the Etruscan Apennines near Moderna in 92 B.C.:

I find in the books of the lore of Tuscany that once a vast and portentous earthquake occurred in the district of Modena; this was during the consulship of Lucius Marcius and Sextus Julius. Two mountains ran together with a mighty crash, leaping forward and then retiring with flames and smoke rising between them to the sky; this took place in the daytime, and was watched from the Aemilian road by a large crowd of Knights of Rome with their retinues and passersby. The shock brought down all the country houses, and a great many animals in the buildings were killed.[81]

Since the region mentioned is not free of extinct volcanic structures, the flames licking heavenward need not have been earthquake lights. But perhaps another report from Pliny's rich store of information suggests a light phenomenon: "Earthquakes are more frequent in autumn and spring as is lightning."

The earthquake at the birth of Alexander the Great, which old texts describe as having been accompanied by thunder and lightning, seems to have been viewed as a divine apparition. When Christ died, the sun became dark at noon, all creation sighed, and the earth quaked amid lightning and thunder. The same combination of natural phenomena is mentioned in the Apocalypse of Saint John. Such phenomena may be the "supernatural" signs behind the genesis of religious concepts. An interesting historical description of an earthquake light comes out of the Byzantine Empire. On January 26, 450, a fiery sign appeared in the sky over Constantinople simultaneously with an earthquake. It shook public morale to such an extent that emperor, senate, and clergy spent several days atoning with prayer and going barefoot.[163]

Earthquake-light lore also lives in ancient Japanese traditions, and a nameless poet speaks of it: "The earth speaks quietly to the mountain, which quakes and lights up the sky." Lights were observed in several of the big Japanese earthquakes of the eighteenth, nineteenth, and twentieth centuries, and 1,500 descriptions of light phenomena were collected after the earthquake of November 26, 1930, in the Idu Peninsula.[164,165] There are 147 eyewitness reports of light phenomena during the Hyuga earthquake of November 2, 1931,[70] and at least 18 such sightings were reported in connection with the Matasushiro quakes between 1965 and 1967.[139] Clear photographs—some in color—were taken of these lights (figure 4). These photographs show hemispherical, glowing white apparitions that touch the ground and that have diameters of 20–200 meters (65–656 feet).[70,139,161] The lights were said to have lasted from 10 seconds to 2 minutes.

Europe, too, offers a rich store of earthquake-light descriptions. The Italian scientist I. Galli collected 148 observations made in Italy in the latter part of the nineteenth century alone.[166] There are also reports of light phenomena during earthquakes from the United States,[167]

Figure 4
A mysterious light of 96 seconds' duration photographed during an earthquake
in the area of Mount Kimyo in Japan. (Fish-eye lens; exposure 36 seconds; F8;
ultraviolet filter; Sakura Colour N film, ASA 100.)

Switzerland,[168] Chile,[169] and Argentina.[170] In the Soviet Union, lights
were observed by scientists during the Tashkent earthquake of 1966.[171]
In China, earthquake lights seem to be taken for granted. The earthquake expert Li Teh-run, describing the successful prediction of the
1975 Haicheng earthquake in an article in the periodical *Earthquake
Fronts*, published in Peking, mentions the earthquake lights only in
passing: "Then the earthquake light flashed and powerful thunderlike
noise pushed out of the ground. . . ."[172] A report in the same periodical
about the successful deployment of earthquake observation groups
says: "When the powerful earthquake of February 4 began, five com-
rades were at their posts, and they nourished a spirit of 'fear neither
need nor death.' One person among them was sent out to observe
the earthquake lightning, and all the others remained with their instruments and were able to take readings by the light of a flashlight."

What exactly did all these observers see? Most who saw the lights
during the earthquake of November 26, 1930, on the Idu Peninsula
compared them with sheet lightning, except that the duration of this
glowing was said to have been decidedly longer.[164] At one spot on the
eastern shore of Tokyo Bay the light appeared in the form of strips
that originated at a particular point on the horizon. Bundles and pillars
of light were seen in several places, and some observers compared
them to the beams of searchlights. Others described these lights as

balls of fire. At Hakone-Mati, near the epicenter, a lightning bolt was seen first in one and then in another place, and as the earthquake reached its climax a straight row of round masses of light was observed in the southwest. Most eyewitnesses described the colors of these lights as pale blue or white, or compared them to ordinary lightning, but a large number maintained that they had a reddish or orange color. The earthquake light in Tokyo was so bright that one could distinguish objects in rooms. It was visible 40–70 miles from the epicenter. Observations of it began even before the quake. It reached its greatest intensity during the tremors and continued after the end of the quake. The light phenomena of the Hyuga quake of November 2, 1931, apparently followed a similar schedule. Twenty-six observers saw lights before the quake, 99 during the quake, and 22 afterwards.[70]

Not infrequently, eyewitnesses report earthquake lights high in the sky. These are said to shine equally strongly in red, blue, or white colors, and there is talk of lightning bolts, balls of fire, and glowing banners. A representative cross-section of the most diverse earthquake lights was sighted during the earthquake of Santa Rosa, California, on October 1, 1969.[173] The observers spoke of heat lightning, electric sparks, Saint Elmo's fire, balls of fire, or meteors. Some even heard explosions.

A vivid description of how impressions can rush at an observer during an earthquake is given by the Italian earthquake researcher Benevilli in connection with the Ligurian earthquake of 1786: "In the moment of the tremors one felt electrified or magnetized and in several places 'sulfur odors' appeared as well as fires moving across the earth. Falling stars and flashing sparks flew through the atmosphere."[160,14] A red cloud that touched the ground and that appeared exactly at the instant of the tremor was reported in connection with the earthquake of Piedmont, Italy, on April 2, 1808.[23] A strong "sulfur odor" was noticed at the same time. Moments before the earthquake in Liguria on February 28, 1887, some residents of the village of Loano observed a red light above the village that resembled a flame. On the evening of November 16, 1894, during a severe earthquake in Calabria, lightning bolts were seen in a clear sky.[23]

Many eyewitnesses reported lights in connection with the earthquake of Valparaiso, Chile, on August 16, 1906.[169] Besides the many observations that might be compared to ordinary or sheet lightning, there were reports of some very strange lights. The police prefect of San Bernardo observed "electrical discharges toward the southeast which emitted an intense red light." Some saw "flames in the form of snakes." Captain Rafael Gonzales in Limache Viejo saw fiery lights in zigzag form, which were very near and appeared close to the ground. Other observers spotted red-violet blotches in the sky during the earthquake. The meteorologists at the Santiago observatory reported that "during the two minutes that the great violence of the earthquake lasted, there were toward the northeast enormous electrical discharges that appeared to cover the entire northeast horizon from the tree tops to an altitude of about 30 degrees. . . ." Interesting, too, was the observation made by the school principal of Rancagua: "When the third shock came, great flames of electric blue color could be seen in the west which rose until they lost themselves in the clouds." An eyewitness from Los Angeles, Chile, reported the following: "During the quake fire and flames could be seen in the sky like heat lightning in the summer. These were also seen in zigzag form which people called fire snakes. . . . The [spectacle] lasted as long as the earthquake."

The strangest light phenomenon reported by eyewitnesses to earthquakes is ball lightning similar to that sometimes seen during thunderstorms, a phenomenon not explained satisfactorily by science. D. Finkelstein of Yeshiva University and J. R. Powell of the Brookhaven National Laboratory, who are now studying the origin of earthquake lights, used to specialize in ball lightning until they noticed that many of the observations of this strange phenomenon were being made in connection with earthquakes.

Ball lightning is very prominent among observations collected by Montessus de Ballore in connection with the 1906 Valparaiso earthquake. He writes: "Bernhard Jensen, currently the first pilot of the ship *Toro* and formerly captain of the ship *Southern Cross* on her expedition to the South Pole, told me that while watching from shipboard he had seen seven or eight fire balls rising from a house that was burning in the hills. Among several houses on fire, this one had been the highest up the mountain. The balls moved a certain distance toward the east and then, as they dropped one after the other, you could hear a detonation each time, as if in a powerful artillery bombardment. The first pilot of a German ship declared that he had seen the same phenomenon."[169] Various members of one family saw fireballs—one of them stationary, as big as the moon, and giving off smaller balls with tails (an explosion?). The residents of Postas Negras saw a fireball that came from the direction of Valparaiso. The police commandant of Curacavi stated that he had seen five little fireballs flying from north to south during the second tremor. They seemed smaller than the moon. In Chimbarongo, large falling balls radiating phosphorescent light aroused considerable attention. Glowing balls were also sighted in Curico, Tongoy, and Constituciòn. Another interesting description of lights during this earthquake is that given by J. M. Munoz Hermosillo, a teacher from Valdivia: "Toward the east in the mountain range of the Andes, colossal electrical discharges were observed that were so persistent that the entire sky seemed directly illuminated. The thunder was barely noticeable, but at the same time two or three bluish lights like giant balls were visible toward the mountain range."[169]

Japanese earthquake literature, too, has incredible-sounding descriptions of large, usually ball-like fiery objects that moved through the air and resembled ball lightning. A document on the Shinshu earthquake of 1847 contains this information: "Under dark skies a fiery cloud appeared in the direction of Mt. Iduna. It was observed making a turning motion and then disappeared. Immediately thereafter a howling noise was heard which was followed by severe earthquakes."[165,42] On the evening of the Edo earthquake of 1855, a group of 18 persons went to sea. Just before the earthquake, there suddenly appeared from the northeast a glow so bright that the color patterns of their clothes could be made out. Shortly after this, a fearsome growling was heard coming from beneath the sea; it sounded as if a large mass of gravel were hitting the underside of the boat. At the same time a mass of flames flew across the sky, accompanied by noises.[42]

The many reports of UFO sightings that caused a great stir in the popular press of Japan and Latin America because they coincided with earthquakes[174] would probably enrich this collection of observations of earthquake lights.

There are reports of light phenomena appearing over the ocean during earthquakes. In Playa Ancha, a coastal village in Chile, various people saw fire coming out of the sea.[169] Similar reports have come from California and Japan. During an earthquake off the California coast in January 1922, a glow seen above the ocean surface was at first believed to be a burning ship. During a quake in October 1926 in the Bay of Monterey in California, one person observed a bolt of lightning over the ocean that was like a transformer explosion.[70] Alexander von Humboldt mentions a similar phenomenon: "Seven miles from Lisbon, near Colares, during the terrible earthquake of November 1, 1755, flames and a thick cloud of smoke were seen bursting out of a rocky cliff near Alvidras and, according to several eyewitnesses, from the sea itself."[54e]

It is not out of the question that unexplained explosions of glowing lights at sea may be traceable to submarine quakes. Of 70 sea captains' reports of light appearances at sea which were evaluated by Kurt Kalle of the German Hydrographic Institute in Hamburg, 19 described a kind of light-ball bombardment from the ocean depths.[175] Small, glowing balls, about a meter across, rose up from the depths and burst soundlessly on the ocean surface, turning into garish discs of light about 100 meters (328 feet) in diameter and then quickly going out. These phenomena have been reported only from volcanically active tropical ocean regions. Could they have something to do with another enigmatic phenomenon observed in the harbor of Lima, Peru, at the time of the earthquake of March 30, 1828?[16] A hissing sound was heard near the British ship *Volage* as if red-hot iron had been quenched in the ocean. Countless bubbles formed, which then burst and released "sulfur odor." The sea suddenly stirred and untold numbers of dead fish drifted up. When the ship weighed anchor, the anchor chain, which had been lying in muddy bottom, showed signs of melting for a length of about 50 meters (164 feet). Could these "meltings" actually have been signs of an electrolytic dissolution of the iron? Had there been electrical discharges underwater, the same processes that cause light phenomena in the atmosphere? Was chlorine gas, generated by the electrolysis of salt water, what caused the "sulfur odor?"

In view of all these unexplained light phenomena, it behooves us to remember Pliny the Elder's description of the now-familiar electrical discharges of Saint Elmo's fire: ". . . stars alight on the yards and other parts of the ship with a sound resembling a voice, hopping from perch to perch in the manner of birds. . . . All these things admit of no certain explanation; they are hidden away in the grandeur of nature."[8b]

For the purposes of this inquiry it is not essential to take guesses about the exact mechanism that causes these earthquake lights; it is only important to consider whether they exist. If so, then they testify to a physical process by which electric charges become visible, whether these manifestations be similar to sheet lightning or to Saint Elmo's fire or whether they be balls of lightning. The existence of these charges would then confirm the basic hypothesis of this book about abnormal animal behavior if it could also be shown that these light phenomena can appear early enough before powerful earthquakes. This possibility is being definitely rejected by modern science, as is evident from literature[42] and from what I know of the attitudes of several earthquake researchers.

Among the documents of the Imperial Earthquake Investigation Commission of Japan[51] is the following memorable report: "In the case of the Genroku earthquake of 1703 (force $M = 8.2$) which caused horrible damage in an area south of Edo, glowing objects and glowing air were frequently seen during the night that preceded the day of the severe quake, as well as afterwards."[51b] Another document reports the following: At the time of the Kyoto earthquake of 1830 it was said that during the night before the earthquake glowing objects were seen over the entire sky and some of them were so powerful that they could have been compared to daylight."[51c] At the time of the North Izu earthquake of 1930 it was reported that a watchman on a fire watchtower in Tokyo saw a light flash about 10 minutes before the tremors. Some fishermen who had been launching their boats before the earthquake observed a spherical glowing object west of Mount Amagi which was moving northwest with considerable speed.[42] It is an old popular tradition in Japan to predict earthquakes from unusual light phenomena, and many human lives are supposed to have been saved that way.[165] A reliable old Japanese document mentioned in the inquiry reports of the Imperial Earthquake Commission reports that, on the evening before the Genroku earthquake of 1703, Sukeraemon Shibukawa, the astronomer of the shogun (the governor and imperial general heading the government for the powerless emperor) had delivered a definite earthquake warning to the shogun's residence.[165] Since he was always watching the sky and would warn of a coming earthquake or heavy thunderstorm, he must have seen light phenomena in the sky.

The Chinese have also learned that light phenomena precede severe earthquakes. Why else would peasants be instructed to look for "lights above their fields" in order to predict earthquakes?[176,5] Chinese literature contains reports that unequivocally mention unusual lights as precursors of certain earthquakes. An example of this is the scientific work of the Lanchow Seismological Brigade, which deals particularly with ground noises before earthquakes: "Another example is the great earthquake of magnitude 8.5 in the Shihaiku region [Haiyuan earthquake, December 16, 1920]. According to the [official] newspaper of the Kuyuan district, people living in the mountains would occasionally see flashing fire and would hear reverberating noise in the water ditches around midnight before the earthquake."[32]

Other parts of the world also have their share of similar reports of glowing earthquake precursors. While I was at Columbia University's Lamont-Doherty Geological Observatory, my attention was directed to a notice that had been sent from Pakistan by the seismologist Wayne Pennington on May 13, 1975. It concerned the Pattan earthquakes of December 28, 1974 (magnitude 6.1) and of April 7, 1975 (magnitude 5.2). The note relates the following incidents: "At least three independent and unsolicited reports about visual observations (a glowing in the sky) in the direction of the earthquake, observations made several days prior to the main quake, were collected (one by me, two by UNESCO) and a report of a similar sighting two to four days before the aftershock of magnitude 5, four to five months after the main quake, was given to me before the observer had been made aware that there had been an aftershock."

The seismologist Ambraseys documents a similar observation made in connection with a severe earthquake in Iran on September 1, 1962.[177] Thirty-nine people living east of Ishtahard and in the direction of Ab-i-Garm (that is, in the epicenter) directed his attention to a red-to-orange glow in the sky visible in the direction of the Rudak region, which appeared before the earthquake and remained visible during it. The light was followed by a noise similar to that of a low-flying airplane. The area in question was free of storm interferences, and there are no electrical conductors there.

Many observations of lights visible in a clear sky before an earthquake have been documented in Europe, too. A remark made by Immanuel Kant in 1756 in reference to the devastating Lisbon earthquake shows that this notable earthquake precursor has long been part of the European store of knowledge: "Powerful lightning bolts in the air and the anxiousness often noticed in animals had been the harbingers of some other earthquakes."[11b] A few reports collected by Taramelli and Mercalli after the Ligurian earthquake of February 23, 1887, give a good overview of the kinds of phenomena that were observed.[22] Around Alassio (a fishing port on the coast), diffuse lightning bolts were observed during the night of February 22–23, even though the sky was clear. This provoked a great deal of fear among the fishermen, who usually would set their nets at night. The earthquake did not happen until 6:20 in the morning. When a fisherman in Bordighera stepped to the window to look at the weather, he saw a dark-colored blue light in the direction of Monaco. This happened a few minutes before the earthquake. From Pietra Ligure comes a report that red light in the form of lightning appeared before the first tremor. In Cervo, a light resembling a lightning bolt was seen in a clear sky immediately before the earthquake. It was also observed that the sky glowed red in the west the evening before the quake, as during the glowing of the northern lights. An exceedingly precise observation is reported from the village of Ponti: "The droning that preceded the first earthquake was accompanied by a white shimmering so that it was possible to distinguish objects in the room." This observation indicates that light phenomena can appear in association with P waves, which also cause earthquake noise.

Alexander von Humboldt describes a light phenomenon that heralded an earthquake in South America and obviously was Saint Elmo's fire:

In Cumana [Venezuela] a half hour before the great [earthquake] catastrophe of December 14, 1797 a powerful "sulfur odor" was noticed at the mountain monastery of San Francisco. The subterranean din which seemed to be rolling from southeast to southwest was strongest at that spot. At the same time, flames were seen shooting out of the ground on the banks of the Manzanares, near the hospice of the Capucins, and in the bay of Caraico near Mariguitar. . . . This fire . . . did not ignite the grass. . . . The people call these reddish flames, strangely enough, "the soul of the tyrant Aguirre." Lopez d'Aguirre, tormented by pangs of conscience, is supposed to be roaming the land which he tarnished with his crimes.[54a]

The earthquake of August 16, 1906 in central Chile produced its share of reports of strange glowing harbingers. M. Alavarrette of Quillon reported the following: "About half an hour before the quake I saw a light glowing east of the main square which resembled a great electrical discharge, and similar phenomena were observed by respected persons in other places."[169]

These documentations of light phenomena before earthquakes gleaned from the literature of three continents show clearly that the experience of people does not agree with current views of scientists. Until recently most of the learned specialists have stubbornly doubted even the existence of earthquake lights during quakes, but without a satisfactory theory of the origin of such lights they have been unable to deal with the precursor lights. We must proceed under the assumption that these lights are not alarm signals that appear regularly, but that they appear only before severe earthquakes and only when the required electrical energy has been built up before earthquake waves are set loose. The appearance of light phenomena before the earthquake proper would prove that a massing of electrostatic charges takes place above the quake. With that another important proof is adduced for the hypothesis under discussion: For animals to react to a change in the concentration of air ions it is of course not necessary that the increase in the charges be so big as to produce a light phenomenon, but the fact that such extreme situations occasionally do occur could mean that a considerably lesser charging of the air above the surface is actually common.

If noticeable light phenomena have occasionally appeared before disastrous earthquakes, then it is not surprising that in Western tradition unusual and inexplicable lights in the sky have been viewed as evil omens ever since antiquity. This was true especially of the ancient Romans, who maintained that nothing unusual ever happened in Rome unless it was first announced by an earthquake[8d]—possibly because earthquakes as well as political misfortunes were relatively common. Pliny gives an interesting rundown:

> There are . . . meteoric lights that are only seen when falling, for instance one that ran across the sky at midday in full view of the public when Germanicus Caesar was giving a gladiatorial show. Of these there are two kinds: one sort are called *lampades*, which means "torches," the other *bolides* (missiles)—that is the sort that appeared at the time of the disasters of Modena. The difference between them is that "torches" make long tracks, with their front part glowing, whereas a "bolis" glows throughout its length and traces a longer path. Other similar meteoric lights are "beams," in Greek *dokoi*, for example one that appeared when the Spartans were defeated at sea and lost the empire of Greece. There also occurs a yawning of the actual sky, called *chasma*. . . . A light from the sky by night, the phenomenon usually called "night-suns," was seen in the consulship of Gaius Caecilius and Gnaeus Papirius and often on other occasions causing apparent daylight in the night. In the consulship of Lucius Valerius and Gaius Marius a burning shield scattering sparks ran across the sky at sunset from west to east.[8e]

If the many reports suggesting that glowing atmospheric phenomena covering vast areas can be produced by such geophysical events as earthquakes should turn out to be true, they represent one of the most mysterious natural phenomena faced by science. Fortunately, spherical light phenomena—ball lightning—are sometimes also sighted during thunderstorms, and now after several hundred well-documented observations they have been freed from the bad reputation of being nothing more than creations of observers gifted with imagination. The mechanism of their origin has been discussed in reputable scientific periodicals. Many models have been suggested, but so far none has dealt with two basic problems: Why is it that so much electrical and electromagnetic energy is concentrated in one fiery ball? How is that ball stabilized so it can fly around in the air?

The reason why science views reports of glowing spherical objects so skeptically and accepts them so reluctantly, and why many observers who are probably totally honest have been branded as fantasizers, lies in the fact that these phenomena do not seem to fit science's concepts. But is it true that they don't fit? For example, none of the theories about the origin of ball lightning advanced so far has considered an energy-conversion phenomenon, well known to physicists, that is capable of amassing energy. A simple experiment can easily be set up to demonstrate this. If we connect a plate capacitor to an electrical oscillator with a coil, and if we change the distance between the plates mechanically (which requires the application of work), we will cause an electrical oscillation to build up in the circuit. If we continue to pump mechanically, the accumulated electrical energy becomes so great that the circuit melts and destroys itself.[178] Such a mechanism is called *parametric energy conversion*, because it is achieved by periodic changes of one of the parameters (in our example, capacitance) that store energy. Parametric amplifiers, which are particularly low in noise and for that reason are used in satellites, work on this principle. They are, of course, not equipped with plate condensers, but with tiny solid-state diodes. They have electrical capacitances that change with the applied voltage. In this way the change in capacitance is manipulated and a signal is amplified parametrically. Instead of connecting many circuits in series, it is enough to have an oblong piece of material with the right voltage-dependent properties. A pumping wave is sent in one end as alternating voltage, and an amplified signal emerges from the other.[179] In this manner it is possible not only to transform voltages, but to transform light into mechanical vibration, mechanical vibrations into light, or light of one frequency into light of another frequency. Such a mechanism for converting energy, labeled nonlinear because of the necessary periodical changes in parameters, could theoretically also appear in connection with earthquakes. Sufficient amounts of pumping energy could be delivered by vibrations accompanying a quake. These vibrations produce periodic pressure changes in the ground, and, as a consequence, electrical oscillations in and above the ground. The periodic changes produced in suitable crystalline rock through pressure waves would amplify light or electric fields parametrically to high intensities.

10

Earthquake Sensitivity and Weather Sensitivity

Weather, animals, and earthquakes

Even without a vivid imagination one might suspect a connection between the unusual animal behavior and the strange atmospheric processes that have been reported to precede earthquakes, but all the collected reports are not nearly sufficient for a persuasive scientific proof. There are no objective means of knowing how often these phenomena have occurred and what their statistical meanings might be. In the first place we do not know how often phenomena actually observed were entered into documents, and in the second place there is the possibility that the reported conjunctions of such phenomena with earthquakes were coincidences. But there are a few reported peculiarities that could help us start the scientific inquiries in the right place.

The following was reported from Spoleto and a few other villages in central Italy that were devastated by a severe earthquake in 1703: In otherwise fair weather, at the time of the earthquake, the moon was red, dark, and surrounded by a lead-colored circle. A gust of wind with a sudden, unusual whistling sound preceded the tremors. Spring water became cloudy. Chickens, ducks, and similar birds raised a cry; pigeons flew up suddenly and kept flying longer than normal. Horses, oxen, and other animals became restless, and dogs began barking. "Sulfur vapors" came out of the ground in several places during the earthquake. Wine that had been stored in well-corked glass bottles with oil poured into the necks turned cloudy after the quake.[222]

In 1737, during a series of earthquakes in Basel and in neighboring Baden-Württemberg, it was noticed that even in the coldest rooms milk had turned sour before the first night was over. Also, unusual lights and excitement among yard fowl were observed.[223] (Microbiological processes that take place in wine and in milk seem to be affected by the atmospherical and physical conditions at the time of an earthquake.)

In the chronicle of Bozen in South Tyrol is the following observation from the momentous earthquake of 1348: "During the earthquake it was dark— while the sun shone."[224]

In 1824 before an earthquake in Tuscany a peculiar kind of fog veiled the sun, which is said to have looked more like the moon.[225]

Sheep fled their pastures and their shepherds before the earthquake in 1682 in French Adijan.[226]

Many severe earthquakes have been accompanied by unusually intense thunderstorms. That was the case in 365–366 A.D., when a violent quake devastated the eastern Mediterranean. About 50,000 people are said to have died in Alexandria alone as a consequence of a tidal wave caused by that earthquake. The Roman Ammianus Marcellinus writes that the learned men could not agree on the nature of the light phenomena that had been observed.[227] Other memorable thunderstorms that coincided exactly with earthquakes have been reported from Würzburg, Germany (1138), from Ferrara, Italy (1570), and from Basel, Switzerland (1704).[228]

Strong electrical activity in the air was also observed on the Ionian island of Zakinthos before an earthquake in 1820. Three or four minutes before the tremor people noticed a kind of fiery phenomenon about 9 kilometers (5.5 miles) from the promontory of Geraca on the southeast part of the island. It was glowing and lingered for 5–6 minutes, as if floating on the sea. Judging by the distance at which it was seen, it seems to have had a diameter of 5–6 feet.[229]

Many lightning bolts, without thunder, were also seen in the eastern Pyrenees on the day of the earthquake of June 18, 1824.[230] "Fire meteors" were seen at the time of earthquakes in Switzerland in 1001 and 1674,[228] and in 1640 in the area of the Rhine and on the North Sea coast.[231] More than 100 years later, in 1756, reports of lightning bolts accompanying earthquakes surfaced again in that same area.[228] At Stavanger, Norway, an unusual light was seen in the east during a strong tremor on March 16, 1752, accompanied by a howling that filled the air.

If people can occasionally recognize these phenomena, then the animals with their more acute senses must find it even easier. As many reports suggest, there is a certain connection between severe earthquakes and electrical phenomena such as appear during thunderstorms. The key to our riddle, then, lies in the search for the conditions that exist before such atmospheric processes become visible.

Charged aerosols and low-frequency fields before weather changes

It would be immensely useful if we could simulate the physical conditions that (according to the ideas advanced in this book) precede an earthquake, while at the same time maintaining animals in their normal living conditions. This simulation would include the setting free of charged suspended particles and the strong alternations of the electric field in the air that go with it, the vertical ion currents flowing through the atmosphere that tend to diminish the charge in the earth's surface, and the low-frequency electromagnetic radiation that would be emitted because of the changing pressures on piezoelectric quartz crystals. Though there have already been numerous experiments proving the biological effects of individual physical factors acting separately, it will be very difficult to repeat the fortuitously observed behavior of animals in villages or in nature before earthquakes under controlled conditions.

Does that mean that we can do nothing except wait patiently for a severe earthquake? What scientist is prepared to wait for years or decades for a big chance that might slip by in the night? By a fortunate coincidence nature has put at the researcher's disposal a large-scale experimental laboratory in which all the desired physical values— electrical charges, electrical fields, and low-frequency electromagnetic radiation—can undergo powerful changes. This is our environment when it goes through drastic weather changes. We cannot, of course, expect that these physical values will remain completely constant before earthquakes and weather changes; the causes of the two phenomena are much too different for that. Yet, in a qualitative sense, certain kinds of phenomena should occur before certain weather fronts that could also be expected to occur just before impending earthquakes.[180]

It has been known for 70 years that with the coming of the *Föhn* the concentration of positive ions in the air rises sharply.[181,130] In at least one species of *Föhn*, the positive charges are produced by the whirling of snow on the ridges of the Alps.[118] A similar rise in positive charges can be observed with the *Sharav*. It can be detected 24–48 hours before any of the other ensuing meteorological changes, such as a rise in temperature or a drop in relative humidity, are perceived.[182,130]

Even in such ordinary weather changes as the buildup and maturing of rain, snowfall, or thunderstorms, noticeable changes in the concentration of electrostatic charges in the air can sometimes occur hours before the bad weather itself arrives. One cause of these variations is the natural radioactivity of the air, which is what usually liberates these charges and which, in turn, is heavily dependent on wind direction, precipitation, and events associated with weather fronts. On the northern slopes of the Alps, for instance, the wind will usually make a turn to the south before cold fronts. Because of this, the wind picks up higher concentrations of radioactive decay products above the Alpine bedrock, which is rich in radioactive radium and thorium. Weather can vary the natural radioactivity of the air, and with that the concentration of free electrostatic charges, as much as twentyfold.[118] High concentrations of electrical charges can also be set free by friction on falling water droplets and ice crystals. This is what brings about the dramatic charging and discharging during thunderstorms. Charges produced in this way can, with suitable air movements, speed ahead of bad weather.

Wherever electrical charges are separated, the electrical fields in the atmosphere change also. At least one kind of *Föhn* is accompanied by extreme variations in the electrical field.[118] Leaps in the strength of fields are, of course, quite vigorous during thunderstorm discharges, but such leaps are also generated in "silent" discharges in rain clouds. These electrical discharges generate a complicated mixture of electrical waves, which spread through the atmosphere and cause crackling in headphones and radio sets far from their source. Near the lightning bolt the precipitous leap of the electrical field predominates, but only 60 kilometers (37 miles) away this leap is very small and the interference spreads as an electromagnetic wave. The frequency of oscillation of these atmospheric waves is comparatively low. Most of them range between 1 and 50,000 hertz. But the distribution of energy is not uniform within this range.

A rise in low-frequency, long-wave electromagnetic radiation from the atmosphere is a rather reliable indicator of an approaching unstable weather front. The intensity of this radiation declines again when the bad weather becomes stabilized or abates. The peak value of the long-wave radiation reaches an observer about 6–15 hours before the bad weather, long before significant meteorological changes can be detected.[118]

An accumulation of electrostatic charges in the air as well as drastic changes in the electrical field and in the intensity of long electromagnetic waves will elicit biological reactions from animals. These physical changes of an electrical nature are considerably more distinct, and can be interpreted with much greater certainty than, say, pressure changes preceding changes in the weather. If the barometer were to fall one millibar per hour before a storm, that change in pressure would correspond to a difference in altitude of about 10 meters (33 feet). It is not likely that animals, which change their locations frequently, can detect a coming change in the weather by such small pressure changes. If animals (and sensitive people) can perceive coming weather changes, they must be doing so, above all, by way of changes in the atmospheric concentration of electrical charges, dramatic electrical-field variations, and long-wave electromagnetic radiation. These exact same physical values ought to change before earthquakes, according to my interpretation of the folklore. If animals react abnormally before earthquakes, then it follows that they would show unusual behavior before weather changes. Animal behavior before storms and earthquakes should even be similar up to a point.

Animals' premonition of storms

Foresters and woodsmen in the northern German plain could tell something was happening on the evening of November 12, 1972. The normally placid forest animals, so steadfast in their habits, were acting remarkably restless, indeed downright panicky. When morning came on November 13, red deer, fallow deer, and roe deer would not go into their familiar, hidden haunts. Even rabbits lingered unusually late in the clearings that morning.

A storm erupted only a short time later. With peak gusts of 170 kilometers per hour (105 miles per hour), it cut a 100-kilometer (62-mile) swath of destruction into northern Lower Saxony. About 130,000 hectares (321,000 acres) of forest were totally destroyed, and about 50–60 million trees were broken by the winds and dashed to the ground.

Despite this massive destruction, the loss of wildlife was surprisingly small. Over a wooded area of about 211,000 hectares (521,000 acres), only three red deer, a dozen fallow deer, seventeen roe deer, three wild hogs, one rabbit, and one badger were found dead. These few forest animals that did come to grief may have been especially stubborn individuals; according to the investigation of D. Stahl, most animals had perceived the coming danger in time and had evaded the falling trees with highly appropriate behavior.[183] Stahl's evaluation of the observations of 88 forestry officers and district hunt masters reveals that deer (especially red deer) left the woods before and at the beginning of the disaster, roamed around in the open plains and broad clearings, and formed herds. This apparently is an instinctual behavior pattern that meets the dangers of storms correctly, but had not been recognized until then. Hoofed game did not always pick treeless plains in their flight from the storm; six forestry officials reported the seeking out of thickets of young trees that provided protection from the wind without danger of falling. There were indications that wild pigs, too, sought out stands of young trees before the storm.

As often happens in emergencies, the animals lost their fear of people during that weather disaster. A herd of fallow deer stayed in a forest clearing close to a group of woodsmen who had also taken refuge there. A large herd of red deer sought refuge under a bridge over the side canal of the Elbe River then under construction and waited there until the gale was over. Roe deer approached houses. Hours and even days after the storm, red, roe, and fallow deer seemed strangely disturbed, and when approached by people they would flee only after some hesitation.

The greatest extremes in weather are encountered by birds that migrate great distances. In 1907, for example, a precipitous temperature drop and a snowfall surprised some northern birds (*Calcarius lapponicus*) just as they were passing through Minnesota. Their frozen bodies were found over an area of 4,000 square kilometers (1,545 square miles). About 75,000 birds were counted at two small lakes alone.[184] To ensure the safety of their dangerous voyages, birds depend on correct estimates of the long-term weather situation. It is not for nothing that peasants often base weather rules on the seasonal arrival or departure of birds. The birds proclaim good weather when they arrive early from the south and bad weather when they start out early on their southward migration. Sometimes when a dangerous weather front is moving in they skip habitual rest breaks in familiar places.

How far did nature get with its instinctive weather service in the heads of animals? Which animals sense weather changes in advance, and how do they behave then? Is it possible to speak of a weather sense of animals? We can put together a rough mosaic of this phenomenon from many observations culled from the rich treasure of the experiences of hunters and farmers.

Some of the peasants in my home village in Friuli have given me the following, and in their opinion reliable, rules about weather: Before the onset of bad weather chickens, cattle, and goats refuse to go into their stalls at the usual hour. They take advantage of the waning light of dusk to take in food (usually very hastily), and they go into their shelters much later than normally. Cows and goats also eat plants that they normally would not touch. Bad weather is also coming when swallows fly low, since insects hover near the ground then. Conversely, nice weather may be expected when the swallows are flying high.

Changes in animal behavior, it is believed, precede any visible meteorological signs of a coming change in the weather.

Inquiries among country people in Germany have confirmed the weather-related flying habits of swallows. Swifts, which also hunt insects, act in a like manner, and fish can often be seen jumping out of the water to catch low-flying insects before a rain. In the Thüringer Woods people count on bad weather when red deer show up in clearings in the daytime, eat hastily and a great deal, and generally act rather carelessly. It is also known that roe deer come out of the woods earlier than usual when there is a change in the weather coming and that they then eat hastily.[25] Fallow deer are also weather-sensitive, but they react differently. From several hours to one day before a rain, they will disappear from their habitual places and await the rain in protected thickets.[25] Some weather-related feeding habits of animals are highly mysterious. Cats, chickens and dogs, we are often assured, eat grass before a rain.

According to popular lore, the chaffinch (*Fringilla coelebs*) will call with a monotonous, long, drawn-out whistling sound before rain.[25] The titmouse, too, whistles when rain is coming; when the weather prospects are good it twitters. The plover may have gotten its German name *Regenpfeifer* (rain piper) because of a similar habit. Fishermen of the Pacific coast of South America know that seabirds flee into the interior before storms to wait out the bad weather there. These fishermen regard the sight of flocks of screeching gulls flying over their villages toward the back country as a sign of great danger.

Smaller living beings are particularly endangered by heavy rainfalls because the water can sweep them away easily. Thus, an old rule says that rain is coming when the dung beetles disappear from their usual places.[25] Friends from Australia have told me that farmers there watch ants to predict the weather; when they start running back and forth hastily and aimlessly, it is a sign that rain will start in a few hours.

The weather sensitivity of animals and the behavior patterns that protect them from hard times seem to be confirmed by many observations from all parts of the world, even though they have not yet been investigated systematically. There are reports from China, for example, that fish jump from the water before rainfall, that chickens refuse to go into their coops, and that ants change their living quarters.[36] Radio and television weather reports have become rather reliable lately and have contributed to the decline of the animals' role in predicting weather. Did we lose a rich observational treasure in this way? In the old days, animal observations certainly played an important role in weather prediction. Pliny the Elder, an attentive observer of nature, gives the following weather rules:

. . . dolphins sporting in a calm sea prophesy wind from the quarter from which they come, and likewise when splashing the water in a billowy sea they also presage calm weather. A cuttlefish fluttering out of the water, shellfish adhering to objects, and sea urchins making themselves fast or ballasting themselves with sand are signs of a storm; so also frogs croaking more than usual, and coots making a chattering in the morning . . . and the other water birds flocking together, cranes hastening inland, and divers and seagulls forsaking the sea or the marshes. Cranes flying high aloft in silence foretell fine weather, and so also does the nightowl when it screeches during a shower, but it prophesies a storm if it screeches in fine weather, and so do crows croaking with a sort of gurgle and shaking themselves, if the sound is continuous, but if they swallow it down in gulps, this foretells gusty rain. Jays returning late from feeding foretell stormy weather, and so do the white birds when they collect in flocks, and land birds when they clamor while facing a piece of water and sprinkle themselves, but especially a rook; a swallow skimming along so close to the water that she repeatedly strikes it with her wing; and birds that live in trees going to cover in their nests; and geese when they make a continuous clamouring at an unusual time; and a heron moping in the middle of the sands.
    . . . sheep skipping and sporting with unseemly gambols have the same prognostications, and oxen sniffing the sky and licking themselves against the way of the hair, and nasty swine tearing up bundles of hay . . . and bees keeping in hiding idly and against their usual habit of industry, or ants hurrying to and fro or carrying forward their eggs, and likewise earthworms emerging from their holes.[8b]

Many of the behavior patterns of animals before weather changes appear to serve the purpose of giving the creatures a better chance at survival. It would follow, then, that the weather sense evolved because it was useful. Individuals that did not have it would more easily perish from the consequences of disastrous weather. The exact same kinds of physical changes that appear when the electrical conditions of the atmosphere are disturbed by earthquake-related processes in the earth's crust cannot be expected to appear before inclement weather. After all, electrical charges and long-wave radiation before thunderstorms do not come out of ground, but from the atmosphere. Earthquakes, then, would not correspond exactly to the storm model for which animals are evidently instinctually prepared. Still, it can be assumed that before earthquakes many animals react in a way that is qualitatively similar to the way they would react before a dramatic onset of stormy weather.

Animals' fright during solar eclipses

In his report on the 1783 Calabria earthquake, Deodat de Dolomieu mentions an uncommonly interesting observation.

During a solar eclipse, animals perceived an almost identical restlessness. At the time of the annular solar eclipse of 1764 domestic animals exhibited agitation and for part of the time that it lasted they made a great noise; but the eclipse did not weaken the light of the sun any more than a thick black cloud would have if it had covered it completely. The difference in air temperature was barely perceptible. What impression could have made the animals aware of the nature of the body that slid before the sun? How could they ascertain that this was not the same situation when the sun is simply darkened by a cloud that absorbs the light?[15]

This is a good question indeed.

The Romantic writer and painter Adalbert Stifter, in an essay about the solar eclipse of July 8, 1842, gives a description of the terror that animals seemed to feel during the darkening. When the sunlight began to return, he reports, the animals seemed to feel a great sense of relief—"the horses whinnied, the sparrows on the roofs began a joyful shouting, as strident and foolish as they usually do when they are very excited, and the swallows darted up and down, flashing and dashing around in the air."

What geophysical factors other than sunlight change during a solar eclipse? It is easy to pick up the trail of this mystery by pursuing the question of which geophysical factors change in the alternation of day and night. If in an eclipse the moon screens out the intense light and the solar wind (which consists of charged particles—protons and electrons), then the ionosphere is in about the same condition as it is at night when that part of the earth's surface is turned away from the sun. The earth's electrical field, which is maintained by the thunderstorms occurring continually all over the world, varies only slightly in the course of a day with the position of the sun over tropical land areas, such as the Amazon basin, where most thunderstorms are hatched. That field would not be affected significantly by a solar eclipse. The earth's magnetic field varies by about 30 gamma between day and night because of the changing pressures of the solar wind, and a solar eclipse would vary it, at most, in roughly the same order of magnitude. The charged particles of the solar wind, with their speed of about 1,500 kilometers (932 miles) per second, need about 41/4 minutes to cover the distance between moon and earth. This means that during a solar eclipse, the earth's magnetic field would begin to deviate from its normal value only after a slight delay. But it would still vary as a consequence of the solar eclipse. The possibility that animals can detect such changes in the magnetic field cannot be dismissed.

As already mentioned in connection with earthquakes, such sensitivity of animal senses would have no practical value. Animals would sense solar eruptions, which are of no concern to life on earth, as the eruptions produced magnetic storms in the ionosphere. In their wanderings over the surface of the earth, animals would notice even greater variations in the magnetic field within the radius of a kilometer because of changing ground composition. What use would such knowledge be to an animal?

But there is something that does change drastically from day to night and that is also affected considerably by a solar eclipse, as measurements have shown: the propagation properties of the lower-frequency electromagnetic waves. This is because incoming energy-rich light dissociates a significant fraction of atmospheric gases into ions and electrons in a layer that extends from 70 to 1,000 kilometers (43 to 620 miles) above the earth's surface. This "ionospheric layer" becomes a good conductor because of the ionization. These periodic changes in the conductivity of the ionosphere vary with the solar irradiation and are responsible for the fact that medium and long radio waves carry only a short distance during the day and a long distance at night. Measurements taken during the eclipse of June 30, 1954, over southeastern Europe showed that the absorption of long waves in the lower ionosphere decreased a hundredfold during the eclipse and that it was only slightly larger than during nighttime hours.[185] An eclipse, of course, has a similarly favorable effect on the propagation properties of atmospheric electromagnetic waves. As the moon temporarily casts its shadow on the ionosphere, animals may pick up the interference signals of distant thunderstorms. Because of the presence of atmospheric disturbances in the wider surrounding area, the animals would perceive briefly the approach of a nonexistent thunderstorm.

This explanation would confirm nicely the hypothesis that animals in their natural habitats react very sensitively to long-wave electromagnetic radiation. The theory deserves more precise examinations. If scientific experiments were to confirm the eclipse excitement of animals and if the cause could be shown to be the influx of long waves, a fascinating new kind of biophysical phenomenon would be indicated. Since the intensity of atmospheric long-wave radiation varies considerably with the change from day to night, then animals that draw conclusions about weather changes from this radiation would have to react toward it with sensitivities that differed from day to night. This would only be possible if the animals could also sense the diurnal variations. That would mean that under some conditions certain animals have the ability to draw inferences by means of atmospheric electromagnetic waves about the condition of the ionosphere and thus about the position of the sun without actually seeing the sun. Since the reflectivity and the absorption of electromagnetic waves in the ionosphere depend heavily on the wavelength of the radiation as well as on the conductivity of the ionosphere, it would suffice to compare the intensity of different wavelengths of radiation arriving from various directions (provided that certain typical frequencies of the atmospheric radiation are familiar to the animal from experience).

There are still some vital details of the mechanism of bird navigation that have not been explained. For example, carrier pigeons retain a certain measure of ability to navigate even under totally overcast skies. A magnetic sense would not be sufficient for fixing location, because it shows direction only and not position. Perhaps birds can sense the ionization condition of the atmosphere and thus the direction of the sun from the frequency distribution of the atmospheric electromagnetic radiation that is being reflected from the ionosphere down through the clouds.

Could earthquakes mimic hurricanes to animals?

February is the time of steady summer weather in Concepciòn, in central Chile, and February 20, 1835, was no exception until suddenly something inexplicable happened that disoriented the older, more weather-wise people. Around 10 A.M., giant flocks of seabirds flew from the coast into the interior.[58,69] Why were they doing that if there was no sign anywhere that the stable weather was about to end? The answer came an hour and 40 minutes later when a severe earthquake lay Concepciòn in ruins. The flight of seabirds to the interior was also observed before the 1822 earthquake in central Chile[56,42] and the 1868 quake in Iquique, in the north of the country.[69,59]

Let us assume for the moment that it was noises inaudible to humans, coming from the interior of the earth, that disturbed the sensitive birds, or that gentle vibrations of the ground from small forerunner quakes had gotten them excited. That would still make it hard to understand why the seabirds flew into the interior. They would have been that much more exposed to these disquieting alarm signals there, whereas the water of the ocean would have attenuated them. Also, how could seabirds react so dramatically to such weak signals in the vibrational chaos of surf against a sheer coast? The only explanation that makes sense is that the seabirds were interpreting the geophysical changes preceding an earthquake as those of a coming storm. Their instinct then signaled them to form flocks and to leave the endangered coast forthwith. This behavior pattern confirms the electrical nature of the atmospheric changes that precede an earthquake.

Are there more examples of earthquake-related behavior of animals that resembles behavior before the onset of bad weather? Apparently there are many (table 2). According to Chinese reports[21] and Chinese rules of thumb about earthquake precursors, ducks and swans leave the water and refuse to go back in before an earthquake. It was also reported that before a severe earthquake Hebgen Lake in Montana, which is rich in waterfowl, was completely deserted by these birds.[63] This strange behavior is reminiscent of a well-known weather rule, mentioned by Pliny the Elder, that waterfowl leave seacoasts and inland lakes before severe storms. The inclination of some birds to flock together and fly around excitedly has also been observed before the onsets of dramatically severe weather.[34,62,69,22,35] Chickens lack any desire to go into their coops not only before earthquakes[22,36] but also before rainy weather, but the urge to get out into the open is not so strong in the latter case. The oddly timed and strange-sounding calls with which birds announce an earthquake[86,36] might also be compared to their well-known weather calls.

Perhaps the desperate attempts of domestic animals to get out in the open before an earthquake[36,35,22] are really not cases of totally unknown, isolated behavior. Could it be that this behavior reflects something of the instinct that causes these four-legged animals to remain in the pasture longer in order to take up more nourishment before bad weather? The behavior of roe deer coming out of the forest in Friuli, or wild animals losing their fear of people, is strikingly similar to the behavior observed before and during the above-mentioned gale in northern Germany in 1972. Is the instinct that drives forest creatures from the dark and dangerous woods into the clearings the same one that impels domestic animals out of the stables? The movement of ants to new places before earthquakes, and their crowding together,[36] is analogous to their behavior before bad weather. The same holds true for earthworms, which come to the surface before earthquakes[42,11a] much as they do before bad weather. Uncommonly excited bees can be observed not only at times of severe thunderstorms, but also before and during earthquakes.[21,20,36]

Although my inquiries suggest that the electrical properties of the atmosphere go through quantitatively similar changes before earthquakes and dramatic weather changes, two such different natural phenomena cannot be expected to run the same course. In fact, some behaviors of animals before earthquakes can hardly be likened to weather sensitivity. In this category are the tendency of snakes, mice, and rats to leave their holes, the loss of appetite in some animals, and the intense excitement to which animals work themselves up before a severe earthquake. These variant behavior modes suggest an additional mechanism that can evoke biochemical changes that bring on acute nervous complaints. Animals will naturally try to evade these afflictions by appropriate behavior. As suggested above, particles suspended in the air and charged from the ground could satisfactorily explain phenomena of this kind, such as the serotonin syndrome.

If we put all these observations and reflections together, we come to the conclusion that animals might indeed sense the approach of a phantom storm in an approaching earthquake. Therefore, their behavior is, at least in part, shaped by an instinctually predetermined pattern. But added to this pattern are further reactions evoked by the unaccustomed intensity of physical alarm signals, by hormone disturbances, and by the different course that an earthquake takes. This insight throws some light on why there is such a thing as an "earthquake instinct" in animals, even though these animals would seem to have had no chance and hardly any reason to develop such an instinct in the course of evolution. Because of other instincts and because of available sensory capacities, an alarm reaction to earthquakes exists in animals even though no mechanism for it had ever arisen.

Human weather premonition

Not only animals, but sensitive people, too, can feel coming changes in the weather. Who among us does not know of an elderly or ill person who makes weather predictions based on his state of health and is often correct? The weather sensitivity of certain people has always figured prominently in the local weather forecast in rural areas. In the fifth century B.C. Hippocrates mulled over the influence of weather on the illnesses of people, and a thousand years ago there was a law in Friesland [the coastal region from central Holland to southern Denmark—Tr.] that provided for more severe punishment for anyone who struck a weather-sensitive scar in his victim. Goethe had a high estimate of his own weather sensitivities, designating himself "the most definite barometer that ever existed."

The weather sensitivity of people is a complicated physiological phenomenon. Because of the many physical changes that accompany changes in the weather, it has been explained only in rough outline. Most of the observed symptoms can be divided into three groups.[118] In the first are tissue reactions such as wound and scar pains, bone aches, headaches, and rheumatic complaints. In the second are nervous complaints such as general restlessness, anxiety, depression, and disturbed sleep. In the third group are functional complaints such as shortness of breath; nausea; colics of the intestine, gall bladder, or kidneys; asthmatic conditions; attacks of angina pectoris; heart and circulatory complaints; and migraine.

Two lines of research have made special contributions to shedding some light on the complicated physical-chemical interrelationships. One deals with the effect of the smallest charged airborne particles, such as appear in large numbers in certain *Föhn*-like winds; the other examines the effect of long-wave radiation, which appears before various kinds of weather changes. Both approaches have contributed concrete insights. As mentioned above, biomedical studies have traced weather complaints produced by the *Sharav*—migraine, nausea, excitability, and respiratory complaints—to increased production of the nerve hormone serotonin. The weather-dependent causative factor is the concentration of positive air ions, which rises rapidly with the coming of the *Sharav* and other famous winds. Since the concentration of positive air ions increases with altitude as a consequence of the intensified ultraviolet radiation, it is likely that it is the serotonin syndrome (in addition to the lack of oxygen) that causes altitude sickness. Vast differences in ion concentration contribute not inconsiderably to the differential effects of city, sea, and mountain air on the health of people.

Another kind of human weather sensitivity is that associated with the increased incidence of long-wave electromagnetic radiation and with interferences in the electrical field of the atmosphere. Laborious statistical examinations by R. Reiter at the Physical-Bioclimatic Research Institute in Munich have shown that the phantom pains of amputees or the pains in the scars of injured persons appear more intense— more so than by chance—during disturbances of the electrical field of the atmosphere.[118] The pains of brain-damaged people or of people with internal illnesses, and the frequency of hemorrhaging in people suffering from tuberculosis, increase with the heightened incidence of infra-long-wave radiation during the buildups of many unstable weather fronts. The physical effect of these long waves depends on the changes in the electrical field, which in this case are periodic. Most human weather sensors can be found among people with irreparable tissue damages, like chronic joint complaints, sciatica, and rheumatism. These people suffer from weather signals that precede the actual bad weather by 6–15 hours.

Other persuasive proof of human weather sensitivity is the fact that for a whole chain of severe illnesses and functional disturbances, such as myocardial infarctions, pulmonary embolisms, acute coronary death, and severe circulatory disorders, the number of cases rises rapidly before certain weather situations. These numbers, too, agree with the weather-related increases of atmospheric infralong waves. Reiter has also shown that births, deaths, and traffic accidents are more frequent during the same atmospheric-field disturbances.

Even though many details of biometeorology remain unclear, it can be considered proven today that positive electrostatic charges in the air, changes in the electrical field, and long electromagnetic waves influence the health of people — especially those who are particularly well predisposed. This forces the following conclusion in the context of the hypothesis developed in this book: If electrostatic charges do move from the ground into the atmosphere, and if their liberation and neutralization produces long electromagnetic waves and changes in the electric field, then sensitive people must feel the approach of an earthquake.

Human earthquake premonition

Several of the persons who described to me their sensations during earth tremors indicated to me a remarkable phenomenon: One or several minutes before the tremors — shortly before any changes typical of quakes can be felt in the environment — something happens that puts the nervous system in a state of the highest alarm. Sensitive people then can tell right away, even with a small tremor, that it isn't a passing truck or a gust of wind, but that the earth itself is moving. A writer who lived through a severe earthquake in 1822 in Copiapo, Chile, describes the disaster signal as an inexplicable condition of the nervous system that manifests itself before any other sign of the earthquake: "Before we hear the sound, or at least are fully conscious of hearing it, we are made sensible, I do not know how, that something uncommon is going to happen; everything seems to change color; our thoughts are chained immovably down; the whole world appears to be in disorder; all nature looks different to what it is wont to do; and we feel quite subdued and overwhelmed by some invisible power, beyond human control or apprehension."[186] This primal fear did not escape the critical spirit of Alexander von Humboldt, who wrote the following: "Most of all it is not so much the worry over the danger, as the peculiar sensation which excites one so when one perceives even a gentle earth tremor for the first time."[54e]

Before the severe earthquake of Lisbon in 1755, people were suffering from nervous irritability and restlessness.[13,12] The Italian earthquake scientist Luigi Bossi wrote after the earthquake of April 2, 1808, in the valley of Pelice, that the more sensitive people were seized by a peculiar, indescribable restlessness some time before the tremors and that they suffered from some kind of trembling or in some cases a severe pounding of the heart.[18,14] Many reports of health disorders in people are available to us from the Ligurian earthquake of 1887 thanks to the careful inquiries by the seismologists Taramelli and Mercalli.[22] The quake happened on February 23 at 6:20 A.M., but as early as the evening of the preceding day—about the time of the first case of abnormal animal behavior—complaints were voiced by sensitive people. Numerous people in San Remo reported that they had felt a peculiar general malaise since the evening of February 22. Some were seized by nausea. From San Lorenzo al Mare came reports of nervous overexcitement and breathing difficulties. From Villa Talla the reports were of people in foul moods. In Sanfrè an uncomfortable, oppressive feeling of fear was experienced. Anxiety states were reported from the village of Casalgrasso, powerful nervous disorders from Verezzi, and unusual excitement of children from Rivarolo. In Albenga, a strange fatigue and weakness in the legs befell people before the earthquake, and the body was perceived as very heavy. A priest named Ambrogio from Cornigliano Ligure reported that this had also happened in Savona, where he had delivered a sermon. He reports: "During the night from the 22nd to the 23rd . . . a powerful nervous change was noticed in an unusual manner by me and by many others. From midnight to the hour of the quake I felt powerless in an unusual way and perceived a mysterious malaise." In the village of Abbiategrasso a woman was seized by dizziness, nausea, and trembling of limbs 10 minutes before the earthquake.

Certain people whose health has been undermined by illness or addiction seem to be extraordinarily sensitive to an approaching earthquake. It was reported from Castillione Falletto that the condition of people suffering from nervous disorders worsened as the 1887 Liguria earthquake approached, but that they recovered afterwards. A very unusual incident in Oneglia was related to the earthquake investigators and confirmed by Dr. Muraglia, the mayor of the village: An alcoholic teacher, while drunk, is said to have predicted a great disaster and the end of the world around 6 on the evening before the earthquake. When the earthquake happened, he jumped from a window and died.

The Japanese tradition, too, is haunted by reports of abnormal people predicting severe earthquakes. There is, for example, the well-known story of the man said to be possessed by the soul of a fox.[42] On the day of the great Edo earthquake of 1855 this mentally ill man is supposed to have warned his neighbors of a severe earthquake that was to happen that evening; then he began to run back and forth.

That the state of health of people can be influenced by the proximity of an earthquake is shown by a report from the Soviet Union.[74] During 1948, physicians in Ashkjabad near the Iranian border observed a dramatic increase in complaints of heart trouble. But electrocardiograms run on these patients showed no signs of any disorders. In the following two months the area was ravaged by catastrophic earthquakes which took many lives. Immediately afterward, all heart complaints disappeared.

After the Friuli quake of June 6, 1976, many people remembered a feeling of malaise, depression, and nervous disorders.[187]

During a severe earthquake, the sensations of sensitive people escalate greatly. Nausea and the urge to vomit appear frequently, and nervous breakdowns and shock are not unusual.[16] Sometimes people die or go insane from the fear.[14] Understandably, earthquake reports include the most varied descriptions of miracle cures.

Most documents that tell of nausea and nervous disorders caused by an earthquake contain no information as to whether the complaints appeared before or during the quake. The disorders are commonly ascribed to the undulation of the ground or to shock. For instance, a report of the State Earthquake Commission that investigated the California quake of April 18, 1906, indicates that adverse effects on human health were most frequent in the border areas of the earthquake zone, where the earth's movements had been rather weak.[61] Among the examples listed are the following:

In Stockton a considerable number of people suffered nausea and dizziness with headaches for a long time after the shock. In some these unpleasant symptoms lasted all the next day. In Modesto a number of people suffered symptoms resembling seasickness for several hours after the shock. Mrs. E. (San Francisco) was made nauseous by the earthquake and she felt heart pains. . . . In Bear Valley a man became dizzy outdoors and he became nauseous without noticing the ground (the earthquake) at that time. In Gardnerville, Nevada, a number of people complained of nausea as they were sitting at breakfast at the time of the earthquake, but they felt no motions.

Could vibrations whose duration must be measured in seconds evoke nausea and headaches lasting hours, or a whole day? Is it possible that people became nauseous without noticing the supposed cause, the gentle movement of the ground, at all? Perhaps it was not the earth movements that evoked these symptoms, but the same phenomenon that gives animals premonitions and drives them to panic during a quake. Many of the complaints felt by people before earthquakes resemble "weather illnesses" to a marked degree.

11

Discoveries and Rediscoveries

New light on ancient enigmas

The various kinds of natural processes that herald earthquakes can be divided into two groups: phenomena connected with the processes in the ground and those associated with the condition of the atmosphere. The former include underground noises, groundwater changes, murky springs, and the influence of water on earthquakes, which will be described in the next section. Among the latter are numbered abnormal animal behavior, the formation of certain kinds of fog, weather changes, discoloration or darkening of the sun, light phenomena in the atmosphere, the "feel" of earthquake weather, characteristic health complaints from people, and the loss of power from magnets.

The most remarkable result of this inquiry has been that the salient characteristics of all these important phenomena associated with changes in the atmosphere can be traced to the effect of a single basic physical process—the appearance of charged aerosol particles—and with that to an increase in the electricity of the atmosphere before an earthquake.

Suspended charged particles exert a definite influence on physiological processes in living organisms. The nature of these reactions is still not very well researched, but it is considered certain that it depends to a considerable extent on the composition and the electrical sign of the charged particles. Positive charges in the air evoke pathologically intense complaints and might play a decisive role in causing panic reactions in animals and health disorders in people (the serotonin syndrome). One important argument for this hypothesis is that it allows considerable room to maneuver. Depending on the weather situation, the geological composition of the substrata, or the already available amount of suspended particles, the aerosol situation before an earthquake could vary considerably. An absence of alarm precursors before an earthquake does not necessarily contradict the theory.

Under certain favorable atmospheric conditions these electrostatic charges can produce fog, which would be impossible without them because of insufficient moisture in the air. An entire series of atmospheric earthquake precursors become self-explanatory in this way, among them the reddening or darkening of the sun, the forming of strange clouds, and the fog itself. A whole series of light phenomena, from Saint Elmo's fire to lightning bolts that flash under a clear sky also can be explained with the electrostatic charging of the air. Even the loss of attraction in magnets before earthquakes is explained by an electrostatic phenomenon—the mutual repulsion of metal pieces. This electricity in the air was also the idea behind our attempt to explain why earthquake-experienced people associate dry, warm, or *Föhn*-like weather with earthquake danger. Since long-wave electromagnetic radiation appears wherever electric charges are generated or neutralized, and since such charges and electromagnetic waves are bound to give animals the impression that a storm is coming, I think the reasons for the many parallels in animal behavior before storms and before quakes are clear.

The fact that the theory being put forth here explains to a certain extent all important mysterious earthquake precursors connected with processes in the atmosphere lends it some weight. At the same time, it bolsters the credibility of the popular reports about these various phenomena. If it had only been anomalous animal behavior that had been observed before earthquakes, then, if we wanted to come to grips with the aerosol theory, we would have to ask ourselves why no one had ever observed fogs or lightning bolts out of a clear sky. It would seem, then, that all these mysterious observations can, in essence, be traced back to the same cause, which represents an unusual deviation from the normal in nature.

But one of the most persuasive supports for the idea developed here is that in it we can recognize the essential features of the dominant earthquake theory of antiquity, the concept of the *pneuma*. The beginnings of this concept go back to the Greek physicists Anaxagoras and Archelaos of the fifth century B.C. It was enhanced in detail by Aristotle, who used rich observational materials with great shrewdness, and it retained its influence in this form until the Middle Ages. The *pneuma* theory of Aristotle departs from the assumption that the processes that lead to an earthquake are introduced by the liberation of vapors (gas) from the earth. Aristotle imagined the *pneuma* to be like condensed water vapor, but dry and warm rather than moist. We can also conclude from the properties that this gas was said to have that it possesses a certain viscosity. When the *pneuma* emerges from the ground, it effects a series of changes in the atmosphere that can be interpreted as earthquake precursors: formation of characteristic clouds, fog phenomena, and darkening of the sun. Before earthquakes that happen at dawn, according to the *pneuma* theory, it becomes extraordinarily cold and sometimes a perfect calm reigns immediately before the quake. After this preparatory phase, the *pneuma* suddenly flows back into the earth, and the pressures it produces make the earth undulate. After the end of the quake, the *pneuma* escapes from the earth completely and disperses.

The similarity between the *pneuma* and the atmospheric earthquake precursors should leave no doubt that it is identical to the gas of charged aerosol particles suggested by the present hypothesis. The *pneuma* was none other than air electricity, which of course was not known at that time. Based on their experiences with earthquake precursors, the Greek physicists evidently deduced the presence of a ground gas in the atmosphere and tried desperately to make it fit as the cause of the ensuing earthquake. Because their knowledge of things geological was modest, they could not have recognized the true nature of the powers that produced their *pneuma* and the earthquakes. We know how hard Aristotle and other ancient Greek scientists tried to confirm their *pneuma* theory by observations of nature. Having explained the reasons behind it, we can confidently throw antiquity's treasure of earthquake experience onto the balance in favor of the aerosol hypothesis.

The many atmospheric observations that the Greeks collected to prove their *pneuma* theory also supports the hypothesis that charged aerosol particles are set free before earthquakes. Aristotle's mention that occasionally an uncommon chill can be felt before earthquakes that happen at dawn seems to contradict the many reports that it seems to get warmer before earthquakes, and obviously does not agree with the description of *pneuma* as a warm, dry gas. But this contradiction is resolved if we remember that an admixture of aerosol particles in the air is supposed to improve its poor temperature conductivity. This same feature, an improvement of the temperature conductivity of the air by moisture, is responsible for the fact that damp heat and cold can be tolerated less well than the dry kinds. Before dawn, when the ground still draws on the stored supply of warmth from the previous day, air loaded with aerosols would accelerate the heat loss of the body; but in the heat of the day it would make the transfer of warmth from the body more difficult. (Recall von Humboldt's surprise before the earthquake in Cumana when the measured temperature was much lower than he had expected because of the oppressive heat under the influence of the red earthquake fog.[54b])

Should my hypothesis about the change in the aerosol composition of the air before an earthquake be confirmed, it would become necessary to take another look at the prevailing opinion that earthquake research in antiquity was governed by abstract speculations and hardly contaminated with practical observations.

Reservoirs and quakes

On October 9, 1963, a 200-million-ton mass of rock suddenly thundered down from the precipice of Monte Toc into the three-year-old Vaiont Reservoir in the north Italian province of Belluno. The water piled up, spilled over the dam, and roared down an idyllic mountain valley. About 2,500 people in the village of Longarone lost their lives. Between 1960 and 1963 only three earthquakes in the area were registered. These were detected by faraway earthquake stations and probably could be traced to the normal activity of that area. But at the dam site the situation looked altogether different: Soon after the initial accumulation of water, and clearly connected with it, a worrisome wave of small local earthquakes appeared. After periods of rapid rising of the water level, as many as 400 tremors were registered in a few days.[188] Their strength was on the order of magnitude 1. The disastrous avalanche is regarded as a consequence of this microquake activity. The microquakes continued when the impounding of water was resumed after 1965.

Further examples pointing to a link between the storing of water and increased earthquake activity have since become known by the dozens,[189,190] but the following will serve to illustrate the character of this phenomenon: In the area of France where the Monteynard Dam was erected, no perceptible earthquakes were known before the dam's completion in 1963. Just between the first impoundment and 1967, 64 earthquakes appeared. The strongest quakes, which reached the astonishing values of 5 and 4.3, always happened when the greatest water depths were attained. Before the construction of the Koyna Reservoir in western India, the designated impoundment zone had been considered seismically inert. In an observation period of 7 years beginning with the impoundment, thousands of little quakes were registered. The strongest quake, which occurred on December 10, 1967, attained magnitude 6. The Hsingfengkiang Dam in China was built in a region that was seismically relatively safe. But after the first impoundment, increased seismic activity set in—clearly associated with the depth of the water in the basin. In 12 years more than 250,000 quakes were registered.[191] Before the most powerful quake (magnitude 6.2; March 19, 1962) the microquake activity decreased sharply for 20 days. This is a sign that the great quake was indeed associated with the impounded water and the microquakes. An escalation of microquake activity was also observed after the construction of the reservoir of Piave di Cadore, near Vaiont. In 1959 alone 20,000 tremors were counted there. Long experience had suggested that the Zambezi River valley in eastern Africa on the border between Zambia and Zimbabwe, in which the Kariba Dam was built, was earthquake-proof; but since the impoundment of water thousands of quakes have been registered. They culminated in seven tremors with magnitudes ranging between 4.7 and 5.8. Quakes also arose after the erection of the Kremasta Dam in Greece. The activity culminated in a tremor of magnitude 6.2 on February 5, 1966.

Intensive research into the association between dams and earthquakes began after the discovery of this phenomenon in 1945 by the American seismologist D. S. Carder, who described how the filling of Lake Mead in Colorado turned an earthquake-free area into an active one with quakes of magnitudes as high as 5. In adherence to a recommendation by UNESCO,[192] reservoirs in several countries are already being watched seismologically.

It was not difficult to find a sensible explanation for the earthquake-generating effect of stored-up water. All theories advanced thus far hold two mechanisms chiefly responsible: the mechanical tensions released in the substrata by the weight of the water, which can cause movements of rock; and the rising water pressure in the water-logged tiny clefts and cracks, which also has a kind of lubricating effect. It depends, of course, very much on the permeability and the geological makeup of the rock whether earthquakes are produced soon after the impounding of water, or whether there is a time lag. It was inevitable that someone would show that artificial earthquakes could be set off by pumping water into drill holes, as was done in Rangely near Denver, Colorado, and in Matsushiro, Japan. In the meantime scientists occupied themselves with the question of how well-aimed water injections could be used in the future to manipulate earthquakes. The discovery that water seepage into the substrata caused earthquakes was deservedly celebrated as a milestone in the struggle to achieve a better understanding of and perhaps some modest measure of control over earthquakes.

Is this achievement in understanding the connection between earthquakes and the soaking of the ground really new, or was this correlation discovered long ago by careful observations of nature? It was not especially difficult to show that in this case, too, modern seismology had inexcusably passed over ancient knowledge. Independent documents from three continents support this. The ancient experiences, of course, do not concern dammed up water but periods of intense rain that soak the ground through and through or overlong arid spells that remove weight and moisture from the soil. Clearly formulated theories about the earthquake-producing effect of water pressure in the ground can be found as far back as the time of the ancient Greeks. Anaximander (610–546 B.C.) and after him Anaximenes (second half of the sixth century B.C.) assumed that the change from extreme aridity to copious rainfall set off earthquakes. For Democritus (first half of the fifth century B.C.) it was water pressure from above or water running into dry caverns in the interior of the earth that caused earthquakes.[78] Aristotle (384–322 B.C.) also advanced the point of view that earthquakes were stimulated by alternating saturation and drying out of the earth. In retrospect, we must presume that the Greek physicists built their theories on precise observations and many years of experience.

That earthquakes proliferate when the ground is soggy and heavy after an intense rainy period was also familiar to the ancient Chinese. More than 200 years ago this idea was written down in a document concerning a 1739 earthquake in the Yinchuan-Pingluo area of Ningsia province that attained a magnitude of 8 and was followed by countless aftershocks for years. In connection with that quake the following observations have been passed down to us: "There are in Ningsia every year small (in comparison with force 8) earthquakes, and people become used to it. Generally there were more earthquakes in spring and winter. . . . When there was a lot of rain in the fall then earthquakes happened the following winter without exception."[32]

Alexander von Humboldt reported a similar experience from South America around 1800: "When one has lived for a long time in New Andalusia or in the lowlands of Peru one cannot deny that at the beginning of the rainy season, that is precisely at the time of thunderstorms, the appearance of earthquakes is to be feared most. The air and the character of the earth's surface seem to exert an influence on the processes in the great depths in a manner completely unknown to us. . . ."[54g]

Toward the end of the nineteenth century, Mercalli showed a statistical correlation between the frequency of earthquakes and the moisture content of the ground. He examined 1,572 earthquakes that had happened in Liguria and Piedmont between the twelfth and the nineteenth centuries in order to find out how they were distributed over the months of the year. The largest number of earthquakes (336) happened in February, whereas only 57 happened in September. There were 1,063 earthquakes in winter and spring, but only 494 in summer and fall. (For 15 of the earthquakes, the month could not be ascertained.) Mercalli came to the conclusion that the lowest earthquake frequency coincided with the end of the driest and warmest seasons. With the onset of the rainy period earthquakes start to bunch up, and they occur with the greatest frequency toward the end of the wet and cool season. Mercalli points out that similar relationships had been confirmed for Switzerland, where 776 earthquakes fell in winter and spring but only 454 in summer and fall.

Earthquake omens in classical antiquity

More than 1,900 years ago Pliny the Elder summarized four natural phenomena that can announce an impending earthquake.[8a] One of these precursors manifests itself in a slight quaking and tinkling of buildings. It is not difficult to recognize in this the small preshocks that, as already mentioned, frequently escalate in number and intensity before a big earthquake. A second omen noted by Pliny is excited animals: "Even the birds do not remain sitting fearlessly." Water that becomes cloudy in the wells and acquires an obnoxious odor was also mentioned. These three earthquake symptoms, which suddenly became the center of interest of earthquake researchers in Western countries in the last quarter of the twentieth century, are the same ones that enabled Chinese experts to predict the great earthquake of Haicheng in 1975. Pliny's fourth earthquake precursor, the formation of a kind of fog, will also prove relevant, at least to the extent that the charged-aerosol-particles hypothesis developed in this book can be confirmed.

The earlier sources from which Pliny took much of his knowledge yield additional information, even though the writings of most of the ancient Greek physicists who tried to explain earthquakes scientifically have been lost forever. Aristotle knew of earthquake fogs and explicitly mentioned discoloration and darkening of the sun as harbingers of earthquakes. The Greek writer Pausanias (second century A.D.) wrote that changes of the sun's color toward red and even black were earthquake precursors.[193] That wells change in water flow and become cloudy before an earthquake has probably been known from time immemorial. Pherecydes (sixth century B.C.), a Greek physicist and possibly the teacher of Pythagoras, even used this phenomenon to predict an earthquake, which happened 3 days later.[194,8g] Pherecydes's personality (he also composed a theory of the philosophy of life) and the way in which he proceeded leave no doubt that his earthquake prediction was a scientific act, the methodical application of experienced fact: ". . . when he had seen the water dipped from an ever-flowing well, he said that an earthquake was impending."[109c]

Also in the sixth century B.C. another physicist, Anaximander of Miletus (615–520 B.C.), predicted another severe earthquake with great assurance. He asked the Lacedaemonians (Spartans) to leave their houses and the city because a quake was impending, and advised them to await the calamity with their weapons in the open fields. The quake came, and the entire city was destroyed. A giant boulder shaped like the stern of a ship broke off from the Taiyetos Mountains and thundered down.[109c]

The Greek physicist Anaxagoras (fifth century B.C.) is supposed to have learned to predict earthquakes from secret Egyptian writings,[195,78] probably lost forever.

The ancient scientists knew the meaning of prequakes and were familiar with a series of precursors with which we in the West are perforce only now beginning to occupy ourselves because of the most recent Chinese successes in quake prediction. In practical short-term prediction we are certainly no further along than the ancients were. Without a doubt, we have a greater theoretical understanding of relationships among the processes within the earth, but when we reject the treasure of observations made by the people we rob ourselves of the opportunity to effectively collect data about a natural event that happens too rarely to permit exhaustive experimental research within a short time.

An analysis of folklore

Having analyzed a series of mysterious and controversial earthquake precursors and seen that they have been observed for thousands of years, let us now attempt to balance the accounts of this inquiry and determine how open-minded and responsible science has been in examining and evaluating these suggestions and experiences from popular tradition. To give a better overview of the fate of these examples of old folk wisdom, I have assembled them in table 3. I have listed there the oldest traditions known to me and the oldest reports of the use of each phenomenon for purposes of earthquake prediction. Table 3 also reports the uses of these phenomena in the earthquake warning system of modern China and the attitude toward them of modern American, European, and Japanese seismology. Aside from typical earthquake precursors (such as abnormal animal behavior, changes in groundwater, light phenomena, fog formations, and ground noises), table 3 lists the earthquake-producing effect of soaked ground and observations of strange lights during earthquakes. An understanding of these phenomena might reveal interrelationships that would improve the outlook for successful earthquake prediction. The table shows that each of these earthquake phenomena was recognized and described anywhere from centuries to two millenia ago, and that often they were enlisted—with some success—as popular rules for the early recognition of earthquakes.

How, then, does the scientific balance look? Can the scholars prove that the traditions rest on fantasy?

The knowledge that an intense soaking of the ground with water could set off earthquakes was 2,500 years old when scientists regained it after 1945 through the use of artificially dammed-up water basins. Now they are even racking their brains over how impending earthquakes might be set off under controlled conditions by means of water pumped into faults.

Pliny wrote that earthquake noise is a "precursor and companion" of the quake, but 1,900 years later seismologists considered it impossible that there could be earthquake noise before the ground went into perceptible vibrations. And yet around 1800 in Venezuela, according to von Humboldt's reports, people saved themselves by running from their houses in the last seconds before quakes thanks to these phantom noises. In 1975 it was finally shown that noise did indeed appear before an earthquake, and that it was generated by P waves, which cause only slight tremors.

Reports or hints about light phenomena during earth tremors have been haunting literature for two or three thousand years. Around 1930 there were 1,500 eyewitness reports of earthquake lights during a single quake in Japan, so some Japanese scholars began to give some thought to the phenomenon for the first time. It remained a curiosity, given too little credence to warrant scientific inquiry. Not until 1965–1967, during the Matsushiro earthquake series, when amateurs delivered dozens of photographs of earthquake lights free of charge, did this phenomenon begin to emerge gradually from folklore. Even if the reasons behind its origins are still not understood, at least some scientists are now wrestling with them.

The knowledge that enabled Pherecydes to predict a quake 2,500 years ago on the basis of characteristic changes in a spring sank into oblivion, and until the present a valuable treasure of additional information about this phenomenon lay around unnoticed. It took the courageous initiative of the Chinese to apply the ancient lore about changes in groundwater methodically and successfully to earthquake prediction.

It need not be reiterated that the recent efforts of Chinese specialists have boosted science's awareness of abnormal animal behavior before quakes. As a result, more than 2,000 years' worth of popular traditions and reports is being studied seriously in Western scientific circles for the first time.

Of the remaining four mysterious earthquake phenomena, two are definitely rejected by Western science: the appearances of lights before severe earthquakes, and the heralding of quakes by ground noises that sometimes clearly precede them. It is hard to understand why these phenomena are considered impossible when data about them have never been pursued seriously. Because records show that lights and noises have been reported independently of one another on three continents, chances are that there are good explanations for them. The same is true of earthquake fogs and earthquake-sensitive people, with the difference that scientific positions on them have not become known.

The restless chimps at Stanford

Since 1974, Stanford University in California has maintained a semicircular enclosure of about 2 acres for primate research. Divided into two sectors, the facility has numerous observation rooms. Each of the two sectors is inhabited by six adult and two young chimpanzees. Every day, the chimpanzees are selected at random, and each is observed intensively for half an hour at an arbitrarily selected time of day. At intervals of 30 seconds, precise notes are made about what the animal does, where it is located, and with which fellow apes it has contact. The carefully trained and supervised observers classify the behavior according to 167 precisely determined behavior indices, which run from gestures of scratching and tenderness to furious fighting or lazy dozing. The activities are coded and stored in a computer, and this information can then be used to evaluate certain behavior modes statistically—for example, restlessness. In this manner variations are detected that even practiced observers would not notice just by looking. The aim of the research program was to detect slow changes caused by hormones.

When the researchers working on the project evaluated these statistical results for the months of May through July 1975, they got a little surprise. While the average fraction of time that chimpanzees spent in active movements during those three months lay around 24 percent and a restlessness of 35 percent was reached on only two days, one day was out of line: One June 18, 1975, the chimpanzees devoted an average of 55 percent of their time to motion-intensive activities. While as a rule they spent an average of 71 percent of their time in the vicinity of the heated, elevated sleeping places and only 10 percent in a neighboring area of the enclosure, these percentages were 24 and 28 respectively on June 18. Even after this exceptional day, the restlessness of the chimpanzees stayed above average from June 19 to June 24, and it flared up again before July 24 and 25. These great deviations could not have been a statistical aberration. The reasons for them were at first a total mystery, as no special occurrences had been noticed at the time.

Because the Stanford primate research center lies only 3 kilometers (1.8 miles) from the San Andreas fault, and because it had become known that in China the appearance of unusual excitement among animals had been successfully used for early earthquake warnings, Helena C. Kraemer, B. E. Smith, and S. Levine resolved to track down earthquake activity that might have appeared during the period of the chimps' excitement.[196] The result was amazing: On the day after that unusual June 18, there had been more than 20 earthquakes, with magnitudes up to 3.1. Their origin lay about 6 kilometers (3.6 miles) from the primate center. A few isolated quakes had followed until June 24, and a single small one happened on July 25. June 18, the day of maximum animal activity, had been completely free of earthquakes. Eight hours had elapsed between the last observations of the primates and the first earthquake of June 19. When the earthquakes (which the observers did not notice) came, the data of the previous day had been long since stored. Because the animals were exceedingly restless right before the earthquake swarm as well as before the single weak quake of July 25, a connection with the coming earthquakes cannot be denied.

As Kraemer, Smith, and Levine were to find out, the experiments also yielded proof that people change their behavior before earthquakes. In the entire month of June there had been only seven days on which three or fewer obervation series had been conducted. Four of these days were Saturdays or Sundays, on which only skeleton crews worked in the primate colony, but the remaining three days were June 17, 18, and 19—the two days that preceded the earthquake swarm and the earthquake day itself. It was impossible to find any reason for this mysterious coincidence. The statistical chance that the unusual behavior of the observers immediately before the quakes was a matter of co-incidence was calculated by Kraemer and her colleagues as less than 0.001.

The persistence of skepticism

The question must be asked why a reputation for unbelievability and falsification adheres so tenaciously to the popular reports about mysterious earthquake phenomena. Not a single one of the nine phenomena mentioned in most of the popular reports and old traditions can be indicted by science as a baseless invention. On the contrary, most of them have been verified through earthquake research, or at least their credibility has been bolstered by Chinese successes. What right does science have to humiliate many honest observers with mistrust without taking the trouble to devote a proper measure of effort to the reported phenomena? Where might earthquake research be today if science had tried seriously to pursue earthquake precursors with simple experiments as far back as the San Francisco earthquake of 1906? This question is difficult to answer, but it is certain that the suffering that earthquakes cause would have justified great efforts—or at least a little trust in ancient traditions. Now, one-and-a-half million earthquake dead later, seismologists can no longer avoid the tasks of measuring groundwater tables, observing animals, and keeping a lookout for lightning.

12

Earthquakes in Scripture and History

Strange signs + earthquake = supernatural phenomenon

Besides suggesting that earthquake precursors from the vernacular should be taken seriously as events that actually happened and deserve an honest scientific analysis, this inquiry also indicates that these phenomena could have played a decisive role in the origin and evolution of many religions and mythologies because of the trauma of the accompanying or ensuing earthquake. The many tales of the apparitions of gods or demons in the form of lights or in the shape of a serpent or other animal, and of displays of the might of gods in the form of growling thunder, fireworks, or the appearance or disappearance of springs, might in fact go back to ancient experiences. When animals behaving oddly were actually seen, unusual lights like fire signals actually sighted, and springs actually observed in the act of welling forth, perhaps the ensuing earthquakes that had evoked these phenomena also elevated them to the status of supernatural and divine manifestations.

No natural event is more violent, more destructive, and more shocking than a severe earthquake, no natural catastrophe is more unpredictable, and nothing dashes man quite so low spiritually. Almost everybody who has experienced a severe earthquake will admit that he has never felt so helpless before nature. Earthquakes bring shocks to the soul, afflictions of the nerves, and radical reevaluations of life's goals, even in our time. Should we wonder, then, that people in olden times detected in earthquakes and their precursors a forceful demonstration of divine powers? If these reflections are accurate, then earthquake forerunners and accompanying phenomena have to be granted a prominent role in the development of mythology and religion. Beyond that, some views that it was always the soaring fantasies of people that burdened them with divine interventions and judgments will have to be revised; surprisingly often it was natural processes whose interconnections they were unable to fathom and which they interpreted according to their confined imaginations.

In a brief survey of the Bible for revealing episodes, the destruction of Sodom and Gomorrah offers itself straightaway: ". . . the Lord rained down fire and brimstone from the skies on Sodom and Gomorrah, He overthrew those cities and destroyed all the Plain, with everyone living there and everything growing in the ground."[197] People have seen fire in the sky (the earthquake lights described above) during many quakes, and there are persuasive indicators of a smell like sulfur in a whole series of earthquake disasters. Von Humboldt reported that a strong sulfur odor was perceived in Cumana a half hour before the great disaster of December 14, 1797,[54i] and on the occasion of the earthquake of 1783 in Calabria "sulfur odor" was reported from various places. The same is true of various other quakes.[16] What remains enigmatic is where sulfur compounds are supposed to come from in an earthquake if there doesn't also happen to be volcanic activity. We can get closer to the riddle if we remember that the vernacular also speaks of sulfur odor when lightning strikes. What is being smelled as sulfur is obviously nitrogen oxides, which appear during electrical discharges and carry a peculiar, intense odor. This assumption is supported by the fact that, besides sulfur odor, von Humboldt speaks of flames that licked out of the ground but that burned no grass. Also, eyewitnesses have reported sulfur odor in connection with other observations of earthquake lights. Chlorine gases, which are liberated through electrolysis of groundwater, have also been taken into consideration as possible causes.

Earthquakes and Exodus

In the processes that accompanied the appearance of God on Mount Sinai it is possible to distinguish a whole series of typical earthquake phenomena without using too much imagination: Earthquake lightning, earthquake noises of different kinds, fog (in the form of a heavy cloud), and dust: "On the third day, when morning came, there were peals of thunder and flashes of lightning, a dense cloud on the mountain and a loud trumpet blast; the people in the camp were all terrified. Moses brought the people out from the camp to meet God, and they took their stand at the foot of the mountain. Mount Sinai was all smoking because the Lord had come down upon it in fire; the smoke went up like the smoke of a kiln; all the people were terrified and the sound of the trumpet grew ever louder. Whenever Moses spoke, God answered him in a peal of thunder."[198] The simultaneous appearance of earthquakes, thick clouds, lightning, and thunder, all in a desert region in which thunderstorms are exceedingly rare, is too unusual to be due to a coincidence. An earthquake would thus seem to be the cause of all the accompanying phenomena.

An astonishingly good description of an earthquake light is contained in the episode where God appears to Moses in a burning thorn bush and charges him with the mission of leading his people out of Egypt: ". . . the angel of the Lord appeared to him in the flame of a burning bush. Moses noticed that, although the bush was on fire, it was not being burnt up. . . ." The details mentioned clearly indicate that this light phenomenon was an electrostatic discharge—a Saint Elmo's fire like the one von Humboldt described as a precursor of the 1797 Cumana earthquake[54i] and like those observed in connection with many other quakes. This explains easily why the thorn bush did not burn. It also provides an enlightening explanation for why this electrostatic discharge was "burning" in a thorny bush and nowhere else: Electric discharges start at those places where the electric field, as it is building up, is at its most intense. Those are the highest elevations of the ground and its most pointed protuberances. A thorn-studded bush extending above the ground would concentrate a Saint Elmo's fire upon itself.

If we assume that in the burning-bush episode God, as he did later on Mount Sinai, spoke to Moses in a thunder, then we also have earthquake noise. What is most amazing in this scene, however, is that a serpent is brought into play. God commands Moses to throw his staff to the ground, and it turns into a snake; then He demands of the initially fearful Moses that he take the snake by the tail, and it turns again into a harmless staff. With this serpent-staff God gives Moses a magic tool with which he can conjure up the ten plagues on Egypt and part the waters of the Red Sea.

Precisely because Moses' snake appears in connection with other earthquake phenomena—a light and noises—it seems reasonable to associate it with the earthquake premonition of animals. But what would this have to do with the mission given to Moses? When God challenges Moses to seize the snake by the tail and to use it as a weapon against the pharaoh, it could mean that the superiority of Moses is to consist of his ability to foresee earthquake disasters in time.

Did the plagues that Moses wished down upon the Egyptians have anything to do with earthquakes? Superficially, there seems to be no connection, and no earthquake is mentioned. The water in the Nile becomes blood red, the fish die and the water becomes undrinkable, frogs overrun the land, swarms of flies appear, and diseases befall animals and people. Other plagues include thunder, hail, and fire from the sky, an invasion of locusts, a darkness that lasts three days, and finally the death of the first-born.

But if we take a second look at the trials of Egypt—a look consistent with this book's analyses of natural phenomena that precede an earth-quake, accompany it, or are a consequence of it—the impression changes considerably. The catastrophes summoned up by Moses' staff fit together like the pieces of a puzzle whose name is earthquake.

Not only have springs and rivers become reddish, yellowish, or whitish (depending on the makeup of the soil) as a consequence of the clay and soil particles set loose by earth motions, but this phe-nomenon has also been observed in shallow seawater. For example, during the Calabrian earthquake of June 11, 1783, the water of two seawater-fed moats around citadels turned yellow and all the fish in them surfaced as if stunned.[23] During the quake of 1348 in Villach, Carinthia, cracks in the form of a cross formed in the main square from which "blood" and then water issued forth. In Concepciòn, Chile, on February 20, 1835, women washing their laundry in the river before the great earthquake were surprised by a sudden appearance of muddy water, which in a short time rose from their ankles to their knees.[57] The Nile becomes red at flood time. An earthquake could also have colored it red. On top of that, the pressure waves generated by a quake, and earthquake illness (which is probably caused by electrical phenomena), could have led to the death of many fish. Several such reports about fish dying have been presented in this book.

Is it surprising that frogs should leave their moist element under the aforementioned conditions? According to Chinese reports, they are among the animals that show unusual behavior before an earth-quake.[21] The earthquake fear of frogs might provide a sensible ex-planation for why the pharaoh should have been intimidated by the great numbers of these harmless (in fact, tasty and welcome) amphibians. The frog invasion evidently was actually observed and interpreted as punishment from God.

The ensuing plague of flies as well as the diseases that befell humans and animals can easily be explained as consequences of an earthquake. Land turned into swamps by flood caused by earthquakes becomes the breeding ground for insects, and the quake's victims decomposing under rubble provide food for them and breeding places for illnesses at the same time. A brief report from the Calabrian earthquake of

1783 supports this conclusion: "Through the creation of so many swamps. . . , diseases of such scope were brought forth that the draining of the same had to be carried out with the greatest sacrifices of money, because the inhabitants were dying like flies. The odor, made unbearable because of the burning summer, which rose from the corpses of 30,000 people and numerous animals in every city and village also weakened the health of the survivors. Another 5,709 people died from the consequences of all this suffering."[16]

An additional plague visited upon Egypt could, at least in the case of a desert land with few thunderstorms, be interpreted as having been caused by an earthquake: "Moses stretched out his staff towards the sky, and the Lord sent thunder and hail, with fire flashing down to the ground. The Lord rained down hail on the land of Egypt, hail and fiery flashes through the hail. . . ." Did the people of Egypt see earthquake lightning and hear earthquake thunder? Was the hail caused by charged aerosol particles? The ensuing invasion of locusts may have been accidental, but after all that has become known about animal behavior in earthquakes, attributing its cause to an earthquake should not be ruled out. It has even been reported from China that the population density of locusts can change drastically as a consequence of an earthquake.[36]

The ninth plague of Egypt, a three-day-long profound darkness, may also be interpreted as an earthquake phenomenon. Numerous examples of earthquake fogs, some of which have heralded disasters and darkened the sun, have been described in this book. Just as numerous are the reports of dense dust clouds that lay over villages, cities, and countryside after a quake or during a series of quakes and sank only slowly to the ground.

Why doesn't the Old Testament mention earthquakes among the plagues of Egypt? That may be because a quake was thought to be the appearance of God Himself. On Mount Sinai God replies to Moses in a thunder and the earth quakes. (However, dialogs between Moses and God are numerous during the trials of Egypt.)

The tenth plague that befell Egypt—the death of the first-born—is probably the only one that cannot be linked to an earthquake, provided one disregards a possible reference to earthquake victims. But the very next miracle, accomplished with Moses' magic staff, is the dividing of the Red Sea. This contributes another piece to the puzzle. On their flight to the sea the people of Moses were already guided by a conspicuous sign in the sky: "And all the time the Lord went before them, by day a pillar of fire to give them light. . . ." Were the Jews following a glow in the sky such as now and then heralds an earthquake? In terms of a natural cause, the dramatic march through the Red Sea in the face of the receded waters would be possible only in connection with a strong earthquake: "Then Moses stretched out his hand over the sea and the Lord drove the sea away all night with a strong east wind and turned the sea-bed into dry land. The waters were torn apart, and the Israelites went through the sea on the dry ground, while the waters made a wall for them to right and to left." An uncommonly widespread receding of the sea and a following destructive flash flood are phenomena that are very often caused by earthquakes. In Moses' time the area of the sea that the Israelites crossed was called the Sea of Reeds, and we may thus assume that it was not especially deep. Shallowness is a good precondition for a perceptible effect of earthquake processes on water levels.

In order to shine more light on the scientific reasons behind the parting of the waters in the Red Sea, it would seem to make sense to search the earthquake literature for eyewitness reports of similar marine phenomena. One observation of a "sea parting" may be found in Giovanni Vivenzio's scientific inquiry into the Calabrian earthquake of 1783.[112,23] He tells of two peasants who, while working on a high bank above the Tyrrhenian Sea, observed that at the first tremor the sea suddenly became calm and then split into two parts in such a way that the sand of the bottom was exposed. How violent the water-level change caused by an earthquake can be is shown by an observation from Chile. A half hour after the earthquake of Concepción in 1835, the water in the Bay of Talcahuano receded so far from the shore that all ships in the bay were suddenly sitting aground, even those that had been able to enter the 11-meter (36-foot) deep bay easily. The wave that next flooded into this bay was so high that its crest was 6 meters (19 feet) above the high-water mark. The walls of water along which the Israelites marched could also have been a real, observed natural phenomenon.

The crews of several ships that were at sea during the 1783 Calabrian earthquake saw two giant waves, as high as a tall ship's mast, arising at a point near the city of Nicotera and rolling away in two different directions—one toward the coast and the other toward the open sea.[23] The strategic role that can be played by a sea receding because of an earthquake and by its destructive resurgence is reported elsewhere besides in Exodus. From antiquity comes the story of a similar fate that befell the army of Artabarus as it was besieging the city of Potidaea. When the sea suddenly receded from the coast and exposed dry ground on the weakly defended sea side of the city, Artabarus saw his chance and attacked from that side. The sea surged back and drowned many of his soldiers.[16]

The hypothesis that the Jews' advantage lay in Moses' anticipation of earthquakes, symbolized by his power over the snake-staff, makes it possible to think of a whole series of miraculous events in terms of natural phenomena: Moses, under the influence of the shock of a severe earthquake, was charged with the task of leading his people out of Egypt. He had the inspiration to observe the precursors of a coming quake and to select them as a signal for getting underway. He prepared carefully, recognized the signs, and took advantage of the general confusion generated in Egypt by a series of quakes to take flight. During the flight he ambushed the pursuing oppressors in an earthquake flood, which he had estimated correctly. Such a hypothesis tends to give weight to Biblical traditions without diminishing the fascination of a story that borders on the miraculous.

Later, at the behest of God, Moses uses his staff to make a spring gush forth from the rock at Mount Horeb. This episode may also indicate an earthquake. As already mentioned, springs often well up or disappear during quakes, and there are suggestions in the literature of antiquity that in the Egypt of Moses' time a body of knowledge about predicting earthquakes existed. The Greek physicist Anaxagoras, according to tradition, predicted earthquakes on the basis of his knowledge of secret Egyptian writings.[195,78]

Balaam's ass

If we accept the premise that in olden times an earthquake was associated with the appearnce of a divine figure, then we can find a detailed description of animal earthquake premonition in Chapter 22 of Numbers. The story concerns the reactions of Balaam's she-ass before an earthquake. The ass refuses to continue on its way, needs to lie down on the ground, and emits fearful sounds:

But God was angry because Balaam was going, and as he came riding on his ass, accompanied by his two servants, the angel of the Lord took his stand in the road to bar his way. When the ass saw the angel standing in the road with his sword drawn, she turned off the road into the fields, and Balaam beat the ass to bring her back on the road. Then the angel of the Lord stood where the road ran through a hollow, with fenced vineyards on either side. The ass saw the angel and, crushing herself against the wall, crushed Balaam's foot against it, and he beat her again. The angel of the Lord moved on further and stood in a narrow place where there was no room to turn either to right or left. When the ass saw the angel, she lay down under Balaam. At that Balaam lost his temper and beat the ass with his stick. The Lord then made the ass speak, and she said to Balaam, "What have I done? This is the third time you have beaten me." Balaam answered the ass, "You have been making a fool of me. If I had had a sword here, I should have killed you on the spot." But the ass answered, "Am I not still the ass which you have ridden all your life? Have I ever taken such a liberty with you before?" He said, "No." Then the Lord opened Balaam's eyes: he saw the angel of the Lord standing in the road with his sword drawn, and he bowed down and fell flat on his face before him. The angel said to him, "What do you mean by beating your ass three times like this? I came out to bar your way but you made straight for me, and three times your ass saw me and turned aside. If she had not turned aside, I should by now have killed you and spared her."

The ass's reactions are comparable to those mentioned in many earthquake reports by eyewitnesses. What is noteworthy in this description is the express suggestion that the ass recognized the mortal danger earlier than the man did. The description of three different patterns of reaction of the animal, each time in somewhat different surroundings, admits of the conclusion that the precursors preceded the earthquake at least by several minutes.

The Trojan Horse

The story of how Troy was tricked by a handful of Greeks hidden in the belly of a giant wooden horse left behind as a trophy and dragged within the walls of the city has become world famous. Children still learn about it in school and marvel at the bold cunning of the Greeks. Classicists, on the other hand, are not enamored of this tradition. The reason is not just that the episode sounds unbelievable from a strategic point of view; what is worse is that certain ancient sources either do not mention this horse at all or give an entirely different description of the reasons for the conquest of Troy.

Virgil attributes the fall of Troy to an earthquake supervised by Neptune, the sea god, and makes no mention of a horse. The sea god of the Greeks, Poseidon, does indeed figure in the conquest of Troy, even in the version with the wooden horse. It is interesting to note in this entire affair that Poseidon was also the god of earthquakes and that he was revered as that in the interior cities of Asia Minor in the form of a mythological horse figure. Thus the classics scholar L. A. Mackay is correct in pointing out that the contradictions in the story could be cleared up if we viewed the Trojan Horse not as an actual instrument of deception, but as a symbol for an earthquake.[199] The conquerors did not penetrate the city of Troy in the belly of a giant wooden horse, but went in over walls suddenly laid in ruins by an earthquake. This earthquake has been confirmed by excavations.

But why was the Greek earthquake god depicted as a horse? A possible answer lies in the fact that in many mythologies around the world earthquakes are said to be caused when giant mythical animals suddenly become active. When horses suddenly went mad without any apparent reason, and when the walls of Troy then collapsed after they had withstood every assault for years, superstitious warriors could easily have explained these events by saying that the earthquake god Poseidon had appeared on earth as a horse and broken down the walls for the benefit of the besieging forces.

Etruscan and Roman auguries

Unusual phenomena of nature were observed carefully in many ancient cultures because people believed that they were precursors of ominous events or announcements of the divine will and pleasure, which they were most anxious to appease. The pyramid texts of the ancient Egyptians mention rain, lightning, thunder, and earthquake—all relatively rare phenomena in the land of the Nile—as omens. The ancient Greeks, early in their cultural history, also took the less common events in nature seriously. Homer, in the songs of the Odyssey, interprets thunder, lightning, and rainbows as divine portents. When an eagle dropped a snake, the superstitious people would take notice. Moreover, specially employed seers would try to draw meaningful conclusions about the future from the flights of birds, the cries of fowl, and other natural observations. But the interpretation of uncommon or incidental natural events gradually lost its importance for the Greeks. Instead, they came to rely increasingly on learning the will of the gods through sacred ceremonies held in specially built oracle temples, such as the one in Delphi.

One people viewed its fate as being tied to nature in a way no other people did, and as with no other people the important decisions affecting the common good were made dependent on unusual phenomena. These were the Etruscans, that enigmatic, artistically gifted people that migrated into Etruria in Italy around 900 B.C. and was absorbed 400–500 years later by the spreading Roman state.

No one knows where the Etruscans came from. Some traces lead back to the pre-Indo-Germanic inhabitants of the eastern Mediterranean; others point to a kinship with Indo-Germanic Thracians. They loved life, and in their magnificent tombs they tried to send their dead on their journeys with some of life's beauty. Their society was organized as a loose federation of twelve of the larger cities and was governed by an aristocracy. The Etruscans' greatest intellectual achievement consisted of the interpretation of unusual natural phenomena, for which they were always on the lookout. Data were collected systematically and passed on to the soothsayer-priests, called *haruspices.* These priests had charge of ancient books (said to have been illustrated) that held the keys for deciphering these signs. These books also listed the measures that would have to be taken to deflect misfortune or to carry out an enterprise successfully.

The Etruscan art of reading auguries would probably have been lost forever if the ancient Romans had not been fascinated by it and if they had not built it into their own complicated procedures for dealing with their gods. Practical and organizationally gifted, but less creative scientifically, philosophically, and religiously, the Romans for centuries would not undertake any important affairs of state without first learning the will of the gods through the interpretation of signs. The whole population was enlisted in the gathering and processing of portents. Anyone could report an unusual phenomenon to government representatives, and such observations were among the prescribed duties of priests. It then became the obligation of the consuls to examine the incoming reports of observations for special signs (known officially as *prodigies*) and to judge their credibility.[200] The consuls presented the observations to the senate, and in rare cases they would also present the relevant witnesses. The senate then had to decide whether the identified prodigies had meaning for the fate of the nation or whether they were of no concern.

When the auguries were familiar, the senate would know from experience what measures to take. However, in the case of extraordinary or portentous prodigies, the priests would be summoned and asked to consult the ancient secret books. Once prodigies were declared to be important, they had to be "provided for," a measure that the Romans called the *procuration.* The purpose of this was to deflect or evade the wrath of the gods. Frequently the means to atone for prodigies were prayer festivals, animal offerings, or plays and theater productions lasting several days. In several cases, such as in 228 B.C. and in the year 16 of the same century after the defeat at Cannae, humans were sacrificed. Sometimes ritual purification ceremonies were prescribed in which, among other things, sacrificial animals wreathed in garlands were led around the city three times. Most of the unusual auguries that led to official actions have been reported by Roman writers for the years between 218 and 42 B.C., but they have been documented as far back as the fifth century B.C. At certain times (as in 193 B.C., when a series of earthquakes shook the land), prodigies piled up to such an extent that the people became tired of the never-ending atonements and the consuls became so preoccupied with judging the auguries that they could no longer attend to ordinary government business.[94]

Classical scholarship has always taken the Romans' prodigy business seriously, because many important political decisions in the Roman empire were influenced by the appearance of and the concern about mysterious signs. But the belief in such signs, and their interpretation, has never been regarded as anything but a religion. It has never been acknowledged that practical ulterior motives and serious study might have been the bases of the interpretation of prodigies, quite apart from the fact that they occasionally made possible skillful manipulation of the superstitious people. However, in searching the Roman literature for reports of earthquake precursors, I became aware that the collection and interpretation of auguries was originally intended to serve an exceedingly practical purpose: the early recognition of natural disasters, especially earthquakes. The extraordinary natural phenomena mentioned repeatedly in that literature as signs of impending danger are considered sure indicators of impending earthquakes in the popular opinion of other countries and cultures, as well as in the ancient traditions of the Chinese. A passage from Virgil's *Georgics* should stand as a representative example of the many reports of prodigies by Roman historians and writers. The *Georgics*, a collection of instructional poems about agriculture and nature, contain the following report about a series of natural events observed in connection with a wave of earthquakes that happened after the death of Caesar in 44 B.C.:

Nay, he [the sun] had pity for Rome, when, after Caesar sank from sight, he veiled his shining face in dusky gloom, and a godless age feared everlasting night. Yet in that hour Earth also, and Ocean's plains, and ill-boding dogs and ominous birds, gave their tokens. How oft we saw Aetna flood the Cyclopes' fields, when streams poured from her rent furnaces, and she whirled balls of flame and molten rocks! Germany heard the clash of arms through all the sky; the Alps rocked with unwonted terrors. A voice, too, was heard of many amid the silence of solemn groves—an awful voice; and spectres, pale in wondrous wise, were seen at evening twilight; and beasts—O portent, terrible!—spake as men. Rivers halt, earth gapes wide, in temples the ivory weeps in sorrow, and bronzes sweat. Eridanus, king of rivers, washed away in the swirl of his mad eddy whole forests, and all across the plains swept cattle and stalls alike. Yea, in that same hour, threatening filaments ceased not to show themselves in ominous entrails, or blood to flow from wells, or lofty cities to echo all the night with the howl of wolves. Never from a cloudless sky fell more lightnings; never so oft blazed fearful comets.[201]

In the context of the earthquakes that are unmistakably described here, complete with tremors, cleaving of ground, and volcanic eruptions, earthquake noise or ground noises can easily be recognized in the "clash of arms through all the sky" and the "awful voice" thundering through silent groves. The lightning bolts from a clear sky, the pale spectres in the evening twilight, and the many "fearful comets" can be identified rather clearly as earthquake lights. In the "blood" that flowed from wells we can recognize the muddy spring water that occasionally breaks through the ground. Even the earthquake fog that makes sunlight seem red is not omitted. The prominent formation of droplets on statues could be a consequence of electrostatic charging, which would facilitate the condensation of water.

It is highly interesting that in ancient Rome such natural events were regarded as evil omens. Reports of unusual animal behavior as portents of misfortune are particularly interesting. Among the "ill-boding dogs" and the beasts speaking as men we may readily imagine excited animals giving voice to their fears. By "ominous birds," the Romans meant the anomalous appearance of wild birds (such as eagle owls) in the city.

Even though most of the important precursors of disaster mentioned by Virgil and other Roman writers can be described as typical natural phenomena of the sort that announce an earthquake, and even though Pliny mentions excited birds and muddy springs as unmistakable earthquake precursors it cannot be said that this whole business of auguries played any prominent role in earthquake prediction. The attention of the Romans was concentrated too much on the fate of the nation, whose venturesome conquests and wars kept the citizens in suspense. The Roman rulers were far less interested in predicting earthquakes than in maintaining control over the vastly more dangerous and ever-present political maneuverings. They considered any means fair. Besides Etruscan auguries and viewing entrails, the Romans would also on occasion use the Greek methods of divination collected in the secret Sibylline books. They were not even averse to consulting the oracle at Delphi. The Romans seem to have been more interested in earthquakes as omens of political events than in the omens of the quakes.

In order to learn where knowledge about natural processes as har-bingers of disaster originated, we will have to pick up the trail of the

Etruscans, the spiritual fathers of such lore, and reconstruct their store of information from Roman sources. There is ample evidence that the otherwise practical Romans kept having difficulties with interpreting Etruscan omens, which, after all, had not grown out of the Romans' own tradition. Mention is made as early as the fifth century B.C. that Etruscan *haruspices* were consulted in interpreting important-seeming omens, and in 398 B.C. at the siege of the Etruscan city of Veii, the Romans were helpless without them. Because of this the senate decided to send young men from prominent families to Etruscan cities so that they might become thoroughly familiar with the secret knowledge of the diviners who worked there. At the same time, the settlement of Etruscan priests in Rome was encouraged. The fact that several Romans wrote books about Etruscan lore shows the extraordinary interest of the Roman government. With patient labors, the highest-ranking priests of Rome recorded all important events precisely so that future happenings could be compared with precedents.[109] This approach made the procedures of interpreting omens easier for them. Interpretation could involve—in accordance with Etruscan custom—the viewing of animal sacrifices or observations of flights of birds. The methods used in interpreting the omens, and details about the deeper meaning of unusual portents, remained barred to the general public. The people knew only the observed variations from the normal, and they were enlisted in attempts to avert political disasters and to placate the gods. The histories of Livy, Obsequens, Cicero, and Tacitus contain numerous reports about this. The original secret writings about the interpretation of omens by the Romans (not to mention the Etruscans) have all been lost, but information from the historians about how reports of unusual events in nature were handled by the Roman senate and its soothsayer-priests has been preserved. This information is sufficient to strengthen the hypothesis that the Etruscans may have developed systematic augury for earthquake prediction—a purpose to which it can be applied more meaningfully than to political divination.

The one prominent indication that the Etruscans originally meant the observation and interpretation of unusual phenomena to be used in earthquake prediction is the fact that many of the signs the Romans considered most important—the *prodigies*—seem downright tailored for earthquakes, especially if we compare them with precursors known to the Chinese.

It cannot be said of the Romans that they had an excessive respect for snakes. They even liked to keep adders as pets. Even so, the unusual appearance of snakes is mentioned as an ominous sign at least twenty times in Roman literature.[200] It seems certain that snakes in unusual places or in greater than usual numbers were associated with unique circumstances which were made meaningful by many other precursors.[94] Appearances of two snakes are usually mentioned in connection with prodigies, and Livy[202a] and Obsequens[203a] report prodigies involving several snakes.

The appearance of wolves in the cities was considered by the Romans to be an omen of a special kind and of national importance. Between 458 and 16 B.C. at least sixteen cases were reported of individual wolves losing their fear of man and going into such cities as Rome, Capua, and Formia, or into military camps. The sighting of an eagle owl in Rome was recognized as a prodigy in at least fourteen cases. About ten cases of a swarm of bees alighting in a city, in a camp, or on the field standard of a legion were reported, and these were considered serious omens. The invasion of sacred temples by vultures, falcons, swans, or swarms of wasps counted among the highly esteemed omens. Animals "talking danger" or simply "talking" are listed as serious prodigies in at least sixteen cases. Classicists generally regard these reports as imaginative inventions, but it seems to make sense to see in these reports, in the context of other precursors, animals expressing fear with their own voices. These reports frequently mention dogs, cattle, chickens, and smaller livestock, and easily suggest the loud clamor that animals often make before earthquakes. A dramatic proof of the significance ascribed to the behavior of these animals is that during the flowering of the Roman republic conclusions about the future were drawn from the behavior of specially kept sacred chickens.

Also important as precursors were unusual light phenomena in the sky. A glowing of the sky is mentioned as a prodigy at least sixteen times, fireballs or comets more than a dozen times, and clefts or strips in the sky several times.[200] The lightning bolts from a clear sky mentioned in this group of ominous signs could mean earthquake lights. They are expressly mentioned by Cicero[202b] and other writers.[204,205] Observations of a "sun" at night are reported for the years 166, 163, 134, and 113 B.C. In 42 B.C. it is said to have become so bright at night that people in Rome arose to begin their daily work.[203b] There were bright nights in 204 B.C., and in 206 and 197 B.C. the same phenomenon was observed in other cities of the empire, among them Fregellae and Frusino.

The sounds of unknown origin and the thunder under a clear sky that were valued as prodigies could have been earthquake noises, which would also apply to "roaring from the sky"[203c] and the above-mentioned sound of arms clashing. The Romans certainly would have been able to distinguish the unusual noises that they regarded as important omens from the growling of thunder during thunderstorms.

Even the atmospheric signs that could be expected as a consequence of fog phenomena or suspended materials in the air are among the ominous signs recognized by the Roman government. In 203 B.C. a ring around the sun was recognized as a prodigy in Frusino; in 44 B.C. such a ring is reported to have worried the Romans. (As mentioned above, a Chilean proverb still current today says that a ring around the sun precedes an earthquake.) In 147 B.C. two rings around the sun, one red and one white, were observed in Lanuvium.[203d] The sun appeared blood-red at Reate in 212 B.C.[202c] In Privernum, in 200 B.C. and in 44 B.C., only dim sunlight reached the ground for months on end. (This was also the case in the earthquake year 1783.[23]) The phenomenon of two satellite suns is reported for the years 42, 44, 103, 118, 122, and 174 B.C. Livy describes this event together with further atmospheric signs: ". . . a rainbow by day in a clear sky was seen extending over the temple of Saturn in the Forum Romanum, and three suns shone at once, and that same night numerous firebrands glided through the sky. . . ."[202d] Rings around the sun and satellite suns are well-known phenomena today. The rings, which are formed by refraction or reflection of sunlight in ice crystals in the atmosphere, usually measure 22°–42° in radius. Larger crystal wafers or crystal stars produce the satellite suns, which often glow quite brightly and even throw shadows. These large crystals also produce the circumzenithal arc, a rainbowlike multicolored circle about the zenith which Livy describes as a stretched-out arc. Colored rings around the sun are produced by the bending of light in tiny droplets. As many as four color sequences can sometimes be made out. The Roman chroniclers evidently described these atmospheric phenomena accurately, without exaggeration. The reason these phenomena became the most significant omens is probably that they were rarely seen in the area around Rome.

Springs and creeks that become cloudy for unknown reasons, which according to popular reports and Chinese observations can indicate a coming earthquake, are also among the omens that were taken seriously in ancient Rome. It is said, for example, that milky creeks bubbled up from the ground near Tarquinii in 103 B.C. In 207 B.C. the springs of Caere turned bloody red, and so did the ones near Manziana in 214. There are similar reports for the years 223, 213, and 207 B.C. from Picernum, Amiternum, Minturnae, and even Rome.[203e]

It is not only the astonishingly high number of earthquake precursors among the prodigies that suggests conscious, purposeful earthquake prediction by the Roman soothsayer priests. They also took ominous signs much more seriously when they appeared in larger numbers. Sometimes unusual events would qualify as prodigies only after they had been observed several times. (Reports of earthquake precursors coming into Chinese earthquake bureaus are subjected to the same statistical treatment. Only if many similar reports have been logged do they enter into decision making.) But the mcst remarkable thing is that educated Romans knew with certainty that at least some of these prodigies were connected with the danger of earthquakes.

Everything suggests that the Romans had an earthquake warning system based on omens recognized by observers among the people, passed on to the offices of the consuls, and evaluated by the soothsayers. The results were then passed on to the senate for a final decision on any preventive measures. The system seems to have been organized along the same lines as today's earthquake watch in China, whose effectiveness has been well proved. There is only one catch: No earthquakes were predicted that way in ancient Rome. Only the will of the gods was divined, so that their wrath might be deflected by appropriate actions.

Even so, the way the indicators come together points too persuasively at an earthquake warning system to be dismissed lightly. Could it be that the auguries were originally developed by the Etruscans for the purpose of predicting natural disasters and were only alienated from their intended purpose by the Romans, who may have misunderstood them? Is it possible that the highly political Romans forced the adaptation of the auguries to the political realm, which they found far more interesting? (They even valued earthquakes themselves as omens for affairs of state.) Another possibility that ought not to be ignored is that the anointed priests knew from their secret books precisely what the real situation was, but faked religious activities to avoid causing general panic or being exposed to public criticisms if their predictions were to fail.

Whether the Romans adapted the Etruscan auguries or whether they disguised them for political or psychological reasons, we should be able to tell from the measures taken in response to the various omens whether they could protect the citizens in case of an earthquake. What measures did the Roman senate take upon reports of those ominous signs that we now recognize as well-known harbingers of earthquakes? What, for example, happened when news was received of "talking animals" (which we, of course, should not accept literally but metaphorically as describing excited animals making a lot of noise)? The decision that the senate would then make is astonishing indeed:

Pliny wrote that pursuant to such a report the senate would hold its sessions outdoors.[8h,200] Also remarkable are the kinds of atonements that were prescribed when wolves entered the city of Rome or when eagle owls or "fire birds" (possibly a species of owl) were seen during the day. In such cases, symbolic purifications of the city (lustrations) were carried out. The first such ceremony that is known of, held in 458 B.C., was supposed to have atoned for the advance of wolves toward the Capitol.[202e] Did the lustration have something to do with precautions to protect the people from earthquakes? According to reports of Roman historians, a lustration consisted of citizens assembling and walking three times around the city leading garlanded sacrificial animals. After that, the animals were slaughtered amid prayer and dedicated to the gods.[202f] This certainly could have been a religious ceremony, but it can be said without fear of contradiction that while this long outdoor ceremony was going on, hardly anyone could have been hurt in case of an earthquake. What is also noteworthy is that on any day when there was lightning or thunder, no popular assemblies were permitted. Did memories of ground noises and earthquake lightning underlie this regulation? When in 179 B.C. the busts of the gods in the temples were displaced during an earthquake, it was interpreted as an evil omen and public games lasting 10 days were organized.[202g] Could it be that the tremor was considered a prequake, and that the authorities tried to lure people from their dangerous houses into the open arena?

The kinds of accepted omens and the procedures by which they were atoned for suggest that the Etruscan auguries were originally intended for early recognition of natural disasters such as earthquakes and that suitable precautions were taken. If the people were kept in the dark about the real reasons behind such events, that may have been done out of prudence. Wouldn't most people, if they were persuaded that an earthquake was approaching, try to rescue their property from their endangered houses and thus risk their lives? Wouldn't failures in earthquake prediction shake the confidence of the citizens in the art of prediction and thus seriously undermine the effectiveness of a warning system? However, people distracted by the belief that they were being threatened by the wrath of the gods were psychologically prepared for disaster, and at the same time deceived so skillfully that they would not commit any ill-considered or selfish acts.

Perhaps the Romans no longer understood the full meaning of the Etruscan auguries and for that reason had constant problems with this art. Etruscan priests had to be called in constantly to straighten them out. It would not have been the first time that a more profound meaning has been found in religious customs; we need only consider the prohibition of pork for Moslems or the fasting of Christians. But if this hypothesis suggesting a larger purpose for the omens should turn out to be true, then we will have to rethink some of our conceptions about the Romans' religion. After all, the omens announcing disaster refer not only to earthquakes, but to other misfortunes as well. But even these prodigies were often followed by very sensible acts of atonement. For example, the feast of the gods was prescribed in Rome in times of epidemics. It was held for the first time in 399 B.C., when the priests were ordered to consult their secret books during an epidemic. Other such feasts were held during pestilences and epidemics in 392, 364, 348, and 327 B.C.[200] In the space of 8 days, meals were presented to several images of gods. All doors in the city had to be left open. Eating was permitted only in the forecourts, where strangers were fed as if they were guests.[202h] Wouldn't physicians, in the absence of suitable vaccines, be likely to prescribe light and air to both houses and people and to order that those afflicted build up their strength with food?

13

Needless Deaths and a Lost Opportunity

The earthquake of May 6, 1976, struck the people of Friuli out of a clear blue sky. The inhabitants had at times felt slight tremors, and they knew from their history lessons that centuries before there had occasionally been severe earthquakes, but no one even remotely thought that the danger might be acute. The unawareness of the population, and of administrative bodies, is best shown by the fact that whole rows of the most modern buildings collapsed like houses of cards. No one had thought it worth the trouble to build them earthquakeproof. In Japan or Chile an earthquake of intensity 6.5 would have caused hardly any serious damage.

Should the Friuli earthquake have been so unexpected? After the catastrophe, I picked through ancient writings from northeastern Friuli in search of earthquake reports, and I was speechless. There were records of twenty earthquakes strong enough to damage houses, going back to the year 1116. Five of them were powerful enough to collapse many buildings and to cause some serious devastation. Even though it may be hard to gauge the extent of damage in one or another of these quakes precisely, the following list seems fairly reliable: 1116, 1223, 1278 (severe), 1279, 1348 (severe), 1364, 1389, 1472 (severe), 1511, 1690 (severe), 1692, 1700, 1788 (severe), 1790, 1841, 1855, 1876, 1881, 1928, 1976 (severe), 1976.

During the oldest of these quakes that could be called catastrophic, the one of 1278, many houses in Friuli collapsed, according to the chronicles. The quake of 1348 may have been the most severe of all in that region. It destroyed the city of Villach in nearby Carinthia and brought the Villach Alp crashing down. The quake of 1472 also caused serious damage to many houses. The quake of 1690 brought severe devastation to Carinthia. There was also widespread destruction from an earthquake in 1788; about forty houses collapsed in the village of Tomezzo alone.

The average interval among these twenty quakes is 43.26 years, but the time between 1976 and the last previous earthquake was 48 years. Using a simple statistical calculation which assumes the random recurrence of earthquakes, one finds that by 1976 there was a 67.7-percent probability of an earthquake that could damage buildings. If one considers only the five catastrophic earthquakes, one comes up with an average interval of 127.5 years. By 1976, however, 188 years had elapsed since the last severe earthquake, the one in 1788. Thus a catastrophic earthquake was due with a 77-percent probability, and it finally came. The inhabitants of Friuli were sitting on a powderkeg and did not know it. If the geophysicists had shown more interest in earthquake history, they would have noticed an interesting detail: At least three of the reported severe quakes (are the chronicles complete?) were not isolated events but were followed within two years by another quake strong enough to be felt: 1223, 1278 (severe), 1279; 1511, 1690 (severe), 1692; 1700, 1788 (severe), 1790. This pairing of a severe earthquake with one that follows so quickly forces itself to our attention because otherwise the intervals between quakes are 43.26 years.

The earthquake of 1976, like the one of 1278, was preceded by half a century of quiet. But the quake of 1278 had been followed $9 1/2$ months later by a further strong tremor. Would there be a second big quake after the one of 1976? When it was followed 4 months later (on September 15) by a quake of magnitude 6.1, with further death and destruction, the experts were completely baffled. The appearance of such a strong satellite earthquake was depicted as altogether atypical.

These simple examinations presented here ought to prove that it should have been easy for an expert to assign a high earthquake risk to the Friuli region. With that knowledge in hand, it would at least have been possible to establish serious guidelines for earthquake-proof construction and to prepare the people psychologically for the coming shock. More of an initiative could not have been expected in a Western country in 1976. If such disasters had loomed over a Chinese province, the preparations would have been considerably different. At the very least, instruments would have stood ready to register the slightest land deformations and changes in the magnetic fields, to afford some rough clues to the approaching earthquake. But the most important weapon against the violence of nature would have been the endangered people themselves. Well instructed about the various kinds of earthquake precursors they could expect, they would have kept track of the water level in wells and the colors of springs by simple means, or they would have kept a critical eye on their animals.

Would they have had the chance to recognize the impending earthquake in time? They would have had a very real chance without taking even the slightest personal initiative. All that would have been necessary was that they would have had to be enlightened about the nature of the earthquake precursors. (The time interval between serious earthquakes in Friuli was too great to allow the growth of a living native earthquake folklore.) The strange events of the last hours before the earthquake would then certainly have been recognized as the signs of a coming disaster: About 2 hours before the May 6 quake, many dead fish were found drifting on the surface of a pond near Maiano, a village near the epicenter which suffered much destruction. When the cause of the massive dying of fish was sought, it was found that the water had become warm. The incident is said to have been reported to the police, but no one knew what to do with the information or how to explain the incident. The details of this incident, which was much talked about after the disaster, were confirmed for me by G. Matteucig of the University of Naples. Reliable persons who at my request checked into this event at its site were able to confirm this rather unmistakable sign of a coming earthquake. Springs whose waters kept getting warmer as the earthquake approached were not isolated events, according to statements by people living at the epicenter. There were also many reports of spring water becoming suddenly murky. According to information obtained by Matteucig, which was also published in the local paper, *Messagero Veneto,* the water of a spring that feeds directly into a restaurant in Loch di Pulfero became cloudy two to three days before the earthquake.[28] Not until several days after the quake did the spring regain its usual clarity. In the Yugoslavian village of Zaga, near the Friuli border, well water also turned cloudy about 2 hours before the earthquake.

Particularly remarkable was the intensity of a similar phenomenon that the citizens of the small Friuli town of Moggio like to tell in great detail. There is a paper mill in town with its own electric power generating station. On May 6, the day of the earthquake, in perfectly fine weather, the turbines of the generating station were suddenly flooded with thick, muddy water. According to eyewitness reports, the dirty water, together with gravel and sand, welled up out of a nearby spring that fed the power plant. The mud made extensive cleaning operations necessary. The phenomenon is said to have recurred on the day of the second big quake, September 15.

Two or three days before the main quake the people living along the river Ledra, which rises in Gemona near the epicenter, noticed vapors rising from the river, something they had never seen before.

Some time before the quake two students in the cellar of a house in Gemona noticed low-frequency sounds coming from beneath the ground.[206] They appreciated the meaning of this no more than did the many people who shortly before the earthquake were confronted by the inexplicable behavior of their animals. In addition, many witnesses are unanimous about the oppressive heat on May 6, when the thermometer climbed to 30°C (86°F). Also, a strange pink glow lying over the mountains at sunset before the earthquake is mentioned now and then.

With all these prominent earthquake precursors, it is no exaggeration to say that the Chinese system of earthquake prediction would very probably have worked in Friuli if it had been applied. Even if no earthquake watch had been organized, many people could have saved themselves if they had been able to interpret the signs correctly.

14

The Response of Science

Antipathy toward the new hypothesis

What sort of reception would be accorded a modern scientist who collected reports of abnormal animal behavior before an earthquake, tried to interpret them, and then offered his findings to the scientific audience? Such an endeavor might hold up a mirror to attitudes that prevail within expert circles, and might give a clue to the reasons why popular reports about earthquake precursors have been rejected until now.

After the earthquake in Friuli, while looking hard for geophysical causes for the earthquake fear of animals, I happened upon the idea of charged suspended particles and decided that they offered a sensible explanation for some of the manifestations of this mysterious phenomenon. I was sure that I would have to pass on this insight in order to stimulate intelligent experiments by earthquake researchers. There was no personal ambition whatsoever involved in this work. On the contrary: Since I knew the prejudices that many scientists hold against colleagues who busy themselves with questionable natural phenomena, I was a little uneasy to see my name connected with the frequently ridiculed earthquake premonition of animals. But my personal confrontation with the tragedy of an earthquake left me no choice.

I wrote a brief work in which the most important of the mysterious earthquake precursors from Friuli were collected in keyword form and in which I described the chain of proof that had led me to the charged suspended particles. Besides an allusion to similar descriptions of abnormal animal behavior in old documents out of China, I included a summary of the most important additional arguments that speak for electrostatic earthquake precursors: reports of mysterious fogs and earthquake lights, old experiments with electrometers, and theories about atmospheric earthquake precursors that reach back into antiquity. Without offering a mechanism for the liberation of charges, I suggested the piezoelectric effect as a possible geophysical cause.

Only scientifically oriented periodicals that addressed a broad, non-specialized readership and that had policies allowing socially relevant or controversial topics could be considered for publication. One German periodical that seemed to meet these criteria rejected the manuscript without giving any objective reasons. I translated the work and handed it in to an American periodical that I assumed would be receptive to reports about earthquake precursors because of the impending earthquake in California.

In the meantime I wrote to Peter Molnar of the Massachusetts Institute of Technology, who had been on the American delegation to Liaoning. I asked him for some information about detailed documentations of the use of animal observations for predicting earthquakes in China, and explained the reason for my interest. In his reply he encouraged me to write down the observations from Friuli, and I sent him the paper I had already submitted. On the basis of that paper I was invited to lecture at the Department of Earth and Planetary Sciences at MIT, at the Lamont-Doherty Geological Observatory of Columbia University in New York, and at the Earthquake Research Center of the U.S. Geological Survey in Menlo Park, California. Since I had some obligations in the United States anyway and since I was very much interested in discussing this unusual subject with earthquake experts, I accepted.

Meanwhile, the American journal rejected my paper. As usual, it sent along the comments of the anonymous reviewers. The main criticism—which I accepted gladly— was that the arguments I adduced could not prove the connection I suggested between charged aerosol particles and abnormal animal behavior before earthquakes. Aside from that, I was supposed to have reproduced interviews with the peasants in transcript form, discussed in detail all the earthquake precursors that might be relevant as signals for the animals, and worked out precisely the geological preconditions for the liberation of electrostatic charges (which, incidentally, is still in doubt). All that, if at all possible, in less than the eight typewritten pages I had submitted. One reviewer, in support of his arguments, added the comment of a colleague of his whom he described as an "expert on earthquake behavior of animals." This colleague thought he could see by the relatively low number of quotations from literature that I was not familiar with the area of animal behavior. It is still a mystery to me who that person was. I maintain that there is no such expert in the whole Western world today. Because of the dearth of modern scientific studies, someone could have designated himself an expert in animal behavior before earthquakes only if he knew a great many historical reports about this phenomenon, if at all. Apart from an unofficial list of 14 anecdotes about abnormal animal behavior before earthquakes being passed around among seismologists,[13] the first serious attempt to collect such reports from all over the world was not carried out until the conference about this phenomenon in Menlo Park, California, in September 1976. That compendium[114] brought the number of independent reports to 33. (For two of these—Friuli 1976 and Liguria 1887—my unpublished work was cited as the literature source.) The present book, with its collection of 78 reports, offers the most extensive compilation thus far.

I rewrote the rejected work for an international periodical, published in London, that had been recommended to me by a well-meaning American earthquake researcher. In the meantime I had started on my lecture trip to the three well-known American earthquake research centers, and I found the information collected on this trip remarkably useful. The newness of the idea of charged suspended particles and the fact that these particles seemed to explain a whole series of enigmatic phenomena were not the only reasons given for the positive reception of my ideas. There was also a remarkable coincidence: At about the same time that my work was being discussed, a sensational article about the general effect of small airborne ions on living organisms was published.[130] As has already been explained, there were differing opinions about the possible mechanisms for liberating charges before earthquakes; however, there was near unanimity that the promising idea of charged suspended particles should be pursued with scientific measurements.

While all this was taking place, the British periodical rejected the article. One reviewer's comments were sent along. His fundamental reservation about the hypothesis was that charged suspended particles did not, in his opinion, address the survival instincts of animals. The hypothesis could only be accepted if experiments actually showed that aerosol particles were set free by rock under pressure and that they were the unmistakable cause of panic reactions by animals. Passing over my similar and even more ambitious suggestions for experiments, he suggested to me that I study the behavior of mice next to breaking rock as a way of buttressing my thesis before publication could be considered. (The critic did not know that experiments of this sort had already been done.[115]) This reviewer also thought that referring to historical reports of mysterious fogs before earthquakes would be pointless unless reliable statistical proofs could be provided at the same time, and he concluded that the paper had nothing to do with science. Thus, my attempt to preserve potentially valuable earthquake observations by publishing them in a scientific periodical was a failure in the West almost two years after the Chinese had predicted the earthquake of Haicheng by using phenomena that were to some extent still controversial.

The editor of the last periodical, in view of the role played by animal observations in Chinese earthquake predictions, generously left me the opportunity to submit a compromise report about the earthquake signs observed in Friuli. But there was no longer any urgency to do that, since the most relevant details had meanwhile been discussed at the Menlo Park conference.

From the strictly scientific point of view, the reviewers of my paper cannot be faulted. It is their job to protect busy researchers from a flood of incompetent and irrelevant work by being sternly critical. They saw in the author of the article merely one of many researchers who want to prove themselves through scientific work and whose investigations must be put under the magnifying glass.

Still, anyone who had ever experienced an earthquake would find it difficult to understand their attitude. Even if we no longer have earthquake scientists going around and inquiring about unusual incidents and observations before earthquakes, as they used to do in the eighteenth and nineteenth centuries, we should not kill private initiative that generates suggestions for appropriate experiments by making impossible demands. How can an earthquake researcher (probably tax-supported) be expected to tell the victim of an earthquake that his accidental discovery may be very important, but if it is to be passed on he will have to carry out experiments and studies for which even a well-equipped scientific team would need a great deal of time and energy?

These experiences have exposed the mechanism science uses to reject accidentally made earthquake observations. The standards for scientific work are simply too high to allow individuals to make convincing starts in an interdisciplinary field where little-understood geophysical, biological, and psychological events interact. Even qualified researchers have until now been unable to approach likely organizations for support for work in such a suspect subject as the earthquake premonition of animals. As a result, all possible semiscientific insights and observations of this phenomenon which could have stimulated serious studies have been mercilessly eliminated. All that was left was anecdotes in local newspapers. Serious attempts at tracking down scientific connections were condemned to failure from the outset. My inquiry into the connections between charged particles and the earth-quake fear of animals gained access to professional circles—despite rejections by journal referees[207]—only because it coincided with the earthquake predictions in China, which are not yet understood by Western experts. Until then a private initiative of this kind had no chance whatsoever. Even today, if the local press does not through sheer chance report on the precursors of an earthquake, then valuable data about them are condemned to be rejected and forgotten. One argument often quoted in professional circles to disprove the existence of precursors—the comparative rarity of reports—thus weakens itself.

Without the disordered battle lines, without a sense of injustice, without challenge, without defeats perceived as unfair, this book would never have been written. The wisdom of Heraclitus that "struggle is the father of all things" was fortunately proved true in this inquiry. But how many others have failed in similar situations? How many amateur observers have been compelled to believe resignedly, after futile, well-meaning attempts to pass on their earthquake experience, that nobody is really interested in it, that it has become the privilege of scientists to make observations?

New tasks for scientists and amateurs

The idea of the Greek natural scientists of 2,500 years ago that earth-quakes spill over into the area of meteorology has been revived in a certain respect by this inquiry. Research on particles suspended in air, their composition, their charge, and their effects on living organisms has thus far been exclusively a division of meteorology. With the exception of some very old and simple experiments in which the emission of charged suspended particles was detected with electro-meters in the course of a series of aftershocks, seismologists have never been interested in such phenomena. Now they can look forward to a completely new area of knowledge which has the potential of giving scientific reality to many previously mysterious phenomena. The meteorologists have supplied the basis. Sensitive instruments for measuring suspended particles and their charges are available.[208] It is merely necessary to use them for the examination of ground air layers with enough skill to keep the interfering influence of weather and environmental pollution under control.

What would be the specifications for measuring these physical phe-nomena? Under suitable geological conditions the subsurface is sup-posed to emit electrostatically charged suspended particles before a quake. Special attention should be paid to positive small ions in the ground layer of air; they might be the ones that cause the serotonin excitation syndrome in animals. Other phenomena to be expected are a change in the atmospheric electrical fields above the epicenter of the earthquake, a change in the vertical atmospheric ion streams, an increase in long-wave electromagnetic radiation, the appearance of electrical earth currents, and changes of potential in water. Statistically evaluated animal observations (such as have been done in the open habitat at Stanford University) are in principle well-suited to improving the understanding of abnormal animal behavior before earthquakes, but the observation procedure is too laborious and would have to be run continuously. There are much simpler alternatives, such as putting a microphone in a beehive or electrically measuring the weight on the roosting bars in a birdcage. The automatically recorded electrical signals from such setups would be direct clues to the nervousness and excitement of the animals. Many other experiments suggest themselves. How, for example, do experimental animals behave when current pulses are sent through the ground beneath their feet? Is it possible to stimulate earthquake panic in them artificially?

One of the most significant Chinese contributions to the prediction of earthquakes was the creation of thousands of amateur groups, which made it possible to search a huge area for unusual phenomena with a limited financial investment. The composition of these amateur groups and their interlocking with one another have been deftly organized.[2] The backbone of the system are the teams of technically trained persons who service sensitive seismological and geophysical instruments and who keep records of their observations, besides working at their regular jobs. These teams take on minor research tasks at times, and now and then they work up the courage to make earthquake predictions. They are under the direct guidance of experts. The intermediate groups consist of amateurs without special training who often build their own simple instruments and who, in a constant exchange of experiences with neighboring teams, build up a measure of self-reliance. The basic groups consist of teams of two or more persons who watch over the condition of water in wells or observe the animals in their production communes, and are prepared to report such occasional earthquake precursors as ground noises or light phenomena. Generally, the members of an observation group attend the same school or work in the same factory or agricultural enterprise. This communality has a positive psychological effect on their ability to persevere.

If such a system of amateur groups could be introduced into the earthquake-prone regions of Western countries, we could reasonably expect that valuable information about controversial earthquake signs could be collected considerably faster than now. Besides that, these groups could, as they do in China, spread vital information among the people about safety measures to be taken in case of an earthquake. Unfortunately, the all-important scientific-technical guidance of earthquake-research centers would probably not be available to such amateur groups in the near future. Still, amateur groups could make interesting contributions. The sequence of events in past earthquakes could be reconstructed as completely as possible through careful study of local traditions so the earthquake risk could be estimated. Older observations of mysterious earthquake signals from animals or springs could be gathered, and these could provide helpful hints for setting up effective measuring stations and about the phenomena that might be expected. If the earthquake danger in an area is great enough, an attempt could be made to conduct a more thorough geophysical examination that might identify the long-term earthquake precursors for that area. It would pay to begin preparing observation points for the collection of short-term earthquake precursors. Examination of water in springs and electrical measurements in the ground could be carried out with very simple means. Interesting data about abnormal animal behavior could be acquired without much effort from existing sources—the number of eggs laid daily in a chicken farm, the milk production of a large dairy, and the daily catch of a fishing village could all render valuable insights. Perhaps alert middle-school children could, as von Humboldt did in Venezuela once, observe the deflections of simple electrometers.

In support of popular wisdom

Modern research works very effectively and with deliberate aim on almost any imaginable scientific problem. Scientific progress seems able to offer us everything except the knowledge that takes centuries to acquire. Such knowledge either relies on very rare concatenations of coincidences or can only be accumulated by successive generations.

Ancient, unexplored discoveries still offer to the scientific detective a fertile field for research and speculation. This is true of the supplementary earthquake knowledge possessed by some peoples. For example, who would have imagined that the much-admired Inca structures, built of interlocking stones fitted together without gaps or mortar, had evolved as an effective countermeasure against the destructive Andean earthquakes? And who would think it possible that severe earthquakes eventually improve the fertility of the soil? South American Indians believed this[54b] and greeted earth tremors with festive dancing. Old reports from Venezuela[54a] and from Italy suggest the same thing. In Italy, unusually vigorous plant growth has not only been documented for the earthquake year 1808, but has been confirmed in historical reports for several earthquake events of previous centuries.[14,150] Research might lead into a dead-end street, but it also might show that airborne ions inhibit the proliferation of plant pests, as has been observed on bacteria and mushrooms in laboratory experiments.

Observations of nature derived from the vernacular, or reports from other epochs which are in essence based on such reports, could reflect genuine interconnections—especially if they crop up again and again in similar form in different places and times. To ignore them without either contradicting or confirming them is irresponsible in the case of a phenomenon as destructive as an earthquake. This book cannot claim to satisfy the scientific demands that are made of fundamental hypotheses nowadays, because it frequently relies on single observations by scientifically untrained persons, observations whose statistical weight is hard to estimate. But it should make it more difficult for scientists to continue to depict earthquake precursors as products of someone's fertile imagination unless they have proof to the contrary. And some untutored observer somewhere in the world will recognize the value of an earthquake observation made by chance and will preserve it for humanity.

Reactions, developments, and new arguments

The British journal *Nature* finally published a paper of mine about the hypothesis developed in this book.[213] Numerous newspapers then took up the topic of unexplained earthquake precursors. This resulted in interesting discussions, new points of view, and topical suggestions. The most remarkable piece of information was published by Stuart A. Hoenig of the University of Arizona as a letter to the editor in *Nature*. He reported that rocks subjected to high pressures in his laboratory did, in fact, emit electrically charged particles before bursting.[214] Hoenig considered this the first experimental proof of the existence of electrostatic earthquake precursors, which I had deduced from the various popular earthquake traditions. Many scientists who wrote to me about the earthquake hypothesis said they agreed, and in the two years after the paper's publication I became aware of no professional or public attacks. However, some readers have let me know that they consider other explanations for the earthquake foreboding of animals more likely. One suggested the animals' sensitivity to sound, another their perception of changes in the magnetic field—possibilities I have also taken into consideration. I know from some of my scientific contacts that several earthquake experts are now trying very hard to get a grip on the predicted electrostatic earthquake precursors experimentally. I seem to have reached my goal of presenting a persuasive theory and in this way moving the earthquake profession to seriously address the precursors.

In the spring of 1976, after the earthquake in Friuli, when I began to collect arguments for the proposition that the precursors were real, science had an attitude of total rejection. Information of this kind was received with amusement. It was interesting to see the situation change gradually. The Stanford Research Institute in Menlo Park, California, under contract to the U.S. Geological Survey (which has been charged with earthquake prediction in the United States), has established a network of animal observers along the San Andreas fault. Leon Otis and William Kautz are in charge of the network. A few hundred selected collaborators are in touch with a central office by way of a constantly manned telephone line, and they pass on precise information using a cleverly devised code system. The observers are keeping an eye on about seventy animal species as part of "Project Earthquake Watch" to see whether these animals can help predict earthquakes.[215]

Similar projects have been initiated in Japan. The Fisheries Experimental Station in Tokyo has begun a systematic watch of catfish, which have played a big role in Japan's earthquake tradition. The experimental team under the direction of Shojiro Nakamura discovered that the ten catfish observed between December 1977 and July 1978 announced 17 out of 20 earthquakes (of a force greater than 1 on the seven-point Japanese scale) by their unusual behavior. Before a severe quake in January 1978, which claimed many victims and destroyed several houses, they circled the basin as many as 60 times a night, whereas normally they would tour it only 5 or 6 times.[216] Also, the general secretary of the Higashijama Park in Nagoya recommended to a meeting of the Japanese Zoo and Aquarium Society that animal observation for the purpose of earthquake prediction be systematically introduced in all zoological parks and aquariums in the country. He pointed out that such observations have already become routine in several zoos, such as the Ueno Zoo in Tokyo.[217]

Anyone following reports of more recent earthquakes would have repeatedly encountered indications of remarkable animal behavior immediately before the disasters.

In the case of a moderately severe quake that shook southern Germany on September 3, 1978, it was said that birds had fallen silent, dogs had become frightened, and cats had become restless. At the zoo in Munich a 2-meter (6-foot) Arapaima (a giant, pikelike tropical freshwater fish) from the Amazon broke through the mesh covering of the aquarium and died. More than seventy letters reporting odd animal behavior in connection with the earthquake were received by the seismological observatory in Fürstenfeldbruck (near Munich) alone.[218,219]

The seismological team that visited eastern Anatolia after a powerful earthquake of magnitude 7.4 on November 24, 1976, asked the people there about unusual animal behavior. No special reactions had been observed among the cattle, but the barking and howling of dogs a few minutes to several hours before the quake was observed frequently in the villages along the earthquake fault.[220]

After a moderately heavy earthquake that happened in the fall of 1979 north of Rome, many Italian newspapers reported a notable event that had happened in Perugia. An hour before the quake the elephants in a circus had began to trumpet wildly, and when the quake came they tore loose and stormed through the town.

An earthquake of magnitude 5.7 near Coyote Lake in California in late August of 1979 happened to strike an area studded with geophysical measuring instruments. To the surprise of the experts, not a single unmistakable precursor could be gleaned. The exceptions were two mysterious phenomena: Changes in the water level of a spring and a slight increase in the number of reports of abnormal animal behavior observed within the framework of "Project Earthquake Watch."[221]

A few letters from readers of the German edition of this book passed along special and interesting old information which probably was never written down and thus probably would have been lost to posterity. The grandson of a man who had worked as a miner toward the end of the last century, when horses were still used in the mines, reported that many rats were always lured into the mineshaft by the presence of draft animals. In those days miners are said to have considered it a sure sign of an impending cave-in when the rats would suddenly flee into the open. Such accidental experiments, which took place under conditions hardly found nowadays, could, if studied carefully, help speed the discovery of the reasons why animals feel the pulse of the earth more clearly than we do.

We probably will never be able to count on recognizing ahead of time all natural events in their most far-reaching effects, but patient observations, careful collecting of information, and modern technology will help to free us from the fear of an inscrutable fate and to guard us against overly great damage.

Tables

Table 1
Reports of unusual animal behavior before earthquakes.

	Place	Length of time before quake[a]	Nature of behavior	Ref.
Europe				
373 B.C.	Helice, Greece	2 days	All animals, especially rats, snakes, weasels, millipedes, and worms, leave city.	7
Dec. 4, 1690	Carinthia, Austria	Shortly	Unusual whining of castle dog at Treffen saves lord of castle and his two sons.	9
before 1794	?	30 min	All animals fearful; horses whinny, tear halters, and flee; dogs bark; rats and mice flee their lairs; birds become frightened.	10
Nov. 1, 1755 (M = 8+)	Lisbon, Portugal	8 days	Earth covered with crawling "worms" near Cadiz (Spanish Atlantic coast).	11a, 12, 13
		20–30 hr	Cattle very excited.	
1771	Liguria, Italy		Animals highly agitated.	14
1783	Calabria, Italy		All animals, especially dogs, geese, and fowl, excited; dogs in Messina bark so much that they are ordered shot.	15
July 26, 1805	Naples, Italy	The night before	Great swarms of locusts crawl through the streets of Naples to the sea.	17, 16

Date	Location	Time before	Animal behavior	Ref.
		Several hours	Ants leave their holes in great confusion.	
		At least a few minutes	Oxen and cows moo; goats and sheep cry, try to break out; dogs howl; geese and fowl make much noise; tied-up horses try to break free; ridden horses stop in street and snort; birds fly up.	
Apr. 2, 1808	Piedmont, Italy	10 min	Many animals excited; horses stamp, kick, and roll on the ground.	18, 14
May 26, 1831	Liguria	Shortly	General unrest among fowl, cats, mules, etc.	14
Aug. 14, 1851	Naples	Up to 10 days	Pigs and other animals uneasy; pigs bite one another.	19, 20
			Constant unusual braying of donkeys, the first animals to announce the quake.	
1870(?)	Lokris, Greece	Several seconds before each tremor	A cat begins to cry.	16
Feb. 23, 1887 (6:30 A.M.)	Liguria	12 hr	Chickens frightened, cannot be driven into coops; cattle act abnormally.	22
		8–9 hr	Dogs bark without letup; donkeys bray; cocks crow all night.	
		3½ hr	Parrot acts strangely.	
		10–30 min	Chickens and birds excited.	

Table 1 (continued)

	Place	Length of time before quake[a]	Nature of behavior	Ref.
March 5, 1892		A few minutes	General panic of domestic animals; fowl try to fly; attempts to break out; unusual cries; chickens break through window panes; coach horses refuse to move on. (Reports from more than 130 localities.)	14
Nov. 14, 1894	Piedmont		Excitement.	
	Calabria	In the nights before the quake	Dogs howl and bark.	23
		Shortly	Horses kick, are excited.	
July 18, 1910 (weak quake)	Landsberg, Bavaria	About 2 min	A goat cries uninterruptedly. All bees leave hives in agitation and return only 15 minutes later.	20
1932	Cephalonia, Zakynthos, Ithaca, Greece	A few hours	Dogs howl, dogs, cats, goats run from houses.	25
April 30, 1954 (M = 7.0)	Sofiadhes, Greece	30 min	Excited storks take to the air, warning many inhabitants.	26
1963	Skopje, Yugoslavia	Night before	Animals in zoo very restless.	76
May 6, 1979 (M = 6.5)	Friuli, Italy	2–3 hr	Roe deer form herds; cats leave homes; chickens won't roost.	90
		15–20 min	Cows moo excitedly, dogs bark.	

China

Date	Location	Precursor time	Animal behavior	Ref.
1789	Yinchuan-Pingluo Ningsia	5–10 min	Birds excited, fly within cages; fowl panic.	32
July 31, 1917 (M = 6.5)	Daguan	1 month	Dogs "barking in unison" regularly herald quakes.	33
			Fish drift to surface.	
		A few days	Thousands of fish jump ashore from Daguan river.	
Dec. 16, 1920	Haiyuan		Abnormal behavior by cows, dogs, wolves, and chickens.	37
March 8, 1966 (M = 6.8)	Hsingtai	3–5 days	Rats run from houses and granaries.	36
		Some days	Snakes crawl on snow-covered ground.	
July 18, 1969 (M = 7.4)	Bohai	2 hr	Abnormal behavior of zoo animals in Tientsin: Panda cries strangely; odd swimming behavior of loaches, blood leeches, and turtles; a yak does not eat and rolls around; swans avoid water and point legs into air.	35
January 5, 1970 (M = 7.7)	Yuxi		Strange fish migrations; fish drift to surface, jump from water.	36

Table 1 (continued)

	Place	Length of time before quake[a]	Nature of behavior	Ref.
May 25, 1970 (M = 4.9)	Tangshan	At least 10 hr	Cattle refuse to enter stables or eat grass.	35
Dec. 30, 1971 (M = 4.75)	Yangtze	2 months	Potato vines bloom.	21
		2 weeks	Yarrow blooms.	
			Chinese cabbage blooms.	
Sept. 27, 1972 (M = 5.8)	Kangting		Chickens panic; pigs refuse to enter sties; horses and sheep run around.	34
Feb. 4, 1975 (M = 7.3)	Haicheng	1½ months	Snakes crawl onto snow; rats are excited, appear in packs, can be caught by hand.	21, 3
		About 6 weeks	Apricot trees bloom in winter.	
		2 days	Pigs aggressive, bite each other.	
		1–2 days	Pigs don't eat, climb walls.	
		1 day	Cows aggressive, attack each other, churn up the ground.	
		8 hr	Stags at red-deer farm break out of corral.	
		20 min	Turtle jumps from water and screams.	

Date	Location	Time before	Observation	Ref.
July 27, 1976 (M = 8.2)	Tangshan	Shortly	Hen flies to treetop; geese honk, won't go into nests, flee.	31
		Several minutes	Dogs bark loudly.	
Japan				
1854	Pacific, off Izu peninsula		Fish leave deep sea; tidal wave washes many deep-sea fish ashore.	42
Nov. 11, 1855 (M = 6.9)	Edo (Tokyo)	2–3 months	Sparrows fail to make annual return to their nesting places.	39, 49
		10 days	Chickens become restless, refuse to go into coops.	
		3 days	Crows fly away noisily.	
		Hours	Many excited catfish are seen.	
			Grass snakes leave their holes and appear on the cold surface.	
1891 (M = 7.9)	Nobi	3–4 days	Many loaches appear in rice paddies.	49, 43
		Several days	Winged ants fly away.	
		1 day	Wild cats scream, pigeons leave nests.	
		Eve of quake	Rats disappear from House of Rats restaurant in Nagoya; many pigeons leave tower of temple.	

Table 1 (continued)

Date	Place	Length of time before quake[a]	Nature of behavior	Ref.
June 15, 1896 (M = 7.1)	Sanriku	3 months	Crows leave rookeries; sparrows leave nests; rats seem very excited.	49, 43, 42
		Days	Unusual migration of tunny (Tokai area).	
		Same day	Trepangs (sea cucumbers) disappear.	
		6 hr	Trout swim up rivers.	
			Crows and other birds leave tree rookeries.	
		20 min	Birds cry till quake starts.	
			Sea snakes swim up rivers; sea urchins appear; eels crowd against shore.	
1896 (M = 7.5)	Rikuu	1 day	Weasels and rats run around in a town (Akiti prefecture).	42
		1 hr	Cocks crow; hens cackle.	
1898 (M = 6.5)	Fukuoka	At least many minutes	Fish jump over crests of waves.	42
Nov. 11, 1918	Omachi (Shinamo)	Shortly	A riding horse lies down and cannot be driven on, even with whipping.	53
Sept. 4, 1923 (M = 7.9)	Kanto	3 months	Mackerel, pike go into nets out of season (off Kinkazan).	43

43, 46, 42

1 month	Eels and char make unusual appearance (off Tokyo), many catfish appear (off Kawasaki).
1 week	Unusual appearances of crabs (Kamakura).
5–6 days	Fish die in muddy water (Yokohama).
Some days	Rats disappear; deep-sea fish (*Nemichthys avocetta*) come to the surface (Hayama).
1–2 days	Great quantities of crabs crawl ashore (Yokohama).
1 day	Great schools of sardines appear (Yokohama Bay); mullets come to surface (Yokohama); catfish jump excitedly in pond (Tokyo); freshwater fish caught out of season (Arakawa River).
Hours	Many fish die amid signs of torment (rivers near Yokohama); plankton comes to surface (Tokyo Bay); unusual school of Katuwa fish caught (Okinosima); bonitos appear unusually close to coast (Tokyo Bay); many deep-sea fish float dead on surface.
Immediately	Many carp caught in Yamanakako Lake.

Table 1 (continued)

Place	Length of time before quake[a]	Nature of behavior	Ref.
		Catfish surface; unusually intensive breeding activity (Saitama); eels disappear (Chiba); bonitos and tunnys cannot be caught, unusually poor fishing (Sagami Bay).	
1927 (M = 7.5)	On morning of quake	Many lobsters and squid caught on surface (Kyoto district); mackerel jump from water.	42
Tango			
March 3, 1933 (M = 8.5)	1 month	Rats disappear, cease to gnaw on rice cakes (Iwate), are uncommonly quiet (Miyagi).	43, 49, 42
Sanriku			
	15–16 days	Unusual kind of crab caught (Iwate).	
	2–3 days	Rats and cats unusually quiet (Iwate); sardines with mud in their stomachs caught (Ishinomaki); many eels crowd against coast, even children can catch them.	
	1 day	Seagulls leave their usual habitats on Kabura Island (Hachinohe); sardines have an unusual species of diatoms in their stomachs.	
	Several hours	A duck refuses to seek out its usual sleeping place.	

1939 (M = 7.0)	Oga peninsula		Tunnys weighing 15 kg (33 lb) crowd against coast; many octopuses, acting as if drunk, in shallow water.	42
1944 (M = 8.0)	Tonankai		Unusually many bonitos caught (Kii peninsula).	42
Dec. 21, 1946 (M = 8.1)	Nankaido	2–3 weeks	Unusual catches of catfish (Kochi).	42, 43
		1 day	Unusually good catches of sardines (coast near Aki).	
		Same day	Chars, lobsters, and squid caught easily.	
		Shortly	Many dolphins appear near shore (off Sanri).	
June 28, 1948 (M = 7.3)	Fukui	4–5 days	Catfish seen in middle of river and at bank (Kuzuryu River).	43, 42
		2 days	Large trout caught in unusual places.	
		Several hours	A fisherman catches 80 sweetfish (Kuzuryu River).	
November, 1963	Niijima	Days	Giant deep-sea fish (*Regalecus glesne*) caught tumbling in shallow water.	50
June 16, 1964 (M = 7.5)	Niigata	About 2 weeks	Catfish rage on surface, are easily caught; largest bream catch in several years.	43
		2–3 days	Unprecedentedly low squid catch (off Fukui).	

Table 1 (continued)

	Place	Length of time before quake[a]	Nature of behavior	Ref.
May 16, 1968 (M = 8.1)	Tokachi-Oki	2 hours	Many dolphins flee Niigata toward Toyama.	43
		8 days	A 1.4-meter-long deep-sea fish (*Alepisaurus borealis*) caught near shore.	
		3 days	A deep-sea eel (*Nemichthys*) caught in only 350-meter (1,148-foot) depth.	
		2 days	A 6-meter (19-foot) deep-sea giant squid (*Architeuthis japonica*) caught.	
August 1968	Uwajima	Eve of quake	Excited groups of fish at surface; two valuable fish specimens (*Regalecus*) caught.	50
The Americas				
1799	Cumana, Venezuela		Restlessness and crying among dogs, goats, pigs.	54a
1811	New Madrid, Missouri	Shortly	Riding horses snort; their heads droop; they rear.	55
1812	Caracas, Venezuela		Spanish stallion breaks out and flees into the mountains.	56, 42
1822	Chile (Valparaiso quake)		Giant flocks of seabirds fly inland.	42, 56

Date	Location	Time before	Description	Ref.
Feb. 20, 1835	Concepciòn, Chile	100 min	Giant flights of seabirds, mostly gulls, fly into interior; dogs flee from Talcahuano.	58, 56
1853	Santiago de Cuba		Pet snakes (*Majita domestica*) flee from indoor nests into the open.	20
1868	Iquique, Chile	Some hours	Flocks of shrieking gulls and other seabirds fly into interior.	69, 60
1906 (M = 8.3)	San Francisco	The whole day before the quake	A mule refuses to eat.	61
		The night before	Dogs howl.	
		Shortly before	Horses are excited, snort, and whinny; 25–30 horses tear loose and run to stablehand; horses that can't tear loose lie down; cows run off in panic.	
			Cattle come down from the hills;	
		10 sec	Dog runs around wildly, jumps out of first-story window.	
1942	San Juan, Argentina	A few hours	Dogs howl mournfully; many run from city.	25
July 10, 1958 (M = 7.9)	Lituya Bay, Situk River, Alaska	2–3 min	Terns and other birds excited, call loudly, circle high in the air; fish bite at each cast.	62
Aug. 17, 1959 (M = 7.1)	Hebgen Lake, Montana	12–6 hr	Aquatic birds completely evacuate a densely populated lakeside habitat.	63, 64

Table 1 (continued)

	Place	Length of time before quake[a]	Nature of behavior	Ref.
May 22, 1960 (M = 8.75)	Valdivia, Chile	10 sec before aftershocks	Ring pheasant cackles loudly.	65
		5 sec before aftershocks	Horses whinny and tremble all over.	
March 27, 1964 (M = 8.5)	Prince William Sound, Kodiak Island, Alaska	A few hours	Cattle, contrary to habit, leave low pastures and wander to higher ones.	66
June 27–29, 1966 (M = 5.0–5.3)	Parkfield, California	2 days	Rattlesnakes flee from hills and are seen in nearby towns.	68, 67, 13
1968	Arenal volcano, Costa Rica		Cattle leave pastures on volcano before people sense trembling.	69
Aug. 2, 1968	Oaxaca, Mexico	1 min	Dog behaves very unusually (Mexico City).	70
1971	San Fernando, California	The night before	Rats flee into street.	71
1972 (M = 6.25)	Managua, Nicaragua	A few hours	Monkeys are very excited.	42
Nov. 28, 1974 (M = 4)	Hollister, California	A few minutes	Horses go wild.	71
Rest of World				
Oct. 12, 1855	lower Egypt, Cairo	2 hr	Dogs bark; donkeys bray.	72, 13
1867	Java		Cocks crow together, emit high-pitched calls, and run away.	69, 60

Date	Location	Time	Behavior	Reference
April, 1905	Lahore, Pakistan	Several hours	Elephants are extraordinarily restless.	60
October, 1907	Karatagh	About 4 hr	Dogs, cattle, horses are very excited.	60
1947	Mt. Hekla, Iceland	Before volcanic eruption	Old dog acts unusually and is frightened.	69
1948 (M = 8.2)	Ashkhabad, Turkmen SSR	Several days	Ants come out of hills; bees out of hives; snakes and lizards crawl from holes.	73
Feb. 28, 1955	Mt. Kilauea, Hawaii	2 days before volcanic eruption	Dogs are excited, dig holes as if chasing small animals.	69
1955–56	Kamchatka, USSR	Some time before quakes and eruptions	Bears leave hibernating dens and seek out safer areas.	74
1965	Taal, Philippines	Hours before volcanic eruption	Dogs, cats, and cattle panic.	69
April 25, 1966	Tashkent, Uzbek SSR	The night before	Goats, antelopes, tigers, and other zoo animals refuse to go into pens.	180, 74
Dec. 4, 1967	Palmer peninsula, Antarctica	Several hours before	Penguins and skuas leave area surrounding scientific station.	75, 13

a. Where time is not specified, report said only that behavior was observed "before" quake.

Table 2
Detailed comparison of unusual behavior of animals before earthquakes and before dramatic weather changes.

Behavior before bad weather	Behavior before earthquakes	Ref. for earthquake behavior
Seabirds fly into interior.	Large flocks of noisy seabirds fly into interior.	Chile, 1822[56,42] Concepciòn, Chile, 1835[56,58] Iquique, Chile, 1868[69,59]
Aquatic birds leave inland lakes.	Waterbirds evacuate lake; swans and ducks leave water, refuse to return.	Montana, 1959[62] China, gen'l rule[21]
Birds are excited, flock together, fly this way and that.	Excited storks take to the air; chickens flock; fowl flutter excitedly; noisy birds fly up and circle excitedly; pigeons fly around without letup.	Sofiadhes, Greece, 1954[26] Java, 1867[69] Liguria, 1887[22] Alaska, 1958[62] China, gen'l rule[35]
Chickens roost late.	Chickens enter coops very reluctantly and late.	Friuli, 1976
	Chickens refuse to enter coops, or break out of them.	Liguria, 1887[22] China, gen'l rule[36]
Many birds have special rain or weather calls.	Remarkable and unusually timed calls; chickens cry, often constantly.	Peruvian folklore[86] Friuli, 1976 China, gen'l rule[36]
Cattle enter stalls late.	Cattle and pigs refuse to enter stalls, or flee from them.	China, gen'l rule[35,36]
	Pets try to flee outdoors.	Liguria, 1887[22]
Roe deer and other game leave the woods, lose shyness.	A herd of roe deer leaves forest and approaches the village.	Friuli, 1976
	Wild animals lose shyness, approach people.	Chilean folklore[77]
Ants are highly agitated, seek safety.	Ants flee their hills, crowd together, change living quarters.	Ashkhabad, USSR, 1970[73] Japanese popular belief[36] Chinese belief[36]
Fish jump from water.	Fish jump from water.	China, 1917[36] Gen'l rule[35]
Bees are very excited, seek protection.	Bees are very excited, swarm.	Chinese wisdom[36,21] Bavaria, 1910[93,20]
Earthworms come out of holes.	Earthworms come out of holes.	Japanese popular belief[42] Lisbon, 1755[11a]

Table 2 (continued)

Behavior before bad weather	Behavior before earthquakes	Ref. for earthquake behavior
Habitual migration time of birds is changed.	Time of return of migratory birds is influenced strongly.	Japanese popular belief[36]
Insects change flight behavior, fly close to ground and water.	Giant swarm of fireflies flew close to the water.	Friuli, 1976[28]
	Insects form swarms.	Japanese popular belief[42]

Table 3
Historical descriptions of the nine most important ancient earthquake insights.

	Earliest reports	Use in earthquake prediction	Role in Chinese warning system	Attitude of international science
Unusual animal behavior before earthquakes	Greece, 373 B.C.[7] Roman empire, first century A.D.[8a] China, more than 2,000 years ago Japan, 1855[49] Venezuela, 1799[54a] Very ancient roots in many mythologies	Roman empire, first century A.D.[8a] China, at least by 1739[32] Japan, 1855[39] Venezuela, 1799[54a]	Important; systematically observed since 1966.	Much skepticism, but now being discussed; first positive proof from Stanford University, 1976.
Springs become murky before a quake; changes in taste and in flow of water (groundwater)	Greece, sixth century B.C.[109c,8g] Roman empire, first century A.D.[8a] Japan, 1751[51d] China, at least by 1739[32] Chile, 1835[57]	Greece, sixth century B.C. (lucky forecast by Pherecydes)[109c,8g] Japan, 1751[51d] China, 1739[32]	Important; systematically observed since 1966.	Varying opinions; possible meaning being examined; first proofs 1968, 1970.[42]
Ground noises noticeable early before quakes in some areas	China, 474[32] Ecuador, 1800[54f] Constantinople, 396[78]	China, 1739[32]	Being developed for prediction of quakes in some areas.[32]	Not recognized
Noise seconds before quake	Roman empire, first century A.D.[8f] Popular reports from many countries	Venezuela, prior to 1799[54a] for salvation in last seconds	People asked to listen for ground noises.	Proved in 1975;[101] until then seen as doubtful folklore.

Light phenomena before quake	Japan, 1703[51a] Europe, before 1756[11b] Venezuela, 1797[54i]	Japan, tradition China, tradition	Peasants asked to look out for them.	Rejected as fantasy.
Light phenomena during quake	Egypt, for more than 3,000 years[162] Greece, hints from second century A.D.[78] Constantinople, 50[163] Italy, 1786[14] Chile, 1906[169]		Considered real companion to earthquakes since amateur photos published in 1967.	Some scientists accept as fact, still doubted by some.[70,42] Mechanism obscure.
Characteristic fogs before quake	Greece, fourth century B.C.[154a] Roman empire, first century[8] Chile, seventeenth century[154,155] Italy, 1706[23] Venezuela, pre-1799[54c] Japan, 1802[51]	Greece, fourth century B.C.[154a] Japan, 1802 and earlier[51] Venezuela, before 1799[54c]	Has been noticed, but apparently plays no role.	Largely unknown.
Soaking of ground causes quakes	Greece, sixth century B.C.[78] China, 1739[32] Italy, 1897[14] South America, before 1800[54g]	Uncertain; possibly China, 1739[32]	Apparently none	Discovered after 1945 in dammed-up reservoirs and now recognized generally.[192]

Table 3 (continued)

	Earliest reports	Use in earthquake prediction	Role in Chinese warning system	Attitude of international science
Sensitive people feel earthquake weather	Portugal, 1755[12] Italy, 1808; old belief[14] Chile, old belief[90] Japan, 1855[42] Soviet Union, 1948[74]	Anecdotes about predictions: Japan, 1855[42] Italy, 1887[22]	Apparently none	Unknown.

References

1. Chinese Seismological Delegation, A brief summary of the work of premonitory observation, prediction and precautionary measures before the Haicheng earthquake, Liaoning province, of magnitude 7.3, *Sci. Geol. Sinica* no. 2: 120–123 (1976) (Chinese). An official translation of this article was distributed in Paris during a UNESCO conference in February 1976.

2. C. B. Raleigh, G. Bennett, H. Craig, T. Hanks, P. Molnar, A. Nur, J. Savage, C. Scholz, R. Turner, and F. Wu, in The Prediction of the Haicheng Earthquake, report by Liaoning Earthquake Study Delegation, U.S.A., 1976.

3. Fung-Ming Chu, An outline of prediction and forecast of Haicheng earthquake of M = 7.3, in Proceedings of the lectures by the seismological delegations of the People's Republic of China, *J. Seism. Soc. Japan* (tr. Jet Propulsion Laboratory, California Institute of Technology), 1976, pp. 11–17.

4. Yingkou Editorial Committee, *The Southern Liaoning Earthquake* (Commercial Press, 1975) (Chinese).

5. Ulrich Grudinski, Verrät die Tierwelt den kommenden Erdstoss? [Do animals announce the coming of earth tremors?], *Frankfurter Allgemeine Zeitung*, March 5, 1975.

6. Plutarch, *Life of Cimon*.

7. Diodorus Siculus, XV: 48–49.

8. Pliny the Elder, *Historia Naturalis*, (a) 2: 84; (b) 18: 87–88; (c) 2: 37; (d) 2: 86; (e) 2: 25–34; (f) 2: 82; (g) 2: 81; (h) 8: 183; (i) 2: 85; (j) 2: 83.

9. C. Gohn, *Geschichte der Stadt Villach* [History of the city of Villach] (Villach, 1901).

10. G.-L. L. Buffon, L'histoire de la terre (Paris, 1749). This contains a reference to Le Gentil's *Voyage autour du monde*.

11. I. M. Kant, *Kants Werke*, vol. 1, *Vorkritische Schriften* [Precritical writings] *I: 1747–1766* (Berlin: Königlich Preussiche Akademie der Wissenschaften, 1910). (a) Von den Ursachen der Erderschütterungen bei Gelegenheit des Unglückes, welches die westlichen Länder von Europa gegen das Ende des vorigen Jahres betroffen hat [On the causes of the earth tremors associated with the misfortune that struck the western countries of Europe toward the end of the previous year]; (b) Geschichte und Naturbeschreibung der merkwürdigsten Vorfälle des Erdbebens, welches am Ende des 1755sten Jahres einen grossen Teil der Erde erschüttert hat [History and scientific description of the

most remarkable of the incidents of the earthquake that shook a large part of the world at the end of the 1755th year].

12. H. O. Wood, The observation of earthquakes—A guide for the general observer *Bull. Seism. Soc. Am.*, 2 June 1911.

13. R. B. Simon, List of 14 observations of unusual animal behavior, Colorado School of Mines, 1976.

14. G. Mercalli, *I terremoti della Liguria e Piemonte* [The earthquakes of Liguria and Piedmont] (Naples, 1897).

15. D. de Dolomieu, *Memoire sur les tremblements de terre de la Calabre pendant l'annee 1783* (Rome, 1784).

16. W. Branco, *Wirkungen und Ursachen der Erdbeben* [Effects and causes of earthquakes] (Berlin, 1902).

17. Anonymous, The mental effect of earthquakes, *Pop. Sci.* 19: 257–260 (1881).

18. L. Bossi, *Rapporto sul terremoto del 2 aprile 1808 nalla vale del Pelice ecc.* ; *Estratto con osservazioni particolari* (Milan: Vassalli-Eandi, 1808).

19. Mallet, *The Great Neapolitan Earthquake* (London, 1862), p. 200.

20. H. von Hentig, Reactions of animals to changes in physical environment. I. Animal and earthquake, *J. Comp. Psychol.* 3: 61–71 (1923).

21. Geological Bureau, *Earthquake Questions and Answers* (Peking: Geology Press, 1975) (Chinese), p. 132.

22. T. Taramelli and G. Mercalli, *Il terremoto Ligure del febbraio 1887,* in annals of Ufficio Centrale di Meteorologia e di Geodinamica (Rome, 1888), part IV, vol. VIII.

23. G. Mercalli, *I terremoti della Calabria Meridionale e del Messinese* [The earthquakes of southern Calabria and Messina] (Rome, 1897).

24. Lutz, *Erdbeben in Bayern* [Earthquake in Bavaria] (Munich, 1921), p. 119.

25. U. Dunkel, *Neben dem Pfirschpfad* [Beside the stalking path] (Berlin, 1969).

26. F. W. Lane, *The Elements Rage* (Philadelphia, 1965), pp. 364 ff.

27. *Kärntner Tageszeitung,* September 25, 1976.

28. G. Matteucig, quoted in *Messagero Veneto* (Udine), September 22, 1976, p. 3.

29. *Corriere di Napoli,* October 9, 1976. p. 3.

30. *Time,* January 24, 1977.

31. ANSA, Report from China, published, e.g., in *Tagesspiegel* (Berlin), July 28, 1976.

32. Lanchow Seismological Brigade Office of Synthesis, Analysis, and Prediction Research, Predicting earthquakes by earth sound, in *Conference I, Abnormal Animal Behavior prior to Earthquakes* (U.S. Geological Survey, 1976).

33. Academia Sinica Seismological Committee, *Chronological Tables of Earthquake Data of China* (Peking, 1956) (Chinese).

34. Y. Y. Liu, A brief introduction of seismological work in the People's Republic of China, *Sci. Geol. Sinica* no. 2: 116–119 (1976) (Chinese). An official translation into English was distributed in Paris at a UNESCO conference in February 1976.

35. Seismological Office of Tientsin, *Earthquakes* (Tientsin: People's Arts Press, 1973) (Chinese).

36. T. P. Wong, *Earthquake Forecasting* (Hong Kong: Tsinghai Publishing Corp., 1974) (Chinese).

37. A. J. Guo et al., Great Haiyuan earthquake on December 16, 1920, *Acta Geophys. Sinica* 19: 42–49 (1976) (Chinese, with English summary).

38. L. Jones and P. Molnar, *Nature* 262: 677 (1976).

39. K. Musha, *Nihon Jishin Shiryo* (Tokyo), 1951.

40. B. A. Bolt, Namazu-e, *Pacific Discovery* XXIX: 10–13 (1976).

41. K. Musha, *Earthquake Catfish* (Tokyo, 1957) (Japanese).

42. T. Rikitake, *Earthquake Prediction* (Amsterdam, 1976).

43. Y. Suyehiro, Catfish's way of detecting earthquakes, *Shoden-sha* (Tokyo), 1976.

44. S. Hatai and N. Abe, The responses of the catfish, *Parasilurus asotus*, to earthquakes, *Proc. Imp. Acad. Japan* 8: 373–378 (1932) (English).

45. S. Hatai, S. Kokubo, and N. Abe, The earth currents in relation to the responses of catfish, *Proc. Imp. Acad. Japan* 8: 478–481 (1932) (English).

46. T. Terada, On some probable influence of earthquakes upon fisheries, *Bull. Earthquake Res. Inst. Tokyo Univ.* 10: 393–401 (1932).

47. Y. Suyehiro, Some observations on the unusual behavior of fishes prior to earthquakes, *Bull. Earthquake Res. Inst. Tokyo Univ.* suppl. 1: 228–231 (1934).

48. K. Musha, Earthquakes and unusual fish behavior, *Zishin (Bull. Seism. Soc. Japan),* ser. 1, 4: 349–362 (1932) (Japanese).

49. K. Musha, Materials on unusual behavior observed before earthquakes, *Zishin (Bull. Seism. Soc. Japan)* ser. 1, 7: 1–22 (1935) (Japanese).

50. Y. Suyehiro, Unusual behavior of fish before earthquakes, *Sci. Rep. Kaikyu Aburatsubo Marine Park Aquarium* 1: 4–11 (1968) (Japanese and English).

51. Dai Nihon Jishin Shiryo [Imperial Japanese Earthquake Investigation Commission], (a) 1: 509; (b) 1: 285; (c) 1: 583; (d) 1: 360. This collection of documents (in Japanese) appeared in 1904 and was reprinted in 1973. It was later edited, supplemented with many recently discovered documents, and published under the title *Zotei Dai Nihon Jishin Shiryo.* An abbreviated version appeared under the title *Nihon Jishin Shiryo.*

52. Y. Suyehiro, Unusual behavior of fish before earthquakes—second report, *Sci. Rep. Keikyu Aburatsubo Marine Park Aquarium* 4: 13–14 (1971) (Japanese with English summary).

53. F. Omori, Pheasant as seismoscope, *Bull. Japanese Imperial Earthquake Investigation Commission* 11: 1–5 (1923) (English).

54. A. von Humboldt, *Reise in die Aequinoctalgegenden des neuen Kontinents* [Journey into the equinoctial regions of the new continent] (Stuttgart: H. Hauff, 1859): (a) 1: 231; (b) 2: 59; (c) 1: 234; (d) 1: 245; (e) 1: 236; (f) 2: 65; (g) 2: 207; (h) 2: 225; (i) 2: 232.

55. Alice Ford (ed.), *Audubon, by Himself: A Profile of John James Audubon* (Natural History Press, 1969).

56. J. Milne, *Earthquakes and Other Movements* (Philadelphia, 1939) (rewritten after Milne's work of 1883).

57. A. Moorehead, *Darwin and the Beagle* (Penguin Books).

58. R. FitzRoy, *Narrative of the Surveying Voyages of H.M.S. Adventure and Beagle between the Years 1826 and 1836* (1838), vol. II.

59. Can animals predict earthquakes? *Sci. Am.* suppl. no. 1754: 100 (1909).

60. F. Knapp, *Mitteilungen aus der kubanischen Tier- und Pflanzenwelt* [Reports from the Cuban plant and animal worlds], *Abh. Naturforsch. Ges. Nürnberg* VI (cited in ref. 20 above).

61. A. C. Lawson, The Californian earthquake of April 18, 1906, in *Report of the State Earthquake Investigation Commission* (Washington, D.C.: Carnegie Institute, 1908), vol. I, p. 382.

62. W. M. Adams, *Earthquakes* (Boston, 1964).

63. E. R. Dewey and O. Mandino, *Cycles: The Mysterious Forces that Trigger Events* (Manor Books, 1973).

64. U.S. Department of Commerce, *U.S. Earthquakes 1959* (Washington, D.C.: U.S. Government Printing Office).

65. E. Kilian, *Naturwissenschaftliche Rundschau* 17: 135 (1964).

66. E. Engle, *Earthquake — The Story of Alaska's Good Friday Disaster* (New York, 1965).

67. Local press, California, 1966.

68. U.S. Department of Commerce, *U.S. Earthquakes 1966* (Washington, D.C.: U.S. Government Printing Office).

69. C. J. Anderson, Animals, earthquakes, and eruptions, *Bull. Field Museum of Natural History* 44, no. 5: 9–11 (1973).

70. J. Derr, *Bull. Seism. Soc. Am.* 63: 2177 (1973).

71. *Science Digest,* March 1966, p. 61.

72. Boscowitz, *Earthquakes* (New York, 1890), pp. 12 ff.

73. Ulonov, *Earthquakes* (Tashkent, 1970).

74. A. Werner, Russian scientists use animals to predict natural disasters, in *California Superquake,* P. James, ed. (Hicksville, N.Y.: Exposition Press, 1974), pp. 40–43.

75. U.S. Coast and Geodetic Survey, Preliminary Determination of Epicenters, report 84–67.

76. D. Simpson, pers. comm.

77. F. de Montessus de Ballore, Apuntes de folklore sismico [Notes on seismic folklore], *Boletin del Servicio Sismologico de Chile* 11: 311 ff. (1915).

78. *Reallexikon für Antike und Christentum* [Encyclopedia of antiquity and christianity], Theodor Klauser, ed., s.v. "Erdbeben."

79. Ovid, *Metamorphoses,* 15: 669/74.

80. B. Bischoff and W. Kohler, Spätantike Ravennater Annalen [Annals of Ravenna for late antiquity], *Medieval Studies in Memory of A. Kingsley Porter* 125: 38 (1939); see especially 132, illustration 2.

81. J. B. Friedrich, *Symbolik und Mythologie* (1899).

82. *Mythology of All Races,* C. J. A. McCulloch, ed. (1964), s.v. "Finno-Ugric-Siberian."

83. *Handbook of Middle American Indians,* R. Wauchope, ed. (University of Texas Press, 1969), vol. 7, part 1.

84. A. Evans, *The Palace of Minos at Knossos* (London, 1928), 2: 32, 324.

85. E. F. Weidner, Ereškigal als Göttin des Erdbebens [Ereshkigal as goddess of earthquakes], *Arch. Oriental Res.* 13: 231/3 (1939).

86. Local press, Huancayo, Peru, February 22, 1975.

87. F. de Montessus de Ballore, *Ethnografie Sismique et Volcanique* (Paris, 1923).

88. *Messagero Veneto* (Udine), July 6, 1976.

89. Wölffing, Das Erdbeben vom 20. Juli 1913, in *Württembergische Jahrbücher für Statistik und Landeskunde* (Stuttgart, 1919–1920), p. 320.

90. H. Tributsch, pers. info.

91. von Seebach, *Das Mitteldeutsche Erdbeben von 1872* (Gotha, 1875), p. 57.

92. Noeggerath, *Das Erdbeben vom 29. Juli 1846 im Rheingebiet und den benachbarten Ländern* [The earthquake of July 29, 1846, in the Rhineland and the neighboring countries] (Bonn, 1847), p. 6.

93. Lutz, *Erdbeben in Bayern* [Earthquake in Bavaria] (Munich, 1921).

94. G. Wissowa, *Paulys Real Encyclopädie der klassischen Altertumswissenschaft* (Stuttgart, 1924).

95. A. Nur, *Bull. Seism. Soc. Am.* 62: 1217 (1972).

96. Y. P. Aggarwal, L. R. Sykes, J. Armbruster, and M. L. Sbar, *Nature* 241: 101 (1973).

97. C. H. Scholz, L. R. Sykes, and Y. P. Aggarwal, *Science* 181: 803 (1973).

98. L. Jones and P. Molnar, *Nature* 262: 677 (1976).

99. C. Davison, Earthquake sounds, *Bull. Seism. Soc. Am.* 28: 147, 161 (1938).

100. B. H. Armstrong, Acoustic emission prior to rockburst and earthquakes, *Bull. Seism. Soc. Am.* 59: 1259 (1969).

101. D. P. Hill, F. G. Fischer, K. M. Lahr, and J. M. Wakley, Earthquake sounds generated by body-wave ground motion, *Bull. Seism. Soc. Am.* 66: 1159 (1976).

102. T. C. Kuo, Can earthquakes be predicted? *Pop. Sci.* (Chinese), April 1966.

103. C. Y. Fu, On several problems in earthquake prediction, *Sci. Bull.* (Chinese), March 1963.

104. M. J. S. Johnston, B. E. Smith, and R. Muller, Tectono-magnetic experiments and observations in the western U.S.A., *J. Geomag. Geoelec.* 28: 85–97 (1976).

105. W. G. Moore, Magnetic disturbances preceding the earthquake, in *The Great Alaska Earthquake of 1964* (Washington, D.C.: National Academy of Sciences, 1972).

106. M. J. S. Johnston and F. D. Stacey, Volcano-magnetic effect observed on Mt. Ruapehu, New Zealand, *J. Geophys. Res.* 74: 6541 (1969); Transient magnetic anomalies accompanying volcanic eruptions in New Zealand, *Nature* 224: 1289 (1969).

107. G. Kondo, The variation of the atmospheric field at the time of earthquake, *Mem. Kakioka Mag. Observatory* 13: 11 (1968).

108. C. Bufe and J. Nanevicz, in *Conference 1, Abnormal Animal Behavior prior to Earthquakes* (U.S. Geological Survey, 1976).

109. Cicero, (a) *De Oratore* 2: 62; (b) *De Divinatione;* (c) *De Divinatione* 1: 50.

110. T. K. Kuo, P. Y. Chin, and H. T. Feng, Discussion of the changes of groundwater levels before severe earthquakes, with use of an earthquake model, *Acta Geophys. Sinica* 17: 99 (1974) (Chinese).

111. F. R. Gordon, Water level changes preceding the earthquake of Meckering, Western Australia, 14 October 1968, *Bull. R. Soc. New Zealand* 9: 85 (1971).

112. G. Vivenzio, *Istoria e teoria del tremuoti in generale e in particolare di quello della Calabria e di Messina del 1783* [History and theory of quakes in general . . .] (Naples, 1783).

113. E. R. Lapwood, *Nature* 266: 220 (1977).

114. *Conference 1* (see ref. 108).

115. W. H. Gawthrope, R. Johnson, R. F. Haberman, and M. Wyss, Preliminary experiments on the behavior of mice before rock failure in the laboratory, in *Conference 1* (see ref. 108).

116. M. Burton, *The Sixth Sense of Animals* (London, 1973).

117. A. M. Brown and J. D. Pye, Auditory sensitivity at high frequencies in mammals, *Adv. Comp. Physiol. Biochem.* 6: 1–73 (1975).

118. R. Reiter, *Meteorobiologie und Elektrizität der Atmosphäre* (Leipzig, 1960).

119. L. Schua, Die Fluchtreaktion von Goldhamstern aus elektrischen Feldern [The flight reaction of golden hamsters in electric fields], *Naturwissenschaften* 40: 514 (1953); Wirken luftelektrische Felder auf Lebewesen? [Do airborne electrical fields have any effect on living things?], *Umschau* 54: 468 (1954).

120. W. T. Keeton, Effect of magnets on pigeon homing, in Animal Orientation and Navigation, NASA report SP-262 (Washington, D.C.: U.S. Government Printing Office, 1972), p. 579.

121. T. S. Larkin and W. T. Keeton, *J. Comp. Physiol.* 110: 227 (1976).

122. C. Walcott and R. P. Green, Orientation of homing pigeons altered by a change in the direction of an applied magnetic field, *Science* 184: 180 (1974).

123. W. Wiltschko and R. Wiltschko, Magnetic compass of European robins, *Science* 176: 62 (1972).

124. M. Lindauer and H. Martin, Magnetic effect on dancing bees, in Animal Orientation and Navigation (see ref. 120), p. 559.

125. M. F. Barnothy, *Biological Effects of Magnetic Fields* (Plenum Press, 1969).

126. P. D. Thompson and R. O'Brien, *The Weather* (Time-Life Books, 1976).

127. F. Dessauer, *Zehn Jahre Forschung auf dem physikalisch-medizinschen Grenzgebiet* [Ten years of research in the physical-medical border area] (Leipzig, 1931).

128. W. W. Hicks and J. C. Beckett, The control of the air ionization and its biological effects, International Society of Bioclimatology and Biometeorology Congress, Paris, 1956.

129. K. Bisa, Zur Aerosolforschung und Therapie, International Society of Bioclimatology and Biometeorology Congress, Paris, 1957, vol. 6, p. 129.

130. P. A. Krueger and E. J. Reed, *Science* 193: 1209 (1976).

131. P. A. Krueger and S. Kotaka, *Int. J. Biometeorol.* 13: 61 (1969).

132. G. O. Gilbert, *Int. J. Biometeorol.* 17: 267 (1973).

133. J. M. Olivereau, doctoral diss., Université de Paris, 1971.

134. N. Robinson and F. S. Dirnfeld, *Int. J. Biometeorol.* 6: 101 (1963).

135. F. G. Sulman, D. Levy, Y. Pfeifer, E. Superstine, and E. Tal, *Int. J. Biometeorol.* 18: 313 (1974).

136. M. P. Volarovich and G. A. Sobolev, The use of piezoelectric effects in rocks for underground prospecting for piezoelectric materials, *Dokl. Akad. Nauk. SSSR* 162: 556 (1965).

137. E. I. Parkhomenko, *Electrification Phenomena in Rocks* (Moscow, 1968) (Russian).

138. M. Wyss, Stress estimates for South American shallow and deep earthquakes, *J. Geophys. Res.* 75: 1929 (1970).

139. Y. Yasui, A study of the luminous phenomena accompanied with earthquake, part I, *Mem. Kakioka Mag. Observatory* 13: 25–61 (1968); part II, *ibid.* 14: 67–68 (1971).

140. G. A. Sobolev, communication at IUGG XV Conference, Moscow, 1971.

141. D. Finkelstein and J. R. Powell, *Nature* 228: 759 (1970).

142. D. Finkelstein and J. R. Powell, presentation at IUGG XV Conference, Moscow, 1971.

143. D. Finkelstein, R. D. Hill, and J. R. Powell, *J. Geophys. Res.* 78: 992 (1973).

144. *Encyclopedia of Physics* (S. Flugge, 1957), vol. XLVIII, p. 1003, s.v. "physical volcanology."

145. Deng Qui-Dung, Geology Institute, Peking, pers. comm. to L. Jones and P. Molnar, MIT, 1977.

146. A. Hickling and M. D. Ingram, Glow-discharge electrolysis, *J. Electroanalyt. Chem.* 8: 65 (1964).

147. A. R. Denaro and A. Hickling, *J. Electrochem. Soc.* 105: 265 (1968).

148. A. Hickling and M. D. Ingram, *Trans. Faraday Soc.* 60: 783 (1964).

149. Hatakeyama, *J. Meteorol. Soc. Japan* 21: 49, 420, 426 (1943); *J. Geomagn. Geoelectr.* 1, no. 2 (1948).

150. Vassalli-Eandi, Rapporte sur le trembl. de terre qui commence le 2 Avril 1808, dans les vallées de Pelis du Cluson du Po, ecc., *Mem. Acad. Turin* (1808); Sopra il terremoto che da 7 mesi scuote le valli del Clusone e del Po, *Mem. Matem. Fisica Soc. Ital.* XIV (1808).

151. H. Resal, *Compt. Rend.* (Paris) CIV: 950 (1887).

152. H. Israel and G. W. Israel, *Spurenstoffe in der Atmosphäre* [Trace materials in the atmosphere] (Stuttgart, 1973), p. 29.

153. R. O. Faulkner, The Cannibal Hymn, from the Pyramid Texts, *J. Egypt. Archaeol.* 10: 97–103 (1924).

154. F. de Montessus de Ballore, La sismologia de los autores clasicos Griegos y Romanos, *Boletin del Servicio Sismologica de Chile,* 1918: (a) p. 22; (b) p. 94.

155. Fr. R. de Lizarraga, *Historiades do Indias II* (Madrid, 1909), 485, chap. LXXV, p. 649.

156. P. D. Thompson and R. O'Brien, *The Weather* (Time-Life Books, 1976).

157. Aristotle, *Meteorologica,* lib. II.

158. Seneca, *Questiones Naturales,* lib. VI, C 12.

159. P. Molnar, pers. comm. from Deng Qui-Dung.

160. Benevelli, *Sopra il terremoto d'Alba dell autumno 1786* (Asti, 1787).

161. Y. Yasui, Seismo-luminous phenomena at Santa Rosa, *Mem. Kakioka Mag. Observatory* 5: 181–186 (1972).

162. H. Bonnet, *Mitt. Inst. Cairo* 14: 11 (1956).

163. Chron. Pasch. 589, 6; Synax, eccl. Cpel. 425, 1–17.

164. K. Musha, On the luminous phenomenon that attended the Idu earthquake, November 25th, 1930, *Bull. Earthquake Res. Inst. Tokyo Univ.* 9: 214–215 (1931).

165. T. Terada, On luminous phenomena accompanying earthquakes, *Bull. Earthquake Res. Inst. Tokyo Univ.* 9: 225–255 (1931).

166. I. Galli, Raccolta e classificazione de fenomeni luminosi osservati nei terremoti (in Italian), *Boll. Soc. Sis. Ital.* 14: 221 (1910).

167. M. Fuller, The New Madrid Earthquake, bulletin 494, U.S. Government Printing Office, 1912.

168. A. Sieberg, *Erdbebenkunde* [Earthquake science] (Jena, 1923).

169. F. de Montessus de Ballore, *Fenomeni luminosi speciali che avrebbero accompagnato il terremoto di Valparaiso del 16 di Agosto 1906* (Modena, 1912).

170. *La Nacion* (Buenos Aires), May 22, 1936.

171. D. M. Zakharovskaya, ed., *The Tashkent Earthquake of April 26, 1966* (Uzbekistan: F.A.S. Tashkent, 1971), pp. 272–302 (Russian).

172. D. Li Teh-Run, *Earthquake Frontiers,* no. 2 (Peking), pp. 8–9 (Chinese).

173. D. Engdahl, report in Santa Rosa, Calif., *Press Democrat,* November 30, 1969.

174. M. D. Altschuler, Atmospheric electricity and plasma interpretations of UFOs, in *Scientific Study of Unidentified Flying Objects,* E. U. Condon, ed. (New York, 1969), pp. 723–755.

175. K. Kalle, Die rätselhafte und unheimliche Naturerscheinung des explodierenden und des rotierenden Meeresleuchtens [The enigmatic and unearthly natural phenomenon of exploding and rotating sea luminosity], *Dtsch. Hydrogr. Z.* 13: 49 (1960).

176. T. von Randow, *Die Zeit,* August 6, 1976.

177. W. M. Adams, *Earthquakes* (Science Resource Series, 1964), p. 89.

178. N. Minorsky, *Nonlinear Oscillations* (New York: Van Nostrand, 1962), pp. 390, 438.

179. R. Landauer, *J. Appl. Phys.* 31: 479 (1960).

180. F. G. Sulman, in "Wetterbeschwerden," M. Kohnlechner, ed., Heyne, *Medizinsche Ratgeber* (Munich, 1980).

181. P. Czermak, *Mitt. Wien. Akad. Wiss.*, p. 127 (1901); *Phys. Z.* 3: 185 (1902).

182. N. Robinson and F. S. Dirnfeld, *Int. J. Biometeorol.* 6: 101 (1963).

183. D. Stahl, *Z. Jagdwiss.* 22: 2 (1976).

184. R. T. Orr, *Animals in Migration* (London, 1970).

185. K. Sprenger, E. A. Lauter, and K. H. Schmelovsky, Sonnenfinsterniseffekte in der unteren Ionosphere nach Beobachtungen im Mittel- und Langwellenbereich [Effects of solar eclipses in the lower ionosphere according to observations in the middle- and long-wave ranges], *Abh. Met. Hydrol. Dienstes DDR* 69 (1962).

186. Anonymous, The mental effect of earthquakes, *Pop. Sci.* 19: 257 (1881).

187. *Messagero Veneto* (Udine), June 25, 1976, p. 20.

188. H. K. Gupta, B. K. Rastogi, and H. Narain, Common features of the reservoir-associated seismic activities, *Bull. Seism. Soc. Am.* 62: 481–492 (1972).

189. J. P. Rothe, Man-made earthquakes, *Tectonophysics* 9: 215–238 (1970).

190. A. Božović, Review and appraisal of case histories related to seismic effects of reservoir impounding, *Eng. Geol.* 8: 9–27 (1974).

191. B. A. Bolt and W. K. Cloud, Recorded strong motion on the Hsingfengkiang dam, China, *Bull. Seism. Soc. Am.* 64: 1337 (1974).

192. UNESCO, Groupe travail sur les phenomenes sismique associes a la mise en eau de grandes retenues [Working group on seismic phenomena associated with the effects of large impoundments of water], *IUGG Chron.* 95, December 1973.

193. Pausanias 7, 24, 7.

194. Diogenes Laertes 1. 116.

195. Ammianus Marcellinus 22, 16, 22.

196. H. C. Kraemer, B. E. Smith, and S. Levine, An animal behavior model for short term earthquake prediction, in *Conference 1, Abnormal Animal Behavior prior to Earthquakes* (U.S. Department of the Interior, 1976).

197. Genesis 19: 24, 25 (New English Bible).

198. Exodus 19.

199. L. A. Mackay, The earthquake-horse, *Class. Phil.* 41: 150–154 (1946).

200. F. Luterbacher, *Der Prodigienglaube und Prodigienstil der Römer* [Belief in and style of prodigies among the Romans] (Darmstadt, 1904).

201. P. Vergilius Maro, *Georgica.* book 1.

202. Livy: (a) 27, 4, 13; (b) 22, 1, 9; (c) 31, 12, 5; (d) 41, 21, 12; (e) 3, 29, 9; (f) 22, 10, 9; (g) 40, 59, 7; (h) 25, 12, 15.

203. Obsequens: (a) 42; (b) 70; (c) 41; (d) 20; (e) 20, 24, 52, 53.

204. Aug. 95.

205. Act. Martyr. S. Callisti, 1 (Patr. Gr. 10) 113.

206. G. Matteucig, pers. comm. (results of inquiries in Friuli).

207. W. L. Bühl, *Einführung in die Wissenschaftssoziologie* [Introduction to the sociology of science] (Munich, 1974).

208. *Encyclopedia of Physics* (S. Flugge, 1957), s.v. "atmospheric electricity."

209. S. Ling-Huang, Can animals help to predict earthquakes? *Earthquake Info. Bull.,* November–December 1978.

210. C. Lomnitz and L. Lomnitz, Tangshan 1976—A case history in earthquake prediction, *Nature* 271: 109 (1978).

211. J. Needham, *Nature* 274: 832 (1978).

212. Antonio Rutili Gentili, *Riflessioni sulle cause naturali dei presenti terremoti,* presentate al Accademia dei Lincei (convocato nel giorno 5 febbraio 1832 per ordine di Segretaria di Stato) [Reflections on the natural causes of the earthquakes in question, presented to the Academy of Science (called on the day of February 5, 1832 by order of the State Secretariat)] (Rome, 1832).

213. H. Tributsch, *Nature* 276: 606 (1978).

214. S. A. Hoenig, *Nature* 279: 169 (1979).

215. Project Earthquake Watch: Dr. L. S. Otis, Office of Earthquake Studies, MS77, 345 Middlefield Road, Menlo Park, CA 94025.

216. *Der Tagesspiegel* (Berlin), January 18, 1978; March 22, 1979.

217. *Japan Times,* May 27, 1978.

218. *Berliner Zeitung,* September 4, 1978.

219. *Der Tagesspiegel* (Berlin), September 10, 1978.

220. M. N. Toksoz, E. Arpat, and F. Saraglu, *Nature* 270: 423 (1977).

221. R. A. Kerr, *Science* 206: 542 (1979).

222. Coll. acad. T. VI, p. 596 (cited in ref. 228).

223. J. Bernoulli, vol. 4 of his works (cited in ref. 228).

224. Cited in A. Till, Dass grosse Naturereignis von 1348 [The great natural event of 1348], *Mitt. Kais. Königl. Geogr. Ges. Wien* 50: 583 (1907).

225. *Preussische Staatszeitung,* 1824, no. 217; *Arch. des decouv.,* 1824, p. 214.

226. *Journal de Savant,* June 1, 1682, p. 195.

227. Ammianus Marcellinus, lib. XXVI, ch. 10.

228. K. E. A. von Hoff, *Geschichte der durch Überlieferung nachgewiesenen natürlichen Veränderungen der Erdoberfläche* [History of the natural changes in the Earth's surface proved by traditional reports] (Gotha, 1840).

229. Count Mercati, in *Journal de Physique* T. XCII, p. 466; Gilbert's *Annales de Physique* LXIX: 330.

230. *Arch. des decouv.* (1824), p. 213.

231. S. Msc., Pergam. 61, Sigebertus Gemblacensis, Gotha Library.